The Arnold and Caroline Rose Monograph
of the American Sociological Association

Trafficking in drug users

Control of illegal drug use and abuse requires an elaborate network of organizations and professions: medical, legal, political, educational, and welfare. This book explores the way in which these diverse sectors coordinate the control of deviance in a complex society and how they respond to a sudden widespread increase in deviance spanning many institutional and professional domains.

The latter of these concerns, James Beniger argues, affords us a unique insight into the more general question of societal control. He takes as an example of this phenomenon the dramatic appearance of the "drug problem" in America in the Vietnam war era of the late 1960s and early 1970s. Exploiting this as an approximation of an experimentally induced disruption of society, Professor Beniger examines its impact on the interorganizational and professional networks that together constitute a system for the control of social deviance. His study produces the startling finding that as various rewards – raises in salary, promotions, government funds, media exposure, enhanced status – accrued to the new social problem, many drug specialists gained increasing stake in the very deviance they were professionally charged to control. Societal control of the drug problem became transformed – quite literally – into a trafficking by professionals in young drug users.

Professor Beniger's study addresses a question at the very center of sociological theory: How does the self-interested control of events at the individual level influence those relationships – represented by exchanges of professional referrals and feedback of related information and advice – required for control at the community level? His analysis draws widely upon information, communication, and control theory, as well as upon the literature on general systems, interpersonal networks, and social exchange. His book is a valuable contribution to sociological theory and methodology, and will also interest professionals concerned with drug abuse.

Other books in the series

Trafficking in drug users:

Professional exchange networks in the control of deviance

James R. Beniger

Princeton University

Cambridge University Press

Cambridge
London   New York   New Rochelle
Melbourne   Sydney

Published by the Press Syndicate of the University of Cambridge
The Pitt Building, Trumpington Street, Cambridge CB2 1RP
32 East 57th Street, New York, NY 10022, USA
296 Beaconsfield Parade, Middle Park, Melbourne 3206, Australia

© Cambridge University Press 1983

First published 1983

Printed in the United States of America

Library of Congress Cataloging in Publication Data
Beniger, James R. (James Ralph), 1946–

Trafficking in drug users.

(The Arnold and Caroline Rose monograph series of the
American Sociological Association)

Bibliography: p.

Includes index.

1. Drug abuse counseling – United States – Case studies.
2. Deviant behavior. 3. Youth – United States – Drug use.
4. Social structure – United States. 5. Social control.
I. Title. II. Series. [DNLM: 1. Social control, Formal.
2. Social control, Informal. 3. Substance abuse – Prevention and control – United States. WM 270 B4675t]
HV5825.B44   1983   362.2'9386'0973   83–5251
ISBN 0 521 25753 0 hard covers
ISBN 0 521 27680 2 paperback

Contents

Acknowledgments

Work on this monograph began in autumn 1974, soon after I – as a post-generals graduate student in sociology and statistics at the University of California at Berkeley – accepted a position as research associate at the Bureau of Social Science Research in Washington, D.C. The survey of drug professionals that provides much of the empirical basis for my study was then in the analysis stage at BSSR. Michael Crotty, a member of the BSSR staff, asked for my opinions on the 48 directed-flow items discussed here in Appendix B. I soon realized that these data would enable me to test theoretical ideas about social-control systems, interpersonal networks, and exchange that – though far removed from the survey initiated by the National Institute of Mental Health – were nonetheless central to my plans for a doctoral dissertation. In autumn 1975 I returned to Berkeley to pursue the possibilities with my professors.

I am grateful to Albert Gollin, principal investigator on the drug survey, and especially to Carol Sosdian, one of his research assistants, for introducing me to the project's records and materials. The report by Dr. Gollin and Barry Feinberg (1975) provided much background information on the conduct of the survey. I am also grateful to Robert Bower, BSSR director, and to Louise Richards, the federal contract officer, for their kind permission to begin analyzing these data at Berkeley even before the final report was completed. Above all, I am grateful to Albert D. Biderman, associate director at BSSR, for his unswerving support – even from the other side of the country. I am proud to have worked with such a fine social scientist and intellectual as Al Biderman and to acknowledge as among my most important teachers this man who has not chosen the classroom as his profession.

Among the many Berkeley teachers who have helped me, I am most indebted to Neil Smelser and Art Stinchcombe, who between them seemed – at least to an impressionable young graduate student – to know everything. I would like to think that each of their distinctly different approaches to social research is well represented in my work. I am also especially grateful to

Charlie Glock, who gave me a home at Berkeley's Survey Research Center and whose limitless time and patience in introductory methods pointed me in a better direction than I ever intended to go.

The Survey Research Center provided me for five years with as warm and supportive a home as any graduate student could expect. I am especially grateful to Bill Nicholls, the executive director and my boss at SRC; most of what little I know about survey research is due to years spent at his elbow. Others at SRC who helped me with my work include Merrill Shanks, the SRC director, and Margaret Baker, Charlotte Coleman, Karen Olson, Judy Roizen, and Harvey Weinstein of the SRC staff.

That I managed to get through the master's degree program in Berkeley's Statistics Department in preparation for this project was due largely to the efforts of two fine people, Henry Scheffe and Elizabeth Scott. What statistical tools I have managed to bring to the analysis here are also due to several other good teachers: David Brillinger, Steve Casey, Kjell Doksum, and Roger Purves.

Although it is not usual in acknowledgments to cite one's intellectual debts to teachers known mostly through their written work, such people have played an important role in the development of this monograph. In information and control-systems theory, which has interested me since my undergraduate days at Harvard, I was particularly influenced by the popular books of Shannon and Weaver (1949) and Norbert Weiner (1948). The input–output models of Leontief, the book by Ekeh (1974) on social-exchange theory, and the work on the small-world problem and social networks by Mark Granovetter, Stanley Milgram, and Harrison White have helped to guide my thinking relevant to this monograph.

During an early stage of its writing, I profited from invitations to speak about my ideas at eight excellent departments of sociology, those at Chicago, Cornell, Harvard, Indiana, North Carolina, Princeton, Wisconsin, and Yale. Discussions and subsequent correspondence with various faculty and students of these departments greatly influenced my work during perhaps its most formative period. I regret that space does not permit individual acknowledgment of my many debts to these individuals.

In my five years of teaching here at Princeton, during which time this manuscript was completed and extensively rewritten, I owe particular thanks to my chairman, Marvin Bressler, for his gentle prodding, advice, and patience. Another Princeton colleague, Suzanne Keller, has provided many helpful comments on the final draft in her role as Rose Monograph Series editor.

Acknowledgments

To the previous Rose Monograph editor, Robin Williams, who is responsible for the acceptance of this work by the series, I want to pay special tribute. Professor Williams managed to find merit in work that I had buried in a horribly organized and tedious manuscript of almost half again the length here. Few editors would have had Professor Williams's patience in waiting out my revisions over the past two years; my only hope is that the final product in some part repays his confidence in me.

For intellectual stimulation and comfort, which served in equal parts as encouragement, distraction, and assistance, I am indebted to two special friends, Dorothy Robyn and Susan Cotts Watkins. Another friend, John French, who knows as much about drugs and the professional drug community as anyone I have met, has taught me a great deal that has proved useful to this study.

Finally, to my parents, Ralph and Charlotte Beniger, for providing a comfortable refuge in which to rework my manuscript, and for countless other lasting contributions during the previous thirty years, this work is dedicated. My sister, Linda York, and a family friend, Henry Zabel, deserve thanks for their interest and assistance in the preparation of the manuscript.

This research was funded in part by predoctoral fellowship 1 F31 DA 05082–01, awarded by the National Institute on Drug Abuse.

Princeton, N.J.   James R. Beniger

Introduction

This is a case study of one of the most dramatic social changes in American history, the rapid increase in the late 1960s in illegal drug use and abuse, especially among the youth of the nation. Although much has been written attempting to explain this development, I have not even bothered to review the literature and do not care to contribute to it. For me, the phenomenon is interesting only as exogenous change, a sharp, strong disturbance of a society's system for the control of social deviance – about as close an approximation to a laboratory test of such a system that a sociologist is likely to achieve, and hence an unusual opportunity to learn more about how social-control systems work.

It may seem insensitive to speak so abstractly about a major national problem fraught with human suffering. Such language is wholly intentional. Indeed, not only have I chosen to ignore the compelling human aspects of drug abuse by the young, I have largely ignored the young altogether. When I mention them at all, which is infrequent, it is usually as "professional referrals" or, in the aggregate, as "commodity flows to be controlled." I do this not because I am without feeling for the young or their problems, which have in fact touched me personally in several ways, but because I believe such problems can only be a distraction from the aim of my study: to understand the containment of rapid social change by the interorganizational community of professional specialists – medical, legal, educational, and counseling – that constitutes the total system for the control of social deviance.

Members of these professions may take offense at my view, implicit in the title *Trafficking in Drug Users*, that professionals might exchange referrals of young drug users to advance their own careers. I do not adopt this perspective because I think drug professionals are necessarily opportunistic or cynical about their work. My experience has been quite the contrary. What I do intend to show is that professional referrals of young drug users were – at least in the early 1970s – a scarce economic commodity that helped to translate standing in the drug-abuse community across organizational

1

boundaries. This meant that professionals who sought to advance their careers in the community tended to gravitate toward centrality in interpersonal networks of information and referral exchange, quite independently of the particular motives for their behavior. By viewing these exchanges as the central dynamic of a more macro-level social-control system, I believe, we can hope to gain fresh insight into the larger phenomenon, the containment of change by such a system.

Aside from this question, which is of general sociological interest, my more theoretical aims in the study are threefold: First, I want to integrate common elements in the largely separate literatures on cybernetic or control systems, interpersonal networks, and social exchange. Second, I want to develop a methodology for the study of social systems, a topic that – despite widely heralded theoretical work by Talcott Parsons and his students and an interdisciplinary "general systems" movement – has thus far resisted quantitative analysis. Finally, I want to suggest a synthesis of the autonomous-system and purposive-action approaches to social change by showing how system-level disturbances can modify the alternatives and utilities of individual actors toward restoring control at the higher level.

Considering these aims, which preceded my selection of the drug problem as a case study, it should be obvious that I am exploiting the phenomenon for what it might yield in social-theoretical understanding, rather than to contribute to the drug-abuse literature per se. Although I will certainly have failed in large measure if my work does not prove useful to researchers and other professionals working on drug abuse and on social deviance in general, this is not my primary goal.

Despite my interests in contributing to sociological theory, however, I do believe my particular approach to social-control systems suggests new directions for applied sociology and evaluation and policy research. The spending of large amounts of money to counter social problems is often advocated and evaluated in terms of outcomes too narrowly construed, I believe, and may often have much broader and possibly subtler effects on society that are unanticipated and go undetected. One example of such effects is the development of well-integrated interorganizational, interprofessional control networks in response both to mounting drug use and abuse among youth and to the considerable outlays of government resources that followed. Certainly unanticipated and unevaluated, I believe, was the emergence of user referrals as a valued commodity in professional exchange.

Although a few pages of my final chapter are devoted to other applications of my control-systems approach, I make no effort to draw out the further implications for evaluation and social-policy research. This would involve a quite separate line of study, one that I am not the best person to conduct. Considering what the current study reveals about professional networks and exchange of professional referrals, however, I suspect that applications of control-systems methods to evaluation and policy research may prove enlightening. I encourage researchers in these areas to explore the possibilities.

Because a decade has passed since the period covered in this monograph, it may be useful to give a brief outline of subsequent developments. The annual survey for the National Institute on Drug Abuse of drug usage among high school seniors (Johnston, Bachman, and O'Malley 1982) finds that the use of illicit drugs has dropped sharply during each of the past three years. The proportion of students who say they regularly smoke marijuana, still the most widely used substance after alcohol, has fallen to 1 in 14 from a high (in 1978) of 1 in 9. Declining use was also reported for tranquilizers; hallucinogens (particularly PCP – "angel dust"); and amyl and butyl nitrites or "poppers," liquid inhalants usually sold legally. Nearly stable in usage are cocaine (which 16.5 percent of students reported they had tried during the year), barbiturates, LSD, heroin, and methaqualone (also known as "Quaaludes" or "ludes"). Only the use of stimulants like amphetamines continued to rise sharply, up 25 percent over the previous year to an annual rate of 1 in 4. Two-thirds of the class of 1981 had tried at least one illegal drug during the previous year. Use of alcohol was steady at 6 percent daily, about 90 percent for the year, whereas daily cigarette use fell to 20 percent from a high of 29 percent in 1977.

Although the use of marijuana by American youth has been widespread for almost a generation, medical evidence concerning its long-term health effects remains inconclusive due largely to insufficient research. In a recent reevaluation of all the scientific literature on marijuana published since 1975 and selected earlier material, a panel of health authorities formed by the National Academy of Sciences' Institute of Medicine noted: "The Federal investment in research on the health-related effects of marijuana has been small, both in relation to the expenditure on other illicit drugs and in absolute terms. The committee considers the research particularly inadequate when viewed in light of the extent of marijuana use in this country, especially by young people" (National Academy of Sciences 1982, p. 5).

The panel's major recommendation was to call for renewed expenditure of resources, not on the drug counseling, treatment, and rehabilitation programs and block and formula grants that characterized federal spending in the early seventies, but rather on medical and health research: "Our major conclusion is that what little we know for certain about the effects of marijuana on human health – and all that we have reason to suspect – justifies serious national concern. Of no less concern is the extent of our ignorance about many of the most basic and important questions about the drug. Our major recommendation is that there be a greatly intensified and more comprehensive program of research into the effects of marijuana on the health of the American people." This echoes the complaints of scientists and legislators, as early as 1969, that government attention had concentrated too narrowly on law enforcement and penalties rather than on medical research and education (see Chapter 1).

Despite scanty and inconclusive evidence concerning marijuana's long-term effects, the NIDA survey suggests that young people are beginning to take seriously the warnings of counseling and health professionals about the drug's hazards. Nearly 60 percent of the class of 1981 said they believed regular marijuana users faced a "great risk" of harming themselves; three years earlier only 35 percent of high school seniors held that view. The NIDA survey also recorded a pronounced drop in support among students for legalizing the use of marijuana, which was down to 23 percent from 33 percent during the same three-year period.

Federal officials have lost no time in claiming credit for the decline in drug use among the nation's youth. On February 24, 1982, the same morning that the NIDA survey results were made public in Washington, Dr. William E. Mayer, the administrator of the Alcohol, Drug Abuse, and Mental Health Administration (which includes NIDA), cited the survey in testimony before the Senate Labor and Human Resources Subcommittee on Alcoholism and Drug Abuse. Alluding to such efforts as federal drug-abuse programs in the schools, Dr. Mayer claimed the survey findings as evidence that his agency's prevention efforts were bearing fruit.

The survey report itself presented a slightly different picture, but one that could nevertheless justify continued government support for drug counseling, treatment, and rehabilitation efforts. Citing the "conservative" estimate that at least two-thirds of the class of 1981 had tried at least one illicit drug during the year, the report concluded: "We judge these still to be very high levels both in absolute terms and relative to other countries. In fact, they are still probably the highest levels of drug abuse among young people to be found in any industrialized nation in the world. Thus, while some improvements are definitely beginning to emerge, the problems of drug use and abuse are still a very long way from being solved."

Without intending to minimize the very real social problems posed by drug abuse among youth, I note that the issue continues to have symbolic media value to which even national politicians are attracted. In the months before

President Richard Nixon's campaign for reelection in 1972, he called for "a concentrated assault on street level heroin pushers," announced creation of a new office of Drug Law Enforcement in the Justice Department, and reminded voters that he would spend eight times as much on the drug problem as the previous administration. Exactly ten years later, in February 1982, Nancy Reagan, accompanied by almost a dozen Secret Service men, twenty members of the press corps, and three aides, took a two-day tour of four drug programs in Florida and Texas. It was only the second major trip for the First Lady since President Reagan took office, the first being to London to attend the wedding of Prince Charles and Lady Diana Spencer.

Despite the NIDA survey data showing that the use of illicit drugs by high school students had dropped sharply since the 1970s, Mrs. Reagan told an informal news conference aboard her Air Force jet that the problem had reached epidemic proportions among young Americans. Asked if she felt like a crusader, she replied, "Yes, I do, because we are in danger of losing a whole generation" (Nemy 1982).

Some news commentators speculated that the First Lady's trip may have been intended to revamp her public image, shaken in recent months by widespread criticism of her White House redecoration, her purchase of a $209,000 set of china for formal state occasions, and her frequent appearances in designer clothes, some of them gifts from the makers. Whatever her motives, however, the trip did call public attention to drug abuse: A single television appearance in Florida brought 17,000 requests for information. "Super, fabulous," her press secretary, Sheila Tate, said afterward. "Everybody is focusing on the issue and the problem and that's exactly what we wanted them to do" (Hertzberg 1982).

Even though Mrs. Reagan felt that the drug problem among young Americans had reached "epidemic proportions" and that the nation was "in danger of losing a whole generation," it is not at all likely that federal funding for the problem will be increased or even maintained under the Reagan administration. When asked by reporters about the possibility, Mrs. Reagan shook her head and replied, "That's not my area" (Nemy 1982). Three of the four drug programs she visited were privately funded; the fourth was partly funded by the State of Florida.

Nor does the public share Mrs. Reagan's concern over the drug problem. In a Gallup Poll concerning "the most important problem facing this country" conducted a month before the First Lady's trip, too few respondents mentioned drugs to place the problem on the list of eight published by Gallup, despite a cutoff of only 3 percent and the recording of multiple responses (inflation and unemployment led the list). In February 1973, at the height of public concern over the issue, 20 percent of Gallup's respondents cited drugs as the most important national problem. Drug abuse has not made the lists of problems published by Gallup since July 1978.

Although the intentions of the Reagan administration toward its future support of drug programs are not yet clear, early indications are that funds will be reduced. One early sign was the replacement of Peter B. Bensinger, who had served both Presidents Ford and Carter as head of the Drug Enforcement Administration, after Bensinger lobbied against budget cuts proposed by the White House for his agency. Initially, the agency's budget was set at $228 million for fiscal year 1982, but a 12 percent cutback for most Federal agencies would reduce that by $27 million. This would mean the dismissal of 434 employees, including 211 agents. Agency officials were also preparing to ask every employee to take a two-week furlough without pay to meet the budget reduction.

In fiscal 1981, the National Institute on Drug Abuse funneled $160 million to local drug-treatment programs. Under the Reagan administration proposals, these funds would be cut by approximately 25 percent and included in a $491 million block grant also aimed at funding alcoholism and mental-health programs. Because each state would determine how to spend its share of the block, drug workers in the field worried publicly that money formerly channeled through NIDA would no longer go for drug treatment and prevention, but would be diverted to competing causes to be covered by a multipurpose grant. In August 1981, William Pollin, NIDA director and a holdover from the Carter administration, conceded that "certainly there will be a cutback in Federal funds for treatment programs" (Maitland 1981).

In short, most of the conditions prevailing during the period of my case study, 1972–3, appear to have changed. Illicit drug use and abuse by American youth, although high in comparison with other industrial nations, seems to have declined sharply for at least the past several years. Public concern for drug abuse as a national problem has all but disappeared, at least relative to problems like unemployment and inflation, which are seen as the most pressing. Federal support for most drug problems is likely to decrease, despite the interest of Mrs. Reagan in this area. Just about the only aspect of the drug problem that remains unchanged compared to a decade ago is that it continues to provide a potent symbol in national media politics.

Thus aided by the considerable advantage of a decade of hindsight, we embark upon an investigation of how even rapid social change, first perceived as a serious threat to society, comes to be contained by social-control systems, so that what was once a major problem can eventually be treated as just another issue for public discourse.

1. The emergence of the "drug problem": social change versus social control

Midway through the 1960s, the use of psychoactive drugs still drew little notice from the national media and the nation's political leaders. By the end of the decade, illegal drug use and abuse – especially by the young – had not only penetrated the public consciousness, but had become a full-blown national crisis that drew the prolonged attention of both the president and Congress. This emergence in the latter half of the 1960s of a so-called drug problem among the nation's youth remains one of the most rapid and dramatic social changes in U.S. history.

As late as 1964, there were still only 7,000 arrests annually for marijuana-law violations in the United States, roughly the same number as in previous years. The *Readers' Guide to Periodical Literature* that year indexed scarcely a dozen articles under the headings "marijuana," "LSD," and "heroin" combined. The first Gallup survey of drug use on American college campuses was still three years away.

By 1966, the number of marijuana arrests had doubled to 15,000. Surveys by campus newspapers at Yale, Princeton, and Caltech put the number of undergraduates who had at least experimented with marijuana at about 25 percent. The commissioner of the Food and Drug Administration, in a letter to officials at more than 2,000 colleges and universities, urged "concerted action" against the illegal use of drugs by college students.

The following summer, *Newsweek* ran a cover story under the headline, "Marijuana – The Pot Problem." "By all reports," the magazine stated, "marijuana has come downtown from the ghetto and the fringes of the middle class and entered the mainstream of U.S. life." By *Newsweek*'s estimate, "as many as 4.5 million Americans may stay on grass these days – most of them in the under-30 generation." The first Gallup Poll of campus drug use nationwide reported that, in 1967, 5 percent of college students had ever used marijuana, whereas 1 percent had tried LSD and related hallucinogens.

In the first six months of 1968, New York City's drug-related deaths in the 15 to 35 age group totaled 450, compared to 670 in all the previous year – and only 57 in 1950. The national death rate due to accidental drug

7

poisoning was 1.23 per 100,000, nearly triple the rate three years earlier. The *Readers' Guide* indexed nearly three dozen articles under "marijuana" alone in 1968, while marijuana arrests reached 80,000, a tenfold increase over the previous four years. The U.S. Armed Forces Radio began warning troops against the use of marijuana late in 1968.

The following year, a second Gallup Poll reported campus use of marijuana at 22 percent and of LSD and other hallucinogens at 4 percent, both fourfold increases over the previous two years; the use of barbiturates, not previously reported, was recorded at 10 percent. The Massachusetts Poll, conducted for the Boston *Globe*, found that adults in the state worried more about drug abuse among the young than any other problem; 80 percent rated the drug problem "very serious." In September, President Nixon began "Operation Intercept," a concerted program to reduce the smuggling of drugs into the United States from Mexico.

Thus, in a period of only a few years, the use of psychoactive drugs spread from a deviant activity of the socially marginal to a major national problem seen to afflict – or at least threaten – American youth in general.

The impact on organizational control systems

The sudden emergence of a national drug problem had a profound impact on community systems for the control of deviance among youth. Youth are ordinarily the professional responsibility, at least until a legal age limit of 16 to 18, of an educational system. With respect to drugs, youth might be deviant in two distinct ways – one medical (through drug abuse), the other legal (involving the use of illegal drugs). Hence the rapid rise in illegal drug use and abuse among American youth in the late 1960s brought increasing pressures for control on three organizational systems, which together comprise a total system for the social control of youth: the educational system, including both the public and private schools; the health system, both public and private; and the law-enforcement and criminal-justice systems.

The response of this total system to the sudden system "disturbance" constituted by the drug problem is the topic of study reported here. To study the effect of so temporally delimited a social change on such a clearly defined control system is to approximate about as closely as possible – under "real world" conditions – a laboratory test of system perturbation and response. It is also to gain insight into a general social phenomenon.

Life in modern societies is organized and regulated by a number of complex organizational control systems: the social-welfare system, the public-health system, the law-enforcement system, the court system, the school system. These formal control systems provide a measure of stability and continuity in the pursuit of collective goals, including the maintenance of public health and order, the punishment and rehabilitation of criminals, and the socialization and education of youth.

Even dramatic social changes are often routinely accommodated by formal organizations through modification of their goals and activities. This occurs, for example, when changing neighborhood patterns cause a school system to shift its emphasis from college-preparatory to vocational education, when new environmental hazards confound the jurisdictions of public health agencies, when a court decision forces police departments to alter arrest and interrogation procedures, or when changes in federal law-enforcement and funding cause several organizational systems to reexamine their hiring practices.

Not all social change is so easily accommodated within existing organizational structures, however. Certain changes, including seemingly minor ones, can crosscut the existing organizational and functional divisions of complex systems, thereby altering the specialized knowledge and skills required of various professions, forcing shifts in formal and informal status hierarchies, and restructuring the informal networks of communication and exchange that link both organizations and professions.

The sudden rise in illegal drug use and abuse by young Americans in the late 1960s was eventually accommodated by the organizational systems – educational, medical, and legal – responsible for the control of deviance among youth. This did not occur without straining various organizational facilities, strains that reverberated upward from facilities to mobilization channels to norms until they were finally contained by a new balance of "control" relationships. This system response included production of new drug specialists and "experts," incorporation of these experts into networks of information and referral exchange, and elaboration of these networks as an economic commodity system. These responses are discussed at length in the next three chapters.

The response of community systems to the drug problem thus affords an excellent case study of a much more general sociological problem: how complex organizational systems attempt to control exogenous social change. This question will be addressed here primarily in terms of an exchange model of interorganizational control derived from cross-sectional survey data. Despite this static model, however, the dynamic aspects of the analysis – including systemic perturbation and response – should not be overlooked. Without the assumption of prior social change, the cross-sectional analysis – presumably of an equilibrium state – would necessarily be confined to the structural aspects of the larger control system. Because prior change can be assumed, however, cross-sectional analysis can enlighten the dynamic as well as structural features of the social-control system.

The drug problem as an ideal case study

The previous section argued that the drug problem of the 1960s provides a case study of social change and of the response of organizational systems that attempt to control change. If this more general sociological problem is the pressing motivation for this study, rather than interest in the drug problem per se, then it is necessary to address an additional question: Why a case study of the drug problem, rather than of some other example of social change?

As a case of change exogenous to community organizations, but demanding their concerted action to effect containment, the drug problem provides an ideal setting for the study of social-control relationships at the macro level. Consider some of the special features:

1. It was a rapid change, as demonstrated in the opening section, and therefore constitutes as discrete an exogenous stimulus – to the organizational control systems of interest – as is likely to be found short of natural disasters and related phenomena.

2. It was an important change in its consequences, involving potentially serious health complications and stiff legal sanctions for a large segment of the nation's youth and an implied challenge to a wide range of social and political institutions.

3. It had broad implications – for a wide range of organizational spheres concerned with youth, drugs, and crime; among a number of occupations, professions, and professional specialties; at all organizational levels; and in a variety of functional activities (administration, research, treatment, counseling, education, etc.).

4. Its impact was felt at the level of individual communities, which not only makes possible analysis in terms of purposive-action theory (involving actors, their interests, and their control of events, as well as interpersonal networks of interaction and exchange), but also the comparative analysis of different communities (the analysis here will be reinforced by comparisons of Baltimore and San Francisco).

5. It was the subject of considerable and well-funded study at the time of the social change itself; the data available for this monograph are thus both intensive and extensive.

6. It remains wholly unanalyzed – despite mountains of data on the subject – as an instance of social change and as an exogenous factor affecting formal organizations and interorganizational control systems (possibly because it was largely overshadowed – in its effects – by the U.S. involvement in Vietnam).

The next chapter will introduce the community-level interorganizational system for the control of deviance among youth with respect to drugs. Chapter 2 will also propose an analysis of interpersonal exchange in networks as a control system, as a step toward a synthesis of the "autonomous-system" and "purposive-action" approaches to social change. The means by which the self-interested control of information and referrals at the action level can aggregate in the control of drug abuse at the system level is established in Chapter 3. Chapters 4 and 5 treat the functional interrelationships of various specialized components of such macro-level control systems.

It remains, in this chapter, to delineate further the timing, nature, and scope of the social change in question – the sudden emergence of a drug problem among American youth, and this problem's effects on local organizational systems responsible for the control of deviance among youth.

First approximations: the mass-media perception

Reliable measures of any illegal activity are difficult to obtain, and illegal use and abuse of drugs by youth is no exception. As will be shown in the next section, a variety of approximate indicators can be used to chart the course of the "drug problem" among American youth in the late 1960s and early 1970s. Before these more objective and quantitative measures are considered, however, it is useful to make a first approximation – based on the perceptions of major mass media – of the widespread use of drugs by youth. Much of the organizational response to social change, for example, the shift of government money and other resources to the new problem, may be related more to public perceptions as generated by – or reflected in – mass-media coverage than to more objective measures of the problem.

The development of the drug story was chronicled by at least four major types of mass media: newspapers, periodicals, radio, and television. Of these, three can be rejected as less useful sources of the desired indicators. Although several U.S. daily newspapers might be considered potentially national in coverage and readership, none (with the possible exception of *The*

Wall Street Journal) is uncontaminated – for research purposes – by coverage of local events and trends. Radio and television network news coverage largely avoids this bias, but radio news broadcasts have not been archived in readily usable form, whereas material on television news, although archived in the *Television News Index* (published by Vanderbilt Television News Archive), exists for only the latter years of coverage of the drug problem.

Of the nation's periodicals, two weekly newsmagazines, *Newsweek* and *Time*, might be considered to reflect national opinion and to affect the perceptions of a national audience. Insofar as these two national periodicals are highly imitative of – and imitated by – other periodicals and types of mass media, they might stand as approximate indicators of media coverage in general.

From 1966 to 1972, *Newsweek* and *Time* together ran seven cover stories on illegal drugs and their use and abuse. Whether these stories accurately reflected social trends, or widely held misconceptions, or were fabricated to sell magazines, it is likely that they – and the other mass-media coverage that accompanied them – molded public perceptions of the youth drug problem. Such changes in public perceptions, perhaps even more than changes in drug use, affected the shift of attention and resources to the new problem.

The first cover story on the drug problem by one of the major newsmagazines appeared in the May 9, 1966, issue of *Newsweek*, which bore on its cover a youthful face distorted by colored lights and the headline, "LSD and the Mind." The accompanying story stressed that the use of such drugs was not widespread: "The number of Americans who have ever tasted LSD, mescaline, psilocybin and the other hallucinogens is small compared with users of such other mind drugs as the amphetamines ("uppies") that provide users with psychic energy, the barbiturates ("downies") that put them to sleep, and the tranquilizers that allay their anxieties and fears . . . " (Clark 1966).

Fourteen months later, *Newsweek* prepared a second cover story on drugs, which appeared in its July 24, 1967, issue. The cover photograph featured a male hand passing a joint of marijuana to a female hand, with the caption: "Marijuana – The Pot Problem." Marijuana use was now presented as widespread and growing, although *Newsweek* still had no hard figures on its prevalence: "No one knows for certain how many Americans have taken this trip. Health officials in Washington, guessing in the dark, estimate that 20 million Americans may have tried pot at least once and that anywhere from 300,000 to 4.5 million smoke it regularly" (Zimmerman 1967, p. 46).

Interest in the drug problem died down following the second *Newsweek* cover story and remained at approximately the same level (as will be seen in the quantitative indicators of the next section) through 1968. By the spring of 1969, interest in drugs began to focus specifically on youth, as evidenced by a story, "The Drug Generation: Growing Younger," in the April 21, 1969, issue of *Newsweek*. The paragraph summary of the story, which appeared in *Newsweek*'s "Top of the Week" column, described the almost two years that had passed since its last cover story: "The use of drugs – from white diet pills that give a Dexedrine high to LSD capsules for mind-bending hallucinations – has spread through the youth population of the U.S. Marijuana can be found in the mess halls of Vietnam, at high schools – and, sometimes, at the elementary school" (*Newsweek* 1969).

The article itself utilized the growing body of research by professionals on the new problem: "Surveying five California campuses, Richard H. Blum, a Stanford University psychologist, found that marijuana use had almost tripled in the 18 months ending December 1968. In a new report, 'Students and Drugs,' Blum states that 57 percent of students at the schools had smoked marijuana at least once, compared with 21 percent a year earlier. About 14 percent were 'regular' users, against 4 percent a year before" (Janssen 1969).[1]

Five months later, *Time* magazine prepared its first cover story on the drug problem, which appeared in its September 26, 1969, issue. The cover featured a youth's face in psychedelic colors, with the caption: "Drugs and the Young." The accompanying article, "Pop Drugs: The High as a Way of Life," portrayed the use of illegal drugs as widespread, citing figures from hastily constituted government research teams – figures that even government officials did not consider accurate. "A recent administration task force "conservatively" estimated that at least 5,000,000 Americans have used marijuana at least once," the story stated. "Dr. Stanley Yolles, director of the National Institute of Mental Health, puts the total far higher: at least 12 million and perhaps even 20 million . . . Yolles estimates that 25 percent to 40 percent of all students have at least tried it; on many college campuses, particularly on the East and West coasts and near large cities, the figure is 50 percent. Last month's Woodstock music festival, where some 90 percent of the 400,000 participants openly smoked marijuana, brought the youthful drug culture to a new apogee" (Cory 1969, p. 69).

This article marked the beginning of a shift in the perception of the increase in marijuana use among youth from a pressing social "problem" to acceptable behavior that might justifiably be deemphasized by law-enforcement officials: "Even if the users who are heavily dependent on drugs (perhaps somewhat less than 2,000,000) are combined with addicts (about 100,000), the sum is smaller than the estimated national total of 6,000,000 alcoholics. Some experts even maintain that the 'drug problem' has become the 'drug problem problem' – one more distorted priority diverting attention from real national needs" (Cory 1969, p. 68).

That this attitude might not have represented a developmental shift in public perceptions, but merely a difference in the editorial position of *Time* compared to *Newsweek*, was disproved a year later in a cover story by the latter newsmagazine. The September 7, 1970, cover of *Newsweek* featured a closeup of a burning joint of marijuana and the caption question: "Marijuana: Time to Change the Law?" The "Top of the Week" summary of the cover story declared: "With the possible exception of speeding cars, marijuana smoking is probably the most widely committed crime in the U.S. today. Is it the law itself that needs reform?" (*Newsweek* 1970, p. 3).

Meanwhile, *Time* had already moved on from marijuana to heroin use among the young. Its March 16, 1970, cover, with a hypodermic needle superimposed on the face of a young boy, carried the banner: "Heroin Hits the Young." The cover story, "Kids and Heroin: The Adolescent Epidemic," emphasized that the problem had worsened dramatically in the 1968–9 period. *Time* relied heavily on government officials and drug "experts" for evidence on this point: "No one knows how many heroin addicts of any age there are in the U.S. But in New York City alone, where most experts think roughly half of the heroin users in the U.S. live, 224 teenagers died from overdoses or heroin-related infections last year, about a quarter of the city's 900 deaths from heroin use. So far this year, over 40 teenagers have died because of heroin. There may be as many as 25,000 young addicts in New York City, and one expert fears the number many mushroom fantastically to 100,000 this summer. Cautious federal officials believe that heroin addiction below age 25 jumped 40 percent from 1968 to 1969" (Johnson 1970, p. 16).

Time presented its "Kids and Heroin" story with uncharacteristic alarm, again bolstering its case with the opinions of drug "experts": "However imprecise the figures, there is no doubting the magnitude of the change, or the certitude that something frightening is sweeping into the corridors of U.S. schools and onto the pavements of America's playgrounds. It has not yet cropped up everywhere, but many experts believe that disaster looms large" (Johnson 1970, p. 16).

The following summer, *Newsweek* ran its first cover story on the rapid increase in heroin use by American youth. The July 5, 1971, cover, with a young boy shooting himself up with a hypodermic needle, introduced a lengthy story, "The Heroin Plague." The summary in *Newsweek*'s "Top of the Week" column set the tone: "Heroin is spreading in epidemic proportions out of the ghetto into white suburbia and through the armed forces" (*Newsweek* 1971, p. 3).

Like the *Time* cover story the previous year, this *Newsweek* story located the onset of the problem in the 1968–9 period, with heavy reliance on official statistics: "In the past three years, the official guess on the scope of heroin addiction alone – and not counting any other drug – has risen to 200,000, then 250,000, finally recently to 300,000 Americans. And it's killing them in record numbers: there were 237 teenagers out of 1,205 total narcotics related deaths in New York City last year, and 16 out of 47 even in a sunny, middle-sized place like Albuquerque" (Boeth 1971, p. 27).

By the following year, when data for the National Institute on Drug Abuse survey used in this study were being gathered in Baltimore and San Francisco,[2] the attention of the newsmagazines had again shifted, this time from heroin use among the young to government control of international drug trafficking. The September 4, 1972, issue of *Time* devoted its cover story to "The Global War on Heroin." The illustration depicted a half face–half skull, overlaid with yet another hypodermic needle, plus a distant view of planet earth – perhaps to remind readers of the larger scope the drug problem had assumed by the end of 1972.

To summarize the evidence, as suggested by the *Newsweek* and *Time* cover stories, public perception of the drug problem – as molded by or reflected in the mass media – evolved through four distinct stages:

> *Stage 1* (1966–7). The first indications of an increase in drug use came to the attention of the mass media.
> *Stage 2* (1968). Interest in a possible drug problem waned as media attention turned to other news events.
> *Stage 3* (1969–71). Concern for the problem of illegal drug use and abuse by youth came to a peak in the media.
> *Stage 4* (1972–). Media attention turned from drug use itself, and its effects on youth, to government countermeasures and particularly to the control of international drug traffic.

These four stages can be seen in Figure 1.1, which presents a graphic chronology of the seven *Newsweek* and *Time* covers from 1966 to 1973 devoted to the drug problem. More objective and quantitative measures that further delineate the four stages of the drug problem will be given in the next section.

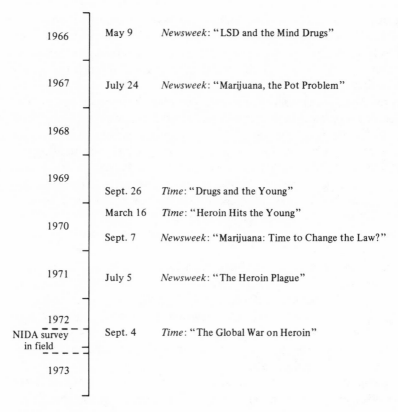

1966	May 9	*Newsweek*: "LSD and the Mind Drugs"
1967	July 24	*Newsweek*: "Marijuana, the Pot Problem"
1968		
1969		
	Sept. 26	*Time*: "Drugs and the Young"
	March 16	*Time*: "Heroin Hits the Young"
1970	Sept. 7	*Newsweek*: "Marijuana: Time to Change the Law?"
1971	July 5	*Newsweek*: "The Heroin Plague"
1972 NIDA survey in field	Sept. 4	*Time*: "The Global War on Heroin"
1973		

Figure 1.1. *Newsweek* and *Time* magazine covers devoted to the drug problem, 1966–73.

Social indicators of the drug problem

The idea that the content of mass-media reporting might serve as an indicator of social change is hardly new.[3] Harold Lasswell may have been the first social scientist to call for the development of social indicators from mass-media measures when, in 1935, he urged a continuing survey of "world attention" – as reflected in trends in media coverage of various social issues – to show the elements involved in the formation of public opinion. Survey research, then in its infancy, could not be an adequate monitor of opinion, Lasswell argued, without simultaneous monitoring of what he called the "symbolic environment." This he sought to establish by outlining general categories for coding media content and by suggesting quantitative indicators based on the resulting data (Lasswell 1935).

The first large-scale collection of mass-media data for use as social indicators, a project that grew out of the U.S. military's interest in mass communication in time of war, was Lasswell's War Time Communication Study at the Library of Congress, 1940–1. Although this study produced certain advances in the methodology of media indicators, it left no institutional heritage (Lasswell et al. 1947). Phillip Stone organized a similarly massive computer-based effort at Harvard University in the early 1960s (Stone 1966), but this, too, failed at institutionalization. The most recent attempt to institutionalize the collection of mass-media data on a large scale is the quarterly *Trend Report* begun in 1969 by the Center for Policy Process (Naisbitt 1976).[4]

Given the potential of mass-media measures to serve as indicators of social trends, and the failure of large-scale efforts fully to exploit this potential, a better strategy might be to develop media indicators on a more modest scale. This can be accomplished, relatively easily and at little cost, using mass-media indexes and guides like the *Readers' Guide to Periodical Literature*. One such effort, the so-called Greenfield Index,[5] has already been elaborated (Beniger 1978b).

The Greenfield Index is based on simple counts of articles indexed in the *Readers' Guide*, and is used to measure trends in mass-media coverage as an indicator of social change. For example, Figure 1.2 charts the Greenfield Index for the *Readers' Guide* classification "Narcotics and Youth" for the 1968–77 period. As can be seen from Figure 1.2, the Greenfield Index strongly confirms the four distinct stages in the development of the drug problem that were listed in the previous section. During the 1966–7 period (Stage 1), when attention turned to other news events, only 12 articles appeared on drugs. During the 1969–71 period (Stage 3), concern for the problem of illegal drug use and abuse by youth came to a peak in the media, as previously stated; the graph in Figure 1.2 clearly peaks during these three years. After 1972 (Stage 4), concern for drugs turned away from youth, as evidenced by the increasingly infrequent use of the "Narcotics and Youth" category.

The Greenfield Index is not necessarily an indicator of actual social change, of course, only of possibly faddish trends in media attention to social issues. This fact has been emphasized by Mueller, who was the first to formalize the Greenfield Index (Mueller 1973): "Much of the fluctuation in the Greenfield Index is, no doubt, due to journalistic fad. A sensational fraud, scandal, or disruption causes theologians, journalists, and other

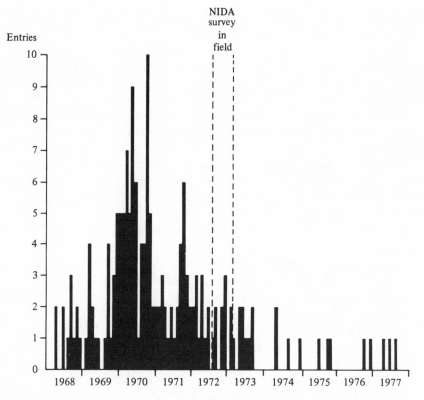

Figure 1.2. Greenfield Index for "Narcotics and Youth," 1968–77 (numbers of *Readers' Guide* entries per month).

intellectuals to sociologize: society itself is sick. Others pick up the idea, and it blossoms into a full moral crisis. In a year or two the theme no longer sells magazines and the space is filled with other profundities, for example, the generation gap. Fraud, scandal, and disruption continue, but the moral crisis eases" (p. 237). To bolster this view, Mueller notes that more objective indicators of public morality (he specifically cites studies of crime rates, church attendance, and sexual practices) do not fluctuate with the extremes of the Greenfield Index (Mueller 1973, p. 237).

Even if an index of mass-media coverage is a poor measure of actual change, however, such an index may nevertheless be more useful as a social indicator than more objective measures in that it better captures public attitudes and opinions about the relative importance of various social issues.

Much of the organizational response to social change, such as the shift of government money and other resources to a new problem, may be related more to public perception – as generated by or reflected in media coverage – than to more objective measures of the problem. This is because attitudes and opinions of government leaders and their constituencies do not necessarily correlate with objective social conditions, but they *are* likely to be related to media coverage – not only because it is in the commercial interests of the media to reflect the personal perspectives of their audiences, but also because of the converse relationship, namely, the so-called agenda-setting function of the media.

The agenda-setting hypothesis, which has drawn increasing attention in the communications literature over the last 10 years (for a review, see McCombs 1976), implies a relationship between the relative emphasis given by the media to various topics and the degree of salience these topics have for the general public. According to this hypothesis, individuals note the distribution of media coverage among topics and thereby weight the salience of each topic for their own behavior (e.g., deciding how to vote among several political candidates). According to the agenda-setting hypothesis, the media do not reflect public priorities so much as they determine them. As this notion was early summarized by Cohen (1963), "[The press] may not be successful much of the time in telling people what to think, but it is stunningly successful in telling its readers what to think *about*" (p. 13).[6]

The implication of such an agenda-setting function for the development of indicators of the drug problem is that media coverage may be more closely associated with public attitudes and opinion than are more objective measures. This possibility is suggested by Figure 1.3, which compares a 15-year Greenfield Index of *Readers' Guide* entries on LSD, marijuana, and heroin to two more "objective" measures of drug use among youth: accidental drug deaths, ages 15–24, as compiled by *Vital Statistics*; and drugs ever tried – separately for marijuana and LSD – by college students, as reported by Gallup polls of this population. Also included in Figure 1.3 is one measure of agenda setting with respect to the drug problem: the percentage of people who see drugs as the most important national problem as measured by the Gallup Poll.[7]

As Figure 1.3 reveals, the two objective measures of the drug problem rose rapidly during the 1966–71 period and tapered off thereafter. Periodical coverage of the problem, as measured by the Greenfield Index, peaked during the 1966–72 period (in 1966 for LSD, in 1971 for marijuana, and the following year for heroin). In the continuing Gallup polls of the most important national problems, however, the drug issue did not peak until mid-

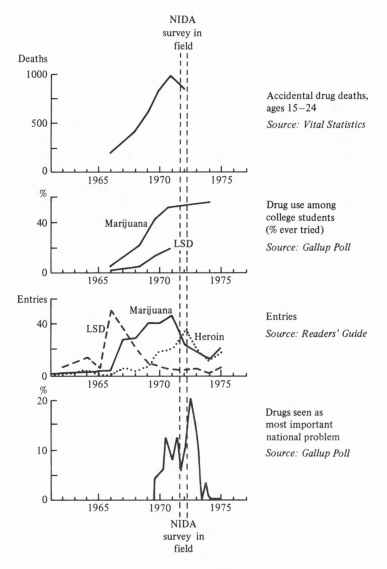

Figure 1.3. Independent measures of the "drug problem" among American youth, 1961–75. (Adapted from Beniger 1978b.)

1973, some two years after the objective and media measures had begun to decline.

In other words, the Greenfield Index lagged only months behind the objective measures (and, in one case, actually led that of periodical reportage and campus use of LSD). The Gallup measure of public concern for the drug problem, by contrast, lagged the objective measure by two years. In at least this case – of the sudden emergence of a drug problem among American youth – the media indicators not only came closer than more objective measures to approximating trends in public attitudes, but also – given the lag in reporting of data like those compiled by *Vital Statistics* – afforded a better means of monitoring the underlying social change.

Similar results are reported by Funkhouser (1973a; 1973b) for a wide range of major issues in the 1960s. His study finds strong correlations between measures of press coverage and national public opinion, but relatively little correlation between these media and public-agenda measures and objective indicators of social trends. Even on those issues (e.g., Vietnam, campus unrest, urban rioting) where media coverage actually peaked well *before* objective trends, public opinion more closely coincided with the media measure (as would be expected under the agenda-setting hypothesis). Similarly, from a correlation analysis of media coverage and public opinion, Stone (1976) estimates that the latter indicators lag the former by approximately two months.

Whatever the nature of mass-media coverage, then, whether it reflects actual social change, or the changing attitudes and opinions of its audience, or is subject to journalistic fads, which in turn help to set the public agenda, its usefulness as an indicator of the drug problem is assured.

The time-series indicators in Figure 1.3 lend further support to the four stages of public perception of the youth drug problem based on *Newsweek* and *Time* magazine covers that were identified in the previous section. In Stage 1, 1966–7, there was an awakening of media interest in the drug problem (particularly in LSD) and a steady increase in the objective measures. In Stage 2, roughly corresponding to the year 1968, in which no *Newsweek* or *Time* cover stories appeared on the problem, objective measures continued to show relatively unchanged increases, while periodical coverage of marijuana held steady and coverage of LSD declined. In Stage 3, 1969–71, when the concern of *Newsweek* and *Time* for the drug problem was at its height, objective measures correspondingly increased more rapidly, periodical reportage on marijuana also peaked, and the drug problem made its first appearance in the Gallup Poll of national problems. In the final stage, after 1972, when the newsmagazines turned to government countermeasures and international controls, objective measures leveled off or began to fall and periodical reportage declined for all three drugs, while national opinion on drugs as a national problem peaked – and then quickly plummeted to near zero.

Given this well-substantiated development of the problem of illegal drug use and abuse among youth, the NIDA survey of drug professionals – which was in the field from August 1972 to February 1973 (as indicated in Figures 1.1 and 1.2) – was ideally timed for the purposes of this study. All the objective and mass-media measures of the drug problem peaked at or shortly before the NIDA survey, while public concern for drugs as a national problem was in its sharpest ascent (and about to peak only months afterward). Thus the NIDA survey permits an almost laboratory test of both an exogenous change that had just run its rapid course and of its impact on organizational systems for the control of deviance among youth with respect to drugs.

The government response: resource shifts

Whenever a previously minor or at least contained social problem suddenly looms large, as illegal drug use and abuse by youth did in the late 1960s and early 1970s, government money and other resources – including research funding – can be expected to shift to the new problem. Such shifts are necessary responses, at the system level, in order to generate the individual behavior required, at the level of purposive action, for the maintenance of organizational control systems.

A full account of governmental responses to the drug problem – and resource shifts to the new problem – would itself require a monographic treatment and is beyond the main focus of this study. The brief outline in this section will be sufficient to establish the link between autonomous social change and system response as generated by individual actors in pursuit of personal self-interests. The link between the system and action levels, in turn, will be developed further in the chapters that follow.

Drug legislation began to move in a new direction in the 1960s with the expansion of federal control over depressant, stimulant, and hallucinogenic drugs (including barbiturates, "pep pills," and LSD). In 1965, Congress passed a law (PL 89-74) amending the Food and Drug Act to require more extensive record keeping and inventory controls in order to try to slacken the illegal flow of drugs; this law was not effective. Passage of the Narcotics Rehabilitation Act (PL 89-793) the following year provided that addicts convicted of drug offenses not be sent to prison, but instead be committed to medical institutions for treatment; it also provided that a relative of an addict could have him or her committed to compulsory treatment. This was a major step in the establishment of a community of health professionals dependent on the problem of drug abuse, which had previously been largely a law-enforcement issue.

Because of the failure of PL 89-74, the Johnson administration requested an amended version in the belief that tougher penalties for violations could decrease the illegal use of drugs. In 1968, Congress passed legislation setting criminal penalties for the illegal possession of stimulant, depressant, or hallucinogenic drugs, including amphetamines, barbiturates, and LSD; President Johnson signed it into law (PL 90-639) on October 24. The major effect of PL 90-639 was greatly to expand the number of drug users, particularly young people, under the governmental purview.

An initial move toward coordinating the enforcement of the various drug laws also came in 1968. President Johnson, through an executive re-organization plan, combined the Bureau of Narcotics in the Department of the Treasury with the Bureau of Drug Abuse Control in the Department of Health, Education and Welfare (HEW). The new agency, the Bureau of Narcotics and Dangerous Drugs, was housed in the Department of Justice. This presidential action further established the drug problem as a subject of concerted federal law-enforcement activity.

The succession of Richard Nixon to the White House in 1969 brought administration calls for channeling additional government resources toward the new problem, but no immediate legislation. On July 14, 1969, in a message to Congress, President Nixon called for a national attack on narcotics abuse and requested more money, personnel, and research. When Attorney General Mitchell submitted the administration drug bill to Congress the following day, however, several scientists and legislators publicly expressed disappointment that the bill focused on law enforcement and penalties rather than on medical research and education (Robbins 1969). Although Congress investigated a variety of drug problems in 1969, it did not clear any major legislation dealing with the matter. One major complication was a jurisdictional question of whether to consider drug abuse the primary responsibility of the Justice Department or HEW.

Meanwhile, after a hiatus in media interest in drugs, the first *Time* cover story on the problem, "Drugs and the Young," appeared in the September 26, 1969, issue. The period from November 1969 to June 1970 brought the most sustained barrage of articles on the problem that has ever appeared (as seen in Figure 1.2). In the middle of this period, on March 11, 1970, President Nixon announced an expanded federal effort to warn school-age youth of the dangers of drugs. His order included a sixfold increase to $12.5 million in annual spending for student and teacher drug-education programs, creation of a National Clearinghouse for Drug Abuse Information within the National Institute of Mental Health, and an expanded public advertising campaign ($50,000 annually for three years) to be run by the Advertising Council. Nixon also modified the federal crime-control program to permit large cities to select drug education as a project for which they could seek federal funds. By this presidential action, educators joined law-enforcement and public-health officials in the federally financed assault on the drug problem.

Congress also acted swiftly, following the burst of media attention to the drug problem, on the legislation proposed by Nixon the previous year and since bogged down in the Senate. The Senate had agreed on a bill sponsored by Senator Thomas J. Dodd in late January, and a compromise version passed both houses a month before the 1970 congressional elections. President Nixon signed the bill into law (PL 91-513) on October 27.

This legislation, the Comprehensive Drug Abuse Prevention and Control Act of 1970, approached the drug problem on a broad scale that encompassed drug research, drug-abuse education, treatment of users, and addict rehabilitation. Not only did the new law unify and revise the patchwork of federal narcotic and drug laws, it also expanded federal support for all drug programs by $409 million in fiscal 1971–4 (see Figure 1.4).

The most significant section of PL 91-513 for local-community drug-abuse prevention and treatment efforts was Title I, a Senate amendment – introduced by Senator Harold E. Hughes – to the administration bill as originally passed by the House. Title I established a national institute for the prevention and treatment of drug dependency within the National Institutes of Health. It gave HEW $189 million in fiscal 1971–3 for states, localities, and projects, and increased the federal drug effort in three major ways:

1. By amending the Community Mental Health Centers Act (Title II of PL 88-164) to increase authorizations for community facilities for the treatment of addicts and drug-dependent persons by $75 million for fiscal 1971, 1972, and 1973 (to $40 million from $30 million for 1971; to $60 million from $35 million for 1972; to $80 million from $40 million for 1973);

2. By amending PL 88-164 to authorize $85 million for grants in fiscal 1971, 1972, and 1973 for special projects in the treatment and rehabilitation of addicts and drug-dependent persons ($20 million for 1971, $30 million for 1972, $35 million for 1973); and

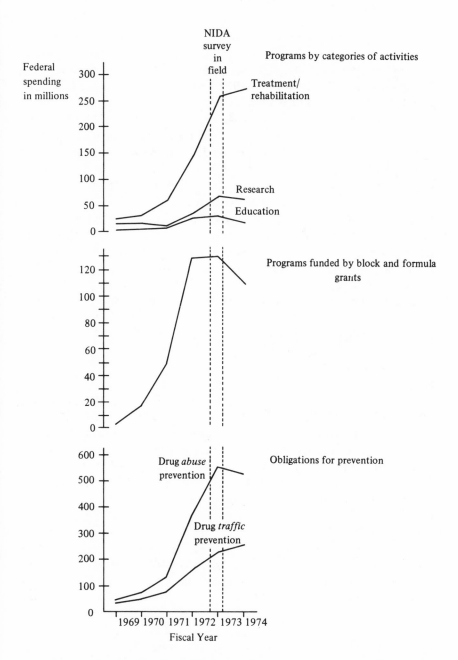

Figure 1.4. Federal drug-abuse programs and obligations for drug abuse and traffic prevention, fiscal years 1969–74. (Source: *Federal Strategy for Drug Abuse and Drug Traffic Prevention 1973.*)

3. By amending PL 88-164 to authorize $29 million for drug-abuse education projects for fiscal 1971, 1972, and 1973 ($3 million for 1971, $12 million for 1972, and $14 million for 1973).

A second piece of legislation, signed into law (PL 91-527) by President Nixon on December 3, further bolstered the educational component of the federal effort against drug abuse. PL 91-527 was designed to alleviate two major problems: a lack of teachers trained to offer drug-abuse courses in elementary and secondary schools, and a lack of scientifically accurate teaching materials. Under the law, the secretary of HEW was authorized to make grants (up to $58 million over fiscal 1971–3) to local educational agencies and other private and nonprofit organizations for community information programs on drug abuse.[8] Grants could be used to develop curricula, disseminate educational materials, provide training programs for teachers and law-enforcement officials, and offer community educational programs to parents and others. PL 91-527 also authorized $29 million ($5 million in 1971, $10 million in 1972, $14 million in 1973) for drug-abuse education programs; equal funding was provided for school-based and community-based programs.

The Comprehensive Drug Abuse Prevention and Control Act went into effect on May 1, 1971. A few days later, Congress passed a bill (PL 92-13) increasing from $1 million to $4 million the authorization for the Presidential Commission on Marijuana and Drug Abuse. The same month, Pentagon officials announced that the Defense Department planned to begin testing every person in military service for drug addiction before discharge into civilian life. The purpose of the check was to identify addicts (then leaving the services at the rate of 20,000 per year) to persuade them to enter Veterans Administration hospitals or to keep them under surveillance by civilian authorities.

On June 1, 1971, President Nixon pledged at a news conference to undertake what he called a "national offensive" to counter the problem of drug addiction among young Americans, including armed-forces members who had become addicted while in Vietnam. This was the first time the problem had been identified with the young in particular. On June 17, in a message to Congress, Nixon declared that drug abuse had "assumed dimensions of a national emergency," and asked for $155 million more for fiscal 1972 for a campaign of rehabilitation, research, education, enforcement, and international control of drug traffic (thus raising the total federal budget for enforcement and treatment to $370 million). He said he would name Dr. J. H. Jaffee to head a new Special Action Office for Drug Abuse Prevention, which combined the tasks of seven domestic agencies.

Congress completed action on Nixon's proposal (which became known as the Drug Abuse Office and Treatment Act, PL 92-255) on March 17, 1972. It created the Special Action Office, which Nixon had called for in his message to Congress, within the Executive Office of the President. The director of the office was given authority to coordinate all federal drug-abuse programs, with the exception of those in law enforcement, and to establish new ones. It authorized slightly more than $1 billion through fiscal 1975 to carry out the director's activities and to provide research funds and state grants. It created the National Institute on Drug Abuse, within the National Institute of Mental Health, plus the National Advisory Council for Drug Abuse Prevention and the National Drug Abuse Training Center. It also established a long-term federal strategy to combat drug abuse.

Meanwhile, President Nixon, who faced reelection that fall, stepped up the frequency of his public statements on drug abuse, which had already begun to peak by objective measures, but which continued to rise in the polls on national problems (Figure 1.3). In Nixon's January 24 message on the fiscal 1973 budget, he proposed an increase in program levels of $120 million; funds for research, education, prevention, treatment, and rehabilitation were to increase from $310 million in 1972 to $365 million in 1973, while obligations for law-enforcement actions were to grow from $164 in 1972 to $229 million in 1973.

Four days later, Nixon ordered what he called "a concentrated assault on street level heroin pushers" and announced the creation of a new office of Drug Law Enforcement in the Justice Department. He named Customs Commissioner Myles J. Ambrose to head the department and empowered him to utilize enforcement personnel from the Justice and Treasury departments; Ambrose was also designated special consultant to Nixon on drug-abuse law enforcement. In the president's March 2 message to Congress on health care, he pointed out that he would be spending eight times as much on the drug problem as was being spent for that purpose when his administration took office.

This, then, was the national climate in which the NIDA survey, which provides the data for this study, was first mailed to respondents in late August 1972. During the survey's five months in the field, Congress cleared another piece of legislation (PL 92-420) requested by Nixon in his 1971 message on drug abuse. This amended the Narcotic Addict Rehabilitation Act of 1966 (PL 89-793) to permit the use of methadone in narcotic addiction treatment programs. Also while the survey was in the field, President Nixon was reelected for a second term.

The following summer brought a peak in the percentage of the public that saw drugs as the most important national problem – the last indicator to show the drug problem beginning to recede. The rhetoric of some government officials, however, continued for some time to dwell in the past. The House Select Committee on Crime, for example, in a report released June 23, 1973, called the drug problem in the nation's schools "an extremely deadly epidemic" that was "leaving a trail of devastation that will take a decade to remedy"; the committee recommended the expenditure of $500 million over the next four years to eliminate the problem. By this time, the mass media had moved on to other problems (as seen in Figures 1.2 and 1.3).

The NIDA survey, in the field from August 1972 through February 1973, would seem well timed to capture the effect of dramatic increases in government spending on the drug problem. Temporal location of the survey measure, relative to shifts in government resources, is summarized in Figure 1.4. The top panel charts federal spending on drug abuse programs by three categories of activity: treatment and rehabilitation, research, and education. As shown by this chart, spending increased dramatically during 1971 and 1972, the years immediately preceding the NIDA survey, and then slowed markedly or fell off.

Federal spending on drug programs through block and formula grants to state and local governments is graphed in the middle panel of Figure 1.4. The federal government funded and operated programs both directly (through the Veterans Administration, Department of Defense, National Institute of Mental Health, etc.) and indirectly (through Housing and Urban Development Model Cities and Law Enforcement Assistance Administration block grant funds, which were used for drug-abuse problems and related activities at local and state discretion, respectively). The data also include reimbursements to drug programs under Medicaid and Titles IV A and B, XIV, and XVI of the Social Security Act. As the chart shows, federal spending via block and formula grants rose sharply from 1969 to 1971, leveled off during fiscal 1973 – the period of the NIDA survey – and then dropped almost as sharply as it had risen.[9]

The bottom panel of Figure 1.4 charts the total amount of federal spending for drug-*abuse* prevention (for which the spending charted in the other two panels is a component) as well as drug-*traffic* prevention. As shown by this chart, spending increased dramatically during 1971 and 1972, the years immediately preceding the NIDA survey, and then slowed or fell off.

In short, Figure 1.4 supports the earlier conclusion: The NIDA survey was almost ideally timed, in the period from August 1972 to February 1973, to capture the full impact of massive shifts in federal resources – both in direct program spending and via block and formula grants – on the systems organized to control illegal drug use and abuse. These shifts included increased resources for professionals in treatment and rehabilitation, research, and education, including those in local programs like Model Cities and in neighborhood drug centers. Such shifts were the system response, on the national level, needed to generate professional behavior that would contain the drug problem at the level of community control systems.

Summary

This chapter has introduced a case study of social change: the sudden emergence of the so-called drug problem among American youth in the late 1960s. As late as 1964, illegal drug use and abuse by the young went relatively unnoticed; by 1969, it was considered one of the nation's most pressing problems – by the mass media, by the president and Congress, and by the American public.

This change, one of the most rapid and dramatic in U.S. history, provides an ideal setting for the study of social-control systems at the macro level. Not only was the change exogenous to the organizational systems responsible for its control, but it demanded their concerted action to effect containment. Specifically, it brought increasing pressures for control on three community systems: education, public health, and law enforcement and criminal justice.

To study the effect of so temporally delimited a social change on such a clearly defined control system is to approximate a laboratory test of system perturbation and response. It is also to gain insight into a more general sociological question: how complex organizational systems attempt to control exogenous social change. Because prior change can be assumed, cross-sectional analysis of a NIDA survey of drug professionals – the major source of data for this study – can enlighten the dynamic as well as structural features of the organizational control system.

The NIDA survey was almost ideally timed, in the period from August 1972 to February 1973, to capture the full impact of the drug problem. This impact involved sharp increases, not only in illegal drug use and abuse by the young, but also in its coverage by the mass media, in public concern over the problem, and in governmental spending devoted to its control.

All the objective and mass-media measures of the problem peaked shortly before or while the NIDA survey was in the field. Public concern over drugs, as measured by the Gallup Poll on the most important national problem, was in its sharpest ascent at the time of the NIDA survey. Much of the organizational response to the drug problem, such as the shift of government resources to the new problem, may be related more to media coverage and public perceptions than to more objective measures.

Federal spending on the drug problem increased dramatically for fiscal 1971 and 1972, the years immediately preceding the NIDA survey. Massive shifts in government resources went to professionals in treatment and rehabilitation, research, and education, including those in community programs and neighborhood drug centers. Such shifts were the control-system response, at the national level, needed to generate professional behavior that would contain the drug problem at the level of community systems.

This suggests a possible link between theories of autonomous control systems and social control as seen in purposive-action theories, a topic that is taken up in the next chapter. This chapter has attempted to show one aspect of that link: governmental monies, the generalized medium by which macro-level response to a problem translates into control of that problem at lower systemic levels. Professional behavior can be influenced by higher-level resource shifts if these, in turn, translate into new positions and local resources and new opportunities for innovation and advancement. In other words, exogenous social change and control-system response, at the macro level, must be played out by individual actors in their pursuit of money, position, and power.

2. Control systems from exchange in networks: toward a synthesis of system and action theory

As suggested by the first chapter, the sudden emergence of the drug problem in the late 1960s might be viewed as a "disturbance" or "perturbation" of the organizational system intended to control illegal drug use and abuse by the young. In other words, the drug problem threatened to disrupt organizational control of deviance with respect to drugs (both medical and legal) in much the same way that, say, a sudden change in temperature threatens the control of a thermostatic system.

Unlike mechanical systems, however, which contain no independently behaving, purposive actors, an organizational control system's response to exogenous change can be seen in either of two analytically distinct ways. One way, what might be called the "autonomous-system" approach, can also apply to mechanical and organic systems. The other perspective, what might be called the "purposive-action" approach, applies in particular to behavioral systems.

The same distinction, between system and action, is reflected in the term "social control," which has two distinct meanings in sociology, each with its own implications for general social theory. Social control can refer to those processes (formal or informal, manifest or latent, coercive or persuasive) by which each member of a society orders and conditions conformity – or identifies and eliminates deviance – in fellow members (the purposive-action viewpoint). Alternatively, social control can refer to a cybernetic property of the larger social system, whereby social processes are maintained in equilibrium by some balance of forces: feedback or other "control" relations (the autonomous-system viewpoint).

Both the system and action perspectives on social control might be applied to the organizational systems – educational, medical, and legal – that attempt to control illegal drug use and abuse by youth, and to those systems' response to the drug problem in the late 1960s. These two perspectives are introduced in the next two sections. Later sections of this chapter elaborate certain theoretical and methodological implications toward a synthesis of the system and action approaches to social theory.

31

The purposive-action perspective

Individual behavior necessary for control to obtain in an organizational system is generated, at the level of purposive action, by shifts in rewards – money, position, prestige, opportunity for innovation and advancement, etc. – at the more macro levels. As seen in the last chapter, federal spending on the drug problem increased dramatically as it burst upon the public consciousness, with massive shifts in government resources to professionals in treatment and rehabilitation, research, and education, including those in community programs and neighborhood drug centers. Such shifts in spending are one predictable response whenever a formerly minor or at least contained form of deviance or other social problem suddenly looms large, with an ensuing strain on various situational facilities.[1]

Shifts of government monies and other resources to the new problem sets off a chain of reactions: Relevant specialties are given higher-level positions and greater prominence in a wide range of organizations; specialists in these areas, suddenly in short supply, command greater salaries; the prestige of the specialties themselves rises relative to that of other subfields. The result is that professionals from a wide variety of related fields scramble to acquire credentials of "expertise" in the new problem. In the case of the drug problem, many social scientists were recruited into the study of social deviance and, within that subfield, into the study of illegal drug use and abuse. One example is provided by the sociologists who worked on the NIDA survey (see Appendix A) and similar research efforts during the early 1970s.

If the motivations for specialization in a new social problem are obvious to those in related professions, so too are the strategies for obtaining the requisite "expertise." In the case of the drug problem, specialization meant first of all a return to the classroom. For the dozen different professions in the NIDA survey of Baltimore and San Francisco, 67 percent of respondents report no drug-specific training as part of their formal professional education, and the percentage is only slightly lower (59 percent) for the hundred or so in each city identified by their peers as drug specialists.[2] Of the same sample, 59 percent report no post degree academic training in drugs either, but the figure for specialists is only 28 percent; 63 percent of this latter group report 11 or more academic credit hours of post degree training on drugs. In other words, specialization in the drug problem implied for many some formal academic training, which was usually obtained well after completion of a professional degree.

Those who chose to specialize in the control of illegal drug use and abuse among youth thus came to acquire a vested interest in a social problem, in effect, not only because of their investment in extraprofessional training, but also because of the personal and material rewards that accrue to experts and specialists in areas of expanding importance. Continued specialization in the problem, however, depended on a steady supply of young drug users (except perhaps for those specialists in the secondary activities of information generation and transmission). Hence young drug users came to acquire many of the system characteristics of a scarce economic commodity. For this reason, power and status tended to accrue to those organizational positions with greatest "nodality" of exchange (i.e., those located at the junctions of referral traffic).

Drug information and advice, in contrast to referrals of drug users, exhibit markedly different commodity properties. As just shown, information essential to the control of illegal drug use, and to drug abuse treatment, largely postdates the formal training for most professions. It is highly esoteric in its technical and subcultural aspects, and is continually changing with both the discovery and development of new drugs and drug habits and the expansion of an extensive and well-funded research effort in this area. Information and advice, under such circumstances, acquires a value in exchange second only to that of drug users themselves. Unlike users, however, information can be contributed multiple times to multiple recipients with relatively little loss (except perhaps in time) to the donor in the exchange.

It is for these reasons that expert status – and resources and power – tend to shift to those specialists whose positions in interorganizational networks of professional exchange are ones of information sources and referral sinks. As will be demonstrated in the next chapter, positional and reputational leaders among professionals in Baltimore and San Francisco were typically sources of drug information and advice – and sinks for referrals of young drug users – in their local drug-abuse communities. The former status appears to be the initial cause of expert standing, at least in the sense that it is temporally prior: There are some experts who are informational sources, many who are both that and referral sinks, but almost none who are only the latter or neither. Recognition as an expert, in turn, is a better predictor than years of training of the various rewards that accrue to drug-abuse professionals.

From the perspective of purposive action, then, professionals were drawn to specialization in the drug problem by shifts in control-system resources – with resultant shifts in prestige, opportunities for innovation and advancement, and power – to the new problem. The result was a scramble to acquire "expertise," which for many professionals meant additional formal training. This investment implied an increased stake in the social problem, which in turn depended upon a steady supply of young drug users and of up-to-date drug information and advice. From this argument we might deduce that, in general, professionals who attempt to capitalize on social change to advance their own careers will control events to become central nodes (sociometric "stars," in an earlier terminology) in networks of information and referral exchange.

The autonomous-system perspective

The social control of deviance described in the previous section can also be viewed, from the perspective of purposive action, as an autonomous or cybernetic control system. This control system includes three major organizational spheres: medical, legal, and educational.

As mentioned in the previous chapter, youth might be deviant with respect to drugs in two distinct ways – one medical (through drug abuse), the other legal (involving the use of illegal drugs). Legal deviance, with respect to both formal law and unwritten police procedures, includes drug possession and use, trafficking, and noncommercial distribution and sales. Medical deviance includes such problems as occasional and chronic illness, psychological and physiological dependence and addiction, psychological and physical injury, and other medical crises demanding emergency treatment or rehabilitation.

The social control of drug use among youth is institutionalized at the community level in two formal organizational systems that correspond to its medical and legal deviant modes: the health system, both public and private, and the law-enforcement and criminal-justice system. The health system includes hospitals, research centers, the public-health department, private health centers, private group and individual medical practices, pharmacies, and programs and units specialized in drug problems. It is staffed by such professions as psychiatrist and physician, pharmacological and medical researcher, pharmacist, and nurse. The community legal system includes federal, state, and local courts; police and probation departments; jails and prisons; and private legal practices. It is staffed by such professions as judge, police and prison administrator, probation and parole officer, and lawyer.

When youth are not deviant in either health or law, they are ordinarily the professional responsibility of a third organizational system, the community-education system. This system includes both the public-school system and private schools, religious and other; it is staffed by such professions as school administrator and counselor, teacher, psychologist, and social worker. Thus the total organizational system for the control of deviant drug-using youth involves not only the police and courts, jails and probation departments, but also hospitals, schools, and other medical and youth-related organizations.

Such a system can be viewed from the purposive-action perspective, of course, in that it is staffed by professionals motivated by personal self-interests like those discussed in the previous section – salary or fees, professional reputation, promotion, power, opportunities for innovation, perhaps to do good. The individual behavior of these separate actors nevertheless aggregates in a macro-level system of social control whereby the social processes governing the use of psychoactive drugs are maintained in equilibrium by some balance of forces.

In terms of the three major organizational spheres, we might expect controlled flows of authority for deviant youths from the educational to the medical and legal spheres and a feedback flow of current drug information and advice back to the educational sphere.[3] This expectation will be tested formally in Chapter 4. As a first approximation of the control of deviance with respect to drugs as an autonomous system, however, it might be helpful to evoke the temporal sequence developed by Smelser (1962, chs. 2 and 3) to explain various forms of collective behavior.

Smelser erects a hierarchy running from values through norms and mobilization in organized roles down to situational facilities (p. 32). "Strain at any level of any component will 'show up' first at the lower, more operative levels," according to Smelser (p. 49). By his model, the first strains in social control resulting from a sudden increase in drug use ought to be felt in the family, the institution with primary responsibility for the socialization of youth. In terms of the three organizational control systems just discussed, the earliest strains are likely to be felt by professionals in the educational system, which has primary *organizational* responsibility for socialization. Administrators, counselors, and teachers will see a form of deviance that they once associated with rebellious and even disturbed youth, lower social and economic strata, and ethnic minorities quite rapidly become the basis for the prevailing youth culture. This strain will appear as what Smelser (1962, following Parsons and Shils 1951) calls an organization's "situational facilities," involving here a lack of knowledge of psychoactive drugs and drug problems, a shortage of personnnel with training and experience in drug abuse by youth, a lack of educational and counseling materials on the subject, etc.

In Smelser's model, the second strain on the control system as the educational system mobilizes to meet the drug problem ought to be on the channels of information and referral exchange between this system and the medical and legal systems. Professionals in the schools will increase their demands on the medical system, for example, for specialized pharmacological knowledge, for training in drug education and rehabilitation, for local emergency treatment, etc. Similarly, they will increase their demands on the legal system for advice from lawyers and for working contacts with law-enforcement and particularly narcotics officials. These strains on the "channels" of the autonomous control system are primarily felt – by individuals – as a perceived lack of contacts in other organizations, particularly those in functionally distinct subsystems.

A third implication of Smelser's model, after contacts are eventually increased across subsystem boundaries and interprofessional referral channels are strengthened, is that informational feedback from higher-level sectors (i.e., those more specialized, in control of deviance among youth with respect to drugs, than the educational one) ought to tend to discourage further increases in referral flows. This is because the other sectors (the medical and legal sectors) are themselves experiencing facility strains, at least while the rate of drug abuse is in its steepest rise. This feedback, combined with an organization's internal facility strains, creates an added strain on norms – on the rules governing acceptable youth behavior, definitions of drug "use" and "abuse," and the decision whether to refer youth to either the medical or the legal subsystems.

The temporal sequence of these three strains on the organizational system for the control of deviance among youth with respect to drugs – strains passing from organizational facilities to mobilization channels to norms – parallels Smelser's sequence for collective behavior. Of course, not all his conceptual apparatus can be made to fit perfectly the organizational response to the drug problem.[4] What is useful about his collective behavior model, however, is his insight that strain begins at the lower material level, that causation runs upward from the objective to the more subjective levels, and that causes later reverberate downward in the opposite direction. Thus "any redefinition of a component of social action necessarily makes for re-adjustment in those components below it, but not necessarily in those above it" (Smelser 1962, p. 33).

This latter type of causation is precisely the dynamic given here to normative change (organizational strains caused by the drug problem appeared to stop short of the value level). Normative change is found to depend on lower-level material changes, that is, on changes in flows of drug information and advice and young-user referrals, and in turn serves to regulate these flows. That community systems for the control of illegal drug use and abuse by the young are indeed control systems in this sense will be tested in Chapter 4. A direct fit of a control-system model to the NIDA survey data will be attempted in Chapter 5.

To summarize this section, then, the organizational system for the control of deviance among youth with respect to drugs can be viewed as an autonomous or cybernetic control system as well as a system of independent, purposive actors. From the autonomous-system perspective, the control of deviance is maintained through the exchange of information and referrals among three organizational spheres: medical, legal, and educational. Controlled flows of authority for deviant youths pass from the educational to the medical and legal spheres, with a feedback flow of current drug information and advice to education. One useful approximation of this system is afforded by Smelser's collective-behavior model, which suggests that strains on control will pass from organizational facilities to mobilization channels to norms, with normative changes in turn serving to regulate information and referral flows through mobilization channels.

System and action theory

As demonstrated by the previous two sections, the same social phenomena can be viewed from radically different analytical perspectives. Information and referral flows among professionals, for example, can be explained as strategies to increase individual rewards, on the action level; the same flows can be viewed as media of feedback and strain, respectively, in an autonomous control system. Such differing views of the same social phenomena suggest the possibility of synthesizing the two alternative approaches to social theory.

These approaches are known by a variety of different names, depending on the theoretical tradition or school, the particular theorists involved, and sometimes the particular treatment or variety of perspective. The autonomous-system approach views social phenomena as a set of abstractable variables, interrelated by a usually complex set of causal relations, which are ordinarily in some state of equilibrium, whether stable or dynamic. The purposive-action approach, in contrast, views social phenomena as involving a finite set of actors, each possessing a set of interests and attempting to control a set of events in furtherance of those interests. Neither of these approaches is more "correct" than the other, of course; each attends to different aspects – different theoretical levels – of any given set of social relations.

The distinction does have certain philosophical implications, however. As Marx (1852/1963) stated the analytical problem, "Men make their own history, but they do not make it just as they please; they do not make it under circumstances chosen by themselves, but under circumstances directly encountered, given and transmitted from the past" (p. 15). Marx's initial independent clause presents the purposive-action perspective, whereas the remainder of his statement gives the autonomous-system or structural view. The question that remains, as it does throughout Marx's writings, is the extent to which human destiny is strictly determined by scientific laws or is the product of free will.

The philosophical issue apparently informed at least the early development of the autonomous-system and purposive-action approaches to social science. Parsons has traced the two types of theory, which he labels the "individualistic" and "collectivistic" orientations of sociology, to British Protestantism and French Catholicism, respectively, beginning in the seventeenth century. Modern sociological theory, Parsons maintains, is the result of a special "marriage" of these traditions (1961a, pp. 86–7). Later Parsons identified the individualistic tradition as one of "English utilitarianism," which he links with "economics, with biological thought and the beginnings of anthropology as a discipline" (1967, p. 642). Stinchcombe also poses the distinction as one between the utilitarian and antiutilitarian traditions (1977, p. 876).

One recent attempt to grapple with these competing approaches is that of James Coleman (1975), who describes his own intellectual development from autonomous-system to purposive-action theorizing. To explain a conflict in his earlier style, Coleman writes, "I would have seen the conflict more nearly as an autonomous process, self-sustaining and with an internal logic and dynamic, which worked itself out. In short, my description of the conflict some years ago would have described the properties of the conflict through time as a dynamic observable phenomenon, much as one would describe the properties of a tornado or other physical phenomenon over time" (1975, p. 77). In Coleman's words, his current approach includes the terms "actors, events, interest and control, [and] views the conflict as inhabited by purposive actors, whose action is predictable from their interests and control and whose joint action gives rise to the dynamic phenomena of proliferation of issues, proliferation of actors, and the like that I might have observed some years ago" (1975, p. 77).

This purposive-action approach was, two generations ago, the dominant paradigm in American sociology, as established by Parsons in *The Structure of Social Action* (1937). This first of Parsons's major works considerably advanced purposive-action theory (see especially the quasi-mathematical summary, pp. 77–82), a fact not lost on Coleman (1975, p. 79). Although Parsons did not abandon the action element in his work, he gradually came to emphasize "emergent" properties of action, particularly role differentiation and integration, and the resultant problems of coordination, hierarchy, control, etc. Such autonomous-system properties are – for most practical purposes – analytically separable from Parsons's early preoccupation with unit acts, means and ends, perfect and imperfect knowledge, etc. (for a related analysis, see Scott 1963).

The autonomous-system model was developed, by Parsons and others, in response to the need to account for a social order that no one, through his or her immediate actions, was directly concerned with maintaining. From this need derives a core assumption about the cybernetic control of a macro-level system, namely, that this is not intended by any particular individual to be control as such. If cybernetic control could be explained by individual motivations, there would be no need for a systems perspective; the purposive-action approach alone would suffice.

Among the autonomous-system approaches to social theory can be included the later work of Parsons (1951, 1960, 1961b), particularly his emphasis on the integrative and adaptive functions of social systems. Distinctly different and separate traditions upholding a systems perspective include general demographic theory (Stinchcombe 1968, pp. 60–79), Ogburn's technological determinism (1922/1966), ecological theories like those of Hawley (1950) and Duncan (1964), the conflict theory of Simmel (1955) and Coser (1956), and the French variety of exchange theory (Levi-Strauss 1949/1969).

Perhaps the most ambitious attempt at autonomous-system theory has been the "general-systems" movement, which grew out of developments in servomechanisms, information and communication theory, and computers after World War II (a more extensive treatment of this development is found in Chapter 4). General-system theory was heralded by some (e.g., Bertalanffy 1968) as a new synthesis of the natural and social sciences. A Society for General System Theory was established at the Annual Meeting of the American Association for the Advancement of Science in 1954, and there have been attempts to incorporate the movement into economics (Boulding 1956a, 1956b), political science (Deutsch 1963), and sociology

(Buckley 1967, 1968). The recent decline of interest in general-systems theory, and alternative possibilities for integrating control-system and network approaches, are discussed in Chapter 4.

Prominent among the purposive-action approaches to social theory, as already mentioned, is the early action theory of Parsons (1937), plus Parsons's later work on actor-orientation (1961a) and his continuing interest in goal attainment and pattern-maintenance. Other early variations on action approaches include social interactionism (Mead 1934, 1956) and theories of psychological and material motivation (Homans 1950).[5] Exchange theory was first advanced along the lines of purposive action by Homans (1961), who stressed that social theory must begin at the level of individual actors (see also Homans 1964); later he lapsed into a behaviorism incompatible with the purposive grounding of exchange theory (Homans 1969). Exchange theory continues along actionist lines in the work of Blau (1964) and Emerson (1972), a topic to be taken up in the next chapter. Limited application of the purposive-action approach can also be found in other social sciences, most notably psychology (Miller, Galanter, and Pribram 1960; Powers 1973), political science (Riker and Ordeshook 1973) and economics (Arrow 1959, Olson 1965).

Comparing the two approaches on change and control

One major difference between the autonomous-system and purposive-action approaches to social theory lies in those phenomena that they choose to ignore or at least give less emphasis. Action theories do not attempt to explain the patterns of control required at the system level, nor the control function of systemwide values and norms. Such theories do address individual behavior in collective interactions and alliances. System theories, in contrast, do not attempt to account for personal motivations and behavior, nor to explain how individual actions aggregate in the control behavior required of a social system. Such theories do predict control relationships among system variables, however, as well as control patterns among component subsystems.

Wallace (1975) declares this the "crucial difference" between the autonomous-system and purposive-action approaches (which he calls "social structuralist theory" and "social actionist theory"): "Social structuralist theory treats purposiveness and other subjective orientational factors as at least secondary and at most irrelevant social phenomena, while these factors are primary in social actionist theory . . . This is the real significance of Peter Blau's point that the social-structural view emphasizes 'differentiation' and 'heterogeneity' and that 'value orientations are taken into account only indirectly . . . ' Differentiation and heterogeneity . . . refer to variability in the things people do, and objectively can do, to each other . . . " (pp. 121–2).[6]

The interface of the system and action approaches lies in the broad area that Merton (1975) has termed "structural analysis" (for discussions, see Loomis and Loomis 1961, Barbano 1968, Wallace 1969, Mulkay 1971, Stinchcombe 1975). "Structural analysis in sociology must deal successively with micro- and macro-level phenomena," according to Merton; "it therefore confronts the formidable problem . . . of developing concepts, methods, and data for linking micro- and macro-analysis" (p. 34).[7]

An analytic summary of the way structural analysis bridges "the micro–macro gap," a way similar to that suggested by Smelser (1977), is given by Stinchcombe (1975): "The core process conceived as central to social structure is the choice between socially structured alternatives. This differs from the choice process of economic theory, in which the alternatives are conceived to have inherent utilities [also true of recent versions of action theory, e.g., Coleman 1975]. It differs from the choice process of learning theory, in which the alternatives are conceived to emit reinforcing or extinguishing stimuli. It differs from both of these in that . . . the utility or reinforcement of a particular alternative choice is thought of as socially established, as part of the institutional order" (p. 197).

Hence the central problem of Mertonian structural analysis, as it translates into a synthesis of the autonomous-system and purposive-action approaches, is to demonstrate how system-level variables (values, norms, institutional arrangements, etc.) structure the alternatives and utilities of individual actors. This task is particularly difficult in explanations of social change, where system changes must be shown to modify individual behavior in a direction consistent with control at the more macro level.

Nowhere do the system and action approaches differ more sharply than in their explanations of social change. Because action theorists view change as a product of purposive behavior, they seek explanations in prior self-interests, power relations, and control of events. Social change is seen, from the action perspective, as a product of purposive actors, whose actions may be predicted from their interests, power, and control relations. These relations generate a temporal progression of individual and joint actions and interactions, alliance formations and dissolutions, assistance and favor exchanges, proliferation of issues, possible addition of actors, etc.

System theorists, in contrast, view society as a self-sustaining process, with an internal logic and dynamic of its own; hence social change is viewed, from the systems perspective, by resort either to change in some variable(s) exogenous to the system, or by an ultimately unexplained change within the system itself. Such changes alter the balance of causal relationships within the system, with one of several possible effects: counter-action by the system ("tension-management," in Parsons's term), movement to a qualitatively different stable equilibrium, initiation of a dynamic or "moving" equilibrium, or total system breakdown and revolutionary change ("morphogenesis," in the biological sense: see Thom 1975).

The containment or control of change is the domain of control-system engineering, including operations research and human engineering. These applied systems sciences grew out of developments in the late 1940s in information theory and cybernetics (Wiener 1948, 1950; Shannon and Weaver 1949) and contemporaneous work on servomechanisms (Bode 1945; James, Nichols, and Phillips 1947; Brown and Campbell 1948); this literature is discussed in Chapter 4. In a control system, change is controlled or contained through restoration of an equilibrium among causal relationships within the system. Control can result from an autonomous process (overcrowding, for example, which may serve to "control" an increased birthrate in a demographic model); it can also result from a purposively designed cybernetic or control process (such as a system for law enforcement, which might attempt to "control" an increase in the rate of crime). In both types of systems, however, the control process is autonomous to the action level.

As suggested earlier, control behavior is the unifying concept shared by both autonomous-system and purposive-action approaches to social theory. Action theories address individual attempts to control events, as well as the aggregation of individual behavior in collective interactions and alliances. System theories, in contrast, predict control relationships among system variables, as well as control patterns among component subsystems. Hence control behavior is directed at other actors and events on the level of purposive action and at changes in exogenous variables and relationships on the system level. Other actors and events, and changes in exogenous variables and relationships, constitute environments to be controlled. A second concept common to both the autonomous-system and purposive-action approaches is that of informational feedback from the environment, with the state of control at time t_0 determining control relations at time t_1.

Considered separately, neither the autonomous-system nor purposive-action perspective provides a wholly adequate framework for the explanation of social change. The action approach cannot account for patterns of control required at the system level, nor for the control function of systemwide values and norms. The system approach, in contrast, cannot account for individual motivations and behavior, nor explain how individual actions aggregate in the control behavior required of a social system. The concept of control of a particular environment – against exogenous change, via informational feedback – does provide the elements, in both systems and action models, for a synthesis of the two approaches.

What would such a synthesis have to accomplish? It would have to show how, as a result of some change in a macro-level control system, the alternatives and utilities of individual actors change so as to restore control at the higher level. This modification of behavior cannot be planned or intended to restore system control, however; if it were, action theory alone would suffice, and there would be no need for an autonomous-system perspective. On the other hand, control of a system cannot be maintained except through the behavior of individuals – so that macro-level control must be an unintended by-product from the viewpoint of individual, self-oriented behavior.

Toward a method

Control-systems engineering, as already mentioned, grew out of information theory and cybernetics. One trend in this development as been the "general-systems" movement, as represented in sociology by the work of Parsons (1951), Buckley (1967), and others (Buckley 1968). The central concept in cybernetic systems is that of *flows* among functionally specialized subsystems that are controlled by opposite flows of informational feedback.

As in any applied science, the success of systems modeling and analysis depends on quantification through precise measurement. This requirement has precluded any wholesale borrowing of control-systems ideas by social scientists. Flows of social information and socially controlled commodities (including social deviance) have proved difficult to conceptualize and have largely eluded measurement and systematic analysis. Renewed hope for a breakthrough has recently arisen from an unexpected source: the rapid developments in what has come to be subsumed under the heading "social networks" (Barnes 1969; Mitchell 1969b; White, Boorman, and Breiger 1976).

Central to the network literature is the representation of social relationships as links between nodes, which represent individual persons, groups, or categories. These links might be considered, in the aggregate, as representing the flows between functionally specialized subsystems in a more macro-level cybernetic system. For example, the level of information and referral exchange among professions is, to the action level, what the level of input–

output flows of goods and services among industrial sectors is to the individual firm, as in the pioneering work of Leontief (1951, 1966). Just as input–output flows are aggregates of values for individual firms, information and referral flows – among professions *qua* professions – must be aggregates of the behavior of individual professionals.

One possible means of constructing a system-level measure of flow is suggested by the literature on an important property of social networks, namely *density*, which is usually defined as the ratio of the numbers of links actually observed to the number theoretically possible (Kephart 1950; Barnes 1969, pp. 61–4). Density has been found to have substantive importance by a number of researchers: Festinger, Schachter, and Back (1950, ch. 5) consider it a measure of small-group cohesion; Bott (1957) treats it as an indicator of group closure (see also Homans 1961); Mayer (1961) uses it to indicate the degree of community modernization (see also Tilly 1969).

Survey-research methods provide an unusual opportunity to determine links, from the perspective of individual respondents, and hence to estimate density in the higher-level social networks. Unfortunately, the practicality of using density as a measure of system-level flow is an inverse function of population size; in systems with only several hundred actors, the large number of potential links makes the measurement of flows intractable except by means of sampling. Sampling methodology in social science has been mostly confined to a peculiarly statistical concept of "population," however; there has been relatively little work on network sampling.

Recent developments in sampling large-scale social networks for survey research (Beniger 1976; Granovetter 1976), as discussed in the next chapter, seem particularly promising as a means to link the social-network literature to empirical work on control systems. Attention to system-level flows, rather than to characteristics of individuals (like positional and reputational status) and individual behavior brings survey research back to what are central sociological questions regarding the structure of relationships among individual actors, questions often ignored by survey researchers (for concurring views, see Coleman 1958; Laumann and Pappi 1976, p. 146).

Because flows at the system level are really aggregates of exchanges among individuals, they are ultimately determined – on the level of purposive action – by principles of social-exchange theory. For example, flows of information and referrals among professions, in the macro-level system for the control of deviance among youth with respect to drugs, must be subject to the norms of restricted and generalized exchange, which Levi-Strauss (1949/ 1969) has likened to "two different forms of mechanical solidarity" (pp. iii–

iv, n. 2). One such norm, of restricted exchange, is what Gouldner (1960) calls "the norm of reciprocity."

It is at precisely this interface, where the norms governing social exchange – on the level of purposive action – regulate flows among functionally specialized components of a more macro-level control system, that a synthesis of the system and action perspectives may be attempted. Purposive interpersonal exchanges aggregate in control-system flows; conversely, requirements of flows in a cybernetic system structure exchanges at the action level.

Attempts at synthesis at this level are not new to social theory. Malinowski's concept of "circular" exchange, for example, which is simultaneously generalized and restricted exchange, does bridge "the micro–macro gap": The restricted exchange of Necklace and Armshell, between any two Kula partners, is accomplished to fill psychological needs; the generalized circular exchange of both items serves to integrate Trobriand society (Malinowski 1922). Similarly, both Homans (1961) and Blau (1964) employ the concept of "indirect exchange," institutionalized behavior in which roles and norms replace individual actors in social exchanges, the "processes by which institutions develop out of elementary social behavior – the increasing roundaboutness of the exchange of rewards, which is sometimes called the increasing division of labor" (Homans 1961, p. 385). Blau especially is concerned with emergent collective phenomena in the development of psychological processes into complex social structures.

What is new about the proposed synthesis of the autonomous-system and purposive-action perspectives is that it enables precise measurement of relevant features and hence systematic modeling and testing. All three constituent approaches – control systems, social networks, and exchange theory – have well-developed methodologies. A major goal of this study, then, is to integrate the separate methods of control, networks, and exchange.

A synthetic model:
interpersonal exchanges as system flows

The crucial question outstanding in the system and action perspectives taken together is how individual actions aggregate in the cybernetic patterns required of a social-control system or, conversely, how such systems communicate – in the broadest sense of that term – the requisite patterns of behavior to individual actors. The answer developed here combines system-level strain and change – in organizational facilities, mobilization channels, and norms – with the pursuit of generalized media of exchange on the action level.

Generalized media of exchange, discussed more fully in the next section, are socially valued commodities like money and authority. In specialized control systems, among specialized individuals, exchange commodities might be as specialized as citations (as in communities of scientists) or professional referrals (among professionals and professions, as with those involved in community systems for the control of illegal drug use and abuse among the young). Individual actors seek such commodities because they constitute generalized media, that is, media that translate status and rewards across organizational, community, and systems boundaries.

The movement of such commodities is also regulated by systemwide norms, defined here as the prevailing rules at decision nodes governing the flow of commodities. Most applications of the term "norm," as most commonly found in sociology, can be modeled in this way. Flows inappropriate to system-level control will either overburden or underutilize system capabilities: This, in turn, will cause normative strain and change among actors supplying commodity flows, with the result of tightening or loosening, respectively, flows of the commodities in question. In this way, normative change – plus such more mundane system variables as convenience in the use of organizational facilities, and burden on channels of exchange and communication – structure the alternatives and utilities of individual actors.

When the environment of any controlling unit (individual or group, system or subsystem) is another such controlling unit, flows become mutually controlled exchanges of both commodities and information about them (feedback in the cybernetic sense). On the action level, individuals and groups will be seen to control commodity exchanges in pursuit of personal self-interests; these exchanges will aggregate in flows essential for the control of commodities at the system level. Informational feedback, a requisite of system-level control, is also exchanged in furtherance of individual goals at the level of purposive action.

It remains to examine whether interorganizational networks of information and referral exchange among professionals, on the community level, constitute a cybernetic system for the control of deviance among youths with respect to drugs. Youths who are deviant – medically, legally, or both – obviously constitute the commodity to be controlled by such a system (in the sense that, say, heat is the commodity controlled by a thermostatic system). At the level of purposive action, in the interpersonal exchanges among professionals, deviant youth become a scarce economic commodity known as "referrals." These referrals constitute a generalized medium that translates status as a drug "specialist" and "expert" across organizational boundaries – increasingly valuable to actors as system resources shift to this problem.

The three spheres of organized activity that have been outlined – educational, medical, and legal – might constitute functionally separate components of a macro-level control system. To do so, the three spheres must manifest two types of flows: (1) a *controlled-commodity flow*, here the flow of authority for deviant youths from the educational to the medical and legal spheres, and (2) a *feedback flow*, here the flow of drug information and advice back to the educational sphere (hence the term "feedback" for this "backward" flow of information). In other words, of the 12 possible directed informational and referral flows among the 3 spheres of organizational activity, empirical investigation ought to find a predominance of 4 flows: user referrals *from* the educational *to* the medical and legal spheres, and informational feedback in the *opposite* directions; the 4 reverse flows ought to be least prominent, with the 4 flows between the medical and legal spheres of intermediate importance (each of these hypotheses is tested in Chapter 4; the control-system model as a whole is fitted to the NIDA survey data in Chapter 5).

Thus control theory serves to explain the *pattern* of information and referral flows, on the system level, among the educational, medical, legal, and counseling spheres of organizational activity. What such a system approach does not explain, however, because it does not account for individual motivations, special interests, and goals, is how and why individuals come to make the information and referral exchanges necessary for cybernetic control of deviance to obtain at the system level.

This question is especially problematical, in the case of referrals of young drug users, because of the organizational factors working *against* their movement, particularly in exchange for drug information and advice. An extensive literature on formal organizations (March and Simon 1958, Blau and Scott 1962, Aldrich 1979) establishes that information tends to enter organizational hierarchies at the top, whereas work with people (as customers, students, patients, etc.) tends to concentrate near the bottom. In other words, organizational information is positively correlated with hierarchical standing, whereas people-commodities (as processed by the organization) are negatively correlated with such standing. These status associations impede both the flows of information downward and of commodity referrals upward. The upward flow of referrals, for example, is minimal, not only because such referrals imply lesser competence of the sender, relative to the receiver, but also because they represent extra, lower-status work for the receiver.

How, then, do school administrators and counselors learn of psychologists and physicians, or of probation officers and lawyers, with specialized knowledge and interest in the drug problems of youth? Why do such specialists accept referrals from the education sphere, and reciprocate with drug-related information? These information and referral exchanges, essential for the control of deviance at the system level, remain problematical at the level of purposive action. It will therefore be necessary to extend control theory to this level, to answer the motivational questions still outstanding.

Professionals are drawn to specialization in a new problem by shifts in control-system resources – with resultant shifts in prestige, opportunities for innovation and advancement, and power. New agencies and programs are instituted from the federal to the neighborhood level; specialists in the problem, suddenly in short supply, can command higher positions and salaries; related specialties gain in prominence in formal organizations working on the problem; the same specialties also gain in status and recruits, relative to other subfields, in a range of disciplines and professions.

For professionals involved with the drug problem, as shown by data presented earlier in this chapter, specialization usually meant additional formal training. Returns on this investment were limited, however, by at least two scarce commodities: the number of high-status positions in local drug-abuse communities, and the number of actual drug users, control of whom is rewarded by the community positions. Even though the number of drug users fluctuates according to the rate of identification activity, and through definitional and normative changes, the supply of users is ultimately limited.

Because users are necessary for professionals seeking similarly limited rewards in the drug-abuse community, control theory predicts that the exchange of user referrals (and drug-related information necessary for their control) will approximate a model of economic competition for scarce resources. As will be shown in the next chapter, standing as a specialist in drug-abuse communities is correlated with the number of professions from which referrals are received, with the number of professions supplied information, and hence with centrality in the interprofessional network of information and referral exchange. This standing, in turn, is correlated with formal positions as treatment and prevention administrators, occupational prestige, and stratification of professions on exchange dominance.

To maximize these returns on personal investments in the drug problem, the strategy for specialists is to exchange drug-related information for user referrals with as many nonspecialists as possible. Such exchanges might be seen as reciprocal control relations between nonspecialist and specialist, or between two specialists in different subject areas (possibly two different professions), with each party to the exchange seeking to maximize its own self-interests. That is, the nonspecialist needs to *make* referrals and seeks to maximize the competence of the specialist to whom they are sent; this typically is someone who has previously supplied the nonspecialist with drug-related information. The specialist, in contrast, needs to *acquire* referrals, to advance standing in the local drug-abuse community; hence specialists seek to maximize their circles of nonspecialist contacts by disseminating specialized information. In exchanges between two specialists, information and referrals will pass in both directions – for the same dual motives of acquiring referrals and maximizing the competency of one's contacts – in double-control relationships.

Thus control theory suggests an answer, on the level of purposive action, to the questions of how and why individuals come to make the informational and referral exchanges necessary for cybernetic control of deviance to obtain on the system level. In the informal drug-abuse community generated by the specialists themselves, through their exchange behavior, information is beneficial to give away, whereas referrals are beneficial to receive (just the opposites of the incentives prevailing in formal organizations). Certain formal positions (head of a police department's juvenile or narcotics bureaus, of the drug-treatment facility at a major hospital, etc.) will ordinarily assure network centrality, and hence facilitate informal exchange behavior. Extra-organizational maneuvering can also secure centrality in local drug-abuse networks, however, and these informal roles may serve as criteria for later hiring in organizational positions. Specialists will therefore attempt to establish themselves as information sources, whether formal or informal, and authority for deviants will readily pass to the specialists in central network positions. In this way, an interorganizational network of individuals establishes both the referral flows – and the reciprocal feedback channels – necessary for the control of social change at the system level.

Generalized media of exchange

Young drug users, as professional referrals, share two characteristics of generalized symbolic media of exchange with the ideal-typical medium, money, as identified by the classical economists early in the nineteenth century (Mill 1909, Marshall 1948). First, drug users – like money – have no value in use, but considerable value in exchange. Indeed, the number of drug users a professional typically deals with directly, and the percentage of work time actually spent with users themselves, are negatively correlated with standing in an organization or with professional prestige (such correlations with "direct client contacts" hold generally in organizations, e.g., in contacts with patrons in a bank or with students in a university). The number of referrals received from other professionals has just the opposite correlations, however, because making a referral carries the implicit acknowledgment of lack of authority, specialization, or expertise (occasionally it may have a contrary connotation, e.g., lack of time by an overburdened expert; but professionals generally are careful to exclude this circumstance from their usage of the term "referral").

The second characteristic of generalized symbolic media that referrals share with money is that both function as measures of value. The number of referrals is an approximate measure of a professional's standing in the drug community, whether his or her functional contribution is as a medical researcher, criminal defense lawyer, or school drug counselor. The number of referrals also serves as a measure of the *relative* severity of problems – and of the urgency of resource reallocation – among widely disparate sectors. Thus referrals serve to integrate the highly differentiated and organizationally scattered components of the total community system for control of illegal drug use and abuse, which is the major function of any generalized medium.

Professional referrals also meet most of Parsons's other criteria for what he terms "generalized symbolic media of interchange," including institutionalization, specificity of meaning, and non-zero-sum character in some contexts (1975, pp. 95–6). One criterion that referrals do not appear to meet is what Parsons calls "circulability": "any medium should be subject to transfer of control from one acting unit to another in some kind of interchange transactions" (p. 96). As already indicated, referrals do not constitute a physical flow; a judge might refer a drug user to a physician, for example, without losing responsibility for the user in a separate sense (legal as distinct from medical).

Wallace (1975) argues, "in explicit difference with Parsons but in accord with classical physics," that media need not circulate as they translate (p. 128), which is the view adopted here. This may indeed be what Parsons means by his criterion that a medium "could not have a zero-sum character attributed to it in all contexts" (1975, p. 96) as, in the previous example, a single user might simultaneously generate referrals of both medical and legal authority. In this case, Parsons's criteria of circulability and non-zero-sum character appear to be mutually exclusive, at least in those contexts where the latter obtains.

Thus referrals of young drug users constitute a generalized medium of exchange, that is, one that translates status and rewards across organizational and system boundaries. This characteristic of user referrals makes them attractive to professionals in much the same way as other generalized media: money, political power, influence, etc. The attraction of referrals as media, in turn, accounts for the problem noted above, namely, that organizational factors work against the flows – of both information and referrals – required for cybernetic control to obtain in the higher-level, interorganizational system.

According to the literature, information tends to enter organizational hierarchies at the top, whereas work with people (as customers, students, patients, etc.) tends to concentrate near the bottom. In relations between organizations, in contrast, professionals seek to diffuse specialized information, and to accept user referrals to advance their own standing in informal local networks. As the next chapter will demonstrate, standing as a specialist in drug-abuse communities is correlated with the number of professions from which referrals are received and with the number of professions supplied with information. Both within and among formal organizations, however, information and referral flows carry opposite connotations: ‚information flow connotes the higher status of the receiver, relative to the sender, whereas referral flow connotes just the reverse. Why, then, are the attitudes toward such exchanges reversed when organizational professionals participate in interorganizational communities?

The answer is that formal organizations have highly institutionalized symbols – formal positions and lines of authority, plus various perquisites (title on the door, Bigelow on the floor, etc.) that translate status and rewards across all organizational contexts; hence, providing information and accepting referrals are not important requirements of individual status and carry few individual (i.e., extra-organizational) connotations in any case. Organizational symbols do *not* mediate well, however, across the many organizational and professional boundaries of informal networks like the drug-abuse community. How is a school administrator to assess the specialized drug training of scores of local psychologists, for example, or a lawyer to choose among hundreds of local physicians for specialized advice?

In contrast to organizational symbols, information and referral flows *do* mediate across organizational and professional boundaries in that they carry connotations of relative expertise – much as citation networks map the relative standing of scientific researchers. Sociologists of science have developed the social fact that flows of information and resources reveal relative standing into a formal methodology; professionals in local drug-abuse communities employ this fact somewhat less consciously, perhaps – but to the same end.

Professional referrals do not necessarily constitute a physical flow, in the sense that drug users themselves move from one organizational system to another, although this may often be the case. If it were always so, physical flows would be approximately equal in each direction in a system for the control of social deviance, because most deviants eventually return – however temporarily – to the nondeviant state or "source" (here represented by the educational sphere among organizations). Professional referrals do involve a flow of responsibility or authority over a drug user, however, with the implicit acknowledgment of lack of authority, specialization, or expertise on the part of the referrer vis-à-vis the recipient.

In this way, referrals serve as the medium – integrating organizations as diverse as research hospitals and high schools, police narcotics bureaus, and church youth groups – by which the needs of one sector are translated into performance in some other sector. Increases in referrals upward *within* an organization communicate lack of knowledge or capability at lower levels (i.e., a strain on "situational facilities") and may signal a need for increased resources. Similarly, rapid increases in user referrals from schools to hospitals, for example, translate the new drug problems of the youth culture into reallocations of medical resources, increased research on psychoactive drugs, etc. (this is not to say that such needs are not communicated in other ways, e.g., through increased government funding, or by increases in emergency cases).

By the same argument, drug-related information is also a generalized symbolic medium of exchange, by which the needs of one organization are translated into performance in some other organization. Organizations that depend on referrals for their existence (e.g., drug-rehabilitation programs), for example, will ordinarily attempt to establish themselves as sources of drug information for professionals and organizations with the potential to reciprocate with referrals. Because many professionals are interested in receiving referrals, for reasons already discussed, the struggle to establish oneself as a source of information to as many others as possible will generally prevail throughout the drug community (much as, for example, academics use citations – really a measure of information transmitted – as one criterion of their relative standing).

In contrast to user contacts, the amount of information possessed is positively correlated with organizational standing and professional prestige, and it is providing information rather than receiving it (just the reverse of referral relationships) that is similarly correlated. Like referrals, however, information has a non-zero-sum character, but not circulability, because information transmitted is not lost (the basic distinction between information and thermodynamic engineering). These similarities and differences among information and referral exchange and other generalized symbolic media suggest that that concept, although crucial to the internal integration of autonomous systems, is much more complicated than present theoretical treatments might indicate and merits further empirical investigation among a wide range of institutional systems.[8]

Summary

Two distinct types of social theory, the autonomous-system and purposive-action approaches, can be applied to organizational systems for the control of deviance and to the response of such systems to exogenous "disturbances" or "perturbations." As a case study of social change and its impact on an organizational control system, the drug problem of the late 1960s and early 1970s has been examined, in this chapter, from both the system and action perspectives.

Individually, neither perspective provides a wholly adequate framework for the explanation of system response to change. The concept of control, however, because it is common to both perspectives, does provide elements for a synthesis of the system and action approaches. Action theories address individual attempts to control events, whereas system theories predict control relationships among system variables. In each case, a particular environment is controlled, against exogenous change, via informational feedback.

Central to a control system is the concept of *flow*, both of the commodity controlled and of information in the opposite direction (the operational definition of "feedback"). System-level flows, in turn, can be measured by the density of interpersonal exchange networks, which might be expected to correlate positively with more direct but elusive measures of flows (numbers of referrals, bits of information, etc.). The network literature treats social relationships as links among nodes; these links might be considered, in the aggregate, as representing flows between functionally specialized subsystems in a more macro-level cybernetic system. Because system flows are aggregates of exchanges among individuals, they are ultimately determined – on the level of purposive action – by norms governing social exchange.

Thus it is at the interface between micro and macro theory, in the broad area that Merton has termed "structural analysis," that the synthesis of the system and action perspectives is attempted. The central problem is, as it was for Merton, to demonstrate how system-level variables (values, norms, institutional arrangements, etc.) structure the alternatives and utilities of individual actors.

The answer suggested here borrows freely from control-system engineering, with compatible elements taken from general-systems, social-network, and exchange approaches to social theory. Individual actors seek the commodities controlled by the higher-level system because these constitute generalized media, that is, media that translate status and rewards across organizational, community, and system boundaries. The movement of such commodities is also regulated by systemwide norms, defined here as the rules prevailing at decision nodes governing controlled flows. Flows inappropriate to system-level control will either overburden or underutilize system capabilities; this, in turn, will cause normative strain and change among actors supplying commodities and thereby tighten or loosen their flows. Thus normative changes structure the alternatives and utilities of individual actors – the solution to the problem of structural analysis.

In the case of the drug problem, the exchange value of young users is determined by their function as a generalized medium, one that translates into status as a specialist or drug "expert." Because the supply of young drug users is ultimately limited, however, control theory predicts that the exchange of user referrals, and of the drug-related information necessary for their control, will approximate a model of economic competition for scarce resources. Professionals who hope to capitalize on the drug problem to advance their careers will attempt to become central nodes in information and referral-exchange networks. Nonspecialists will seek to acquire information and make referrals to competent specialists; the latter will seek to acquire referrals using their specialized knowledge of drugs.

For a specialist on drug abuse to have other professionals asking for information or sending referrals is like money in the bank – in that such flows translate into both status and material rewards in the larger professional community. This explains a common irony of organizational life: The same individuals who cannot find time to diffuse information and who shun referrals within their own organization may actively seek referrals, and devote time to establishing themselves as informational sources, outside their own organization – even at much lower levels. The ranking methodologist in a sociology department, for example, does not ordinarily need problems to solve for faculty and students to maintain status, but will require a flow of queries from outside methodologists, and a flow of manuscripts from major journals, to maintain comparable status in methodology circles and the larger profession, where departmental reputations (for departmental work) do not mediate very well. In the same way, the ranking expert on drugs in, say, a social-welfare agency does not need internal referrals to maintain that status but does need referrals from outside professionals to claim similar status in the larger drug-abuse community.

This, then, is the synthetic model of control systems derived from exchange networks. Purposive interpersonal exchanges aggregate in control-system flows; requirements for the control of such flows structure networks of exchange at the action level. The latter occurs at decision nodes governing flows, where normative strain and change serve to regulate the flow of commodities controlled.

Such attempts at theoretical synthesis are, of course, not new. What is new about the integration of control, network, and exchange theory and methods as proposed in this chapter is that it enables the precise measurement of relevant features and hence systematic modeling and testing. The next chapter will establish a necessary (though not sufficient) condition for cybernetic control at the system level, namely, a means by which the self-interested control of information and referrals aggregates in the social exchanges needed for control of the drug problem to obtain at the system level. The other necessary condition for cybernetic control, the functional interrelationship of various specialized system components, will be the subject of Chapters 4 and 5. These three chapters, taken together, will serve to integrate, in a unified analysis of control through exchange networks, the autonomous-system and purposive-action approaches to social control.

3. Stratification in information and referral exchange

Information and referrals convey opposite statuses in exchange relationships. This simple fact reconciles individual motivation, on the level of purposive action, with the prerequisites of control in the higher-level cybernetic system. With respect to the system, the relationship might be translated: The commodity controlled, and information about that commodity, convey opposite statuses to actors through exchange; information confers higher status on the provider, relative to the receiver, whereas commodity flow confers just the reverse statuses. Conversely, for any pair of actors differing in status, information and referrals are likely to move in opposite directions – information downward, referrals upward.

The importance of this fact for the community control of deviant drug-using youth was suggested in the previous chapter. In the informal drug community generated by professionals themselves through their exchange behavior, information is beneficial to give away, whereas referrals of young users (the commodity controlled by the system) are beneficial to receive. Certain formal positions can assure network centrality in local drug-abuse networks, but extra-organizational maneuvering can also secure centrality – and these informal roles may serve as criteria for later hiring in formal positions. Professionals will therefore attempt to establish themselves as information sources, whether formal or informal, and authority for deviants will readily pass (in the form of professional referrals) to specialists in central network positions.

In this way, an interorganizational network establishes both the referral flows – and the reciprocal feedback channels – necessary for the control of social change at the system level. Reciprocal exchanges are precisely what is required of a cybernetic system, in which the flow of some commodity (like heat in a thermostatic system) is controlled via a flow of information about it in the opposite direction. In the community control of drug-using youth, deviants ought to flow to more specialized components: to drug specialists and administrators, on the individual level; to higher-status professions (with respect to the specialized functions of the control of drug abuse among

56

youth), on a more macro level; to specialized spheres of professional activity (involving medical and legal institutions), on the highest control-system level. Drug information and advice, in contrast, ought to flow in the opposite direction, from more to less specialized individuals, professions, and spheres of activity. This is the system's "feedback," the means by which the more specialized and higher-status professionals inform others about the current states of the system (about new drugs – and new symptoms – to monitor; about new enforcement and treatment procedures; about over-crowding or waiting periods in hospitals, courts, rehabilitation programs, etc.), and thus "control" (against changes exogenous to the system) the flow of drug-using deviants.

What is problematic about this model, as discussed in the previous chapter, is that organizational factors apparently work *against* the exchanges necessary for cybernetic control. The literature on formal organizations suggests that information tends to enter organizational hierarchies at the top, whereas work directly with people (such as youth who have illegally used or abused drugs) tends to concentrate near the bottom. In other words, information is positively correlated with hierarchical standing within a formal organization, whereas people commodities – as processed by the organi-zation – are negatively correlated with such standing. Thus organizational status is likely to impede the exchange of information downward and commodity referrals upward, precisely the flows needed if cybernetic control is to be maintained.

How might these implications of organization theory be reconciled with the requirements of a cybernetic system and with the model of community control of drugs as advanced in this monograph? The solution proposed here is that organizations have highly formal symbols (like positions and perquisites) that translate status and rewards across organizational contexts. Such organizational symbols do not mediate well, however, across the organizational and professional boundaries of interorganizational networks like the drug-abuse community. Here drug information and user referrals serve as generalized media, ones that carry connotations of relative expertise from one formal organization to another. This explains a common irony of organizational life: the same individuals who hoard information and avoid referrals, within their own organizations, may establish themselves as informational sources – and may actively seek referrals – outside their organizations. At a higher level, information and referrals are the media by which the needs of one control-system sector are translated into performance in some other sector.

This view of information and referrals as generalized media of exchange, with status implications the opposite of those that prevail within organizations, is plausible and logically consistent with both control-system engineering and Parsonian social theory. Whether it is empirically correct, however (the literature on formal organizational flows to the contrary), remains to be established. The remainder of this chapter will be devoted to testing these hypothesized implications for stratification of information and referral exchange.

Exchange and stratification: three propositions

Flows of drug-related information and advice, and of professional referrals of young drug users, move through organizational systems for the community control of deviant drug-using youth. These same flows might be seen, on the level of interpersonal relations, as governed by the principles of *social exchange*. This view is particularly useful, because such exchanges often occur outside formal organizational boundaries and rules, for assessing the motives of professionals in sending and accepting drug information and advice and referrals of young users.

Such exchanges of information and referrals can be restricted or generalized (Levi-Strauss 1949, ch. 12).[1] Restricted exchanges are mutual reciprocities between two actors that ordinarily occur because the commodities exchanged have value to those receiving them.[2] In the referral of young drug users, for example, a nonspecialist will find useful the information and advice of an expert on a relatively new or specialized field; the drug expert, in contrast, will value referrals as a means to advance his or her status in the informal drug-abuse community, where more institutionalized symbols of status and reward – formal titles and lines of authority, plus various perquisites of office – do not translate well across organizational boundaries.

At the same time, however, social exchanges of drug information and referrals can also be generalized exchanges, that is, univocal reciprocities involving three or more (usually many) actors.[3] A drug expert might publish in his or her area of specialization, for example, with the expectation that this means of providing many anonymous colleagues with information will eventually bring referrals and other rewards in exchange. The use by sociologists of citation counts to measure standing in the scientific community is an acknowledgment of this form of generalized exchange of information for professional rewards.

This chapter will focus on interpersonal exchanges of information and referrals – both restricted and generalized – among professions involved in local drug-abuse communities. The general hypothesis tested will be that professionals and professions are stratified in information and referral exchange, with opposite flows of these system commodities down and up the hierarchy, respectively. This hypothesis, a necessary (though not sufficient) condition for cybernetic control to prevail on the system level, will constitute one step toward reconciling the autonomous-system and purposive-action approaches to social control.

On the level of individual action, professionals with relatively high status – specialists in the drug field, plus treatment and prevention administrators – ought to provide information to a wider circle of individuals than provides information to them; conversely, they ought to provide referrals to fewer individuals than provide referrals to them. Just the opposite ought to be true of those professionals (nonspecialists in drugs, and those who have not planned or administered drug-treatment or -prevention programs) who have relatively little status in the drug community. These hypothesized relationships may be more rigorously stated in a formal proposition:

> *Proposition 3.1.* High-status individuals provide information to more professions than provide information to them and, conversely, provide referrals to fewer professions than provide referrals to them. The opposite relations hold for individuals of low status.

This is the first of three formal propositions to be tested in this chapter, in an empirical verification of the general hypothesis of stratification of professionals and professions in information and referral exchange.

Because of the status differences in exchange at the action level, as stated in Proposition 3.1, the movement of information and referrals among professions ought to be predominantly in opposite directions, so that whenever one profession is a relative system *source* of information for a second profession, the first profession will also be a relative system *sink* for the second, and conversely for information sinks and referral sources. These hypothesized relationships are more formally stated in a second proposition:

> *Proposition 3.2.* The movement of information and referrals among professions is predominantly in *opposite* directions, so that whenever one profession is a relative information source for a second profession, the first profession is also a relative referral sink for the second, and conversely for information sinks and referral sources, for all pairs of professions.

The fact that information and referral flows, which imply opposite statuses on the individual level (Proposition 3.1), move in opposite directions on the system level (Proposition 3.2) can mean that the professions are themselves stratified by such exchanges. That is, there may exist a strict exchange-dominance hierarchy of professions with respect to information and referral flow, with predominant movement of information down the hierarchy and predominant movement of referrals up the same hierarchy. This hypothesized stratification of professions is more formally stated in a final proposition:

> *Proposition 3.3.* Professions are stratified by reciprocal flows of information and referrals, with predominant movement of information down the hierarchy and predominant movement of referrals up the same hierarchy.

The remainder of this chapter will be devoted to testing, in turn, Propositions 3.1 to 3.3. These propositions will establish necessary (though not sufficient) conditions for cybernetic control at the system level. They will suggest the means by which the self-interested control of information and referrals, at the level of individual action, can aggregate in the social exchanges needed for the control of drug abuse at the system level.

The data set

Propositions 3.1 to 3.3 will be tested using data from the National Institute on Drug Abuse survey of drug professionals. This survey has already been discussed in previous chapters, and its data on formal education and drug-specific training were used in Chapter 2. For further details of the survey not included in this section, see Appendix A.

The NIDA data are based on a personal interview and self-administered mail survey of 3,786 professionals in Baltimore and San Francisco who were either working with youth, or in positions involving potential contact with youthful drug users, from August 1972 through February 1973 (demonstrated in Chapter 1 to be a critical period in the development of the drug problem). The total sample is almost evenly divided between Baltimore (1,839) and San Francisco (1,947), and includes subsamples ranging from 101 to 225 for each of 11 professions in the two cities (except for police, which were surveyed only in San Francisco). A twelfth profession, psychiatrists, can be distinguished among physicians; the sample includes 41 psychiatrists in Baltimore and 26 in San Francisco.

The data set itself is perhaps uniquely suited, among those produced by survey-research efforts, to address the theoretical and analytic questions raised in Chapter 2, in general, and by Propositions 3.1 to 3.3 in particular. The location of the survey in the context of social change – including illegal drug use and abuse by youth, mass-media coverage, public concern, and governmental spending – has already been discussed in Chapter 1. The survey's use of professions as "subgroups," in the sense of sampling social networks (Beniger 1976), permits the measurement of information and referral flows by means of "estimated-density spaces" (EDS), as will be discussed later in this chapter. Particularly useful in the data set itself – and worthy goals of future survey-research efforts along similar lines – are the following five features:

1. The sizes of the samples of professions, by ordinary survey standards, are unusually large. Even within each city, samples exceed by one-third the 1,500-case range typical for major national surveys. All but two of the 23 city-profession categories contain more than 100 cases (the exceptions are psychiatrists in each city); this is well above the minimal allowable subgroup sample size for the type of multivariate categorical analyses conducted here.

2. The survey is of two cities, and cities – along with their component neighborhoods and surrounding suburbs – are the relevant social level and context for the control of illegal drug use and abuse among youth as described here. National and regional surveys on the same topics would not permit similar analysis of social control as a system process. Similarities between Baltimore and San Francisco permit generalization of the results of the analysis beyond the particular local contexts.

3. The survey is limited to 12 professions (11 in Baltimore), which lends the random samples a degree of social structure not found in general population surveys. This structure includes the various characteristics of professions *qua* professions, the interactions within professions in particular urban contexts, and the interorganizational relationships among professions engaged in a common activity of social control. One drawback of the restricted number of professions is that the social system under investigation is undoubtedly not closed in a similar way. Some such restriction is ultimately necessary, however, for theoretical and methodological tractability. The NIDA data set seems to mediate well between the competing needs for simplicity and the dangers of distortion due to oversimplification.

4. Both the dozen sampled professions and the particular survey items were chosen to illuminate an ongoing, well-defined, highly motivated social process, the prevention and control of illegal drug use and abuse by youth.

This gives all the variables – individual, contextual, professional – a unity and salience not found in standard surveys on general or miscellaneous topics.

5. The survey permits analysis in terms of social-structural positions and interrelationships. Nominations by respondents of other professionals (including other respondents) as community drug experts permits the sociometric analysis of professional stratification systems. As already mentioned, the four parallel questions about the giving and receiving of information and referrals permit the measurement of network exchange flows by means of estimated-density spaces (EDS). Both the nomination and the information-referral questions will be discussed further in this chapter.

In short, the NIDA data set is particularly – if not uniquely – suited to answer the various theoretical and analytic questions concerning inter-relationships among functional roles and structural positions, both institutionalized and informal, organizational and interorganizational, that are raised in this monograph. It remains, in this chapter, to apply these data to a test of Propositions 3.1 to 3.3

Proposition 3.1: exchange and status

The most extensive work on stratification in interorganizational networks concerns patterns of community influence; this literature is reviewed by Aiken and Mott (1970); Bonjean, Clark, and Lineberry (1971); and Clark (1973). Researchers of community influence networks have developed two distinct approaches to the identification of high-status individuals, what Bonjean and Olson (1964) call the positional and reputational approaches.[4] The positional approach assumes that those who occupy formal positions of leadership in community organizations play the most influential roles in local activities. Underlying this position is the assumption that control over organizational resources translates directly into leadership. Studies relying on this assumption (on the whole or in part) include Lynd and Lynd (1937), Jennings (1964), and Freeman (1968).

The positional approach was used almost exclusively before 1953, when Floyd Hunter's study of Atlanta (Hunter 1963) challenged the relationship between organizational position and community influence and made problematical the legitimacy of formal leadership structures (Bonjean and Olson 1964, p. 278). Hunter introduced to the study of community influence the reputational approach, which had previously been used to measure social status by Warner (1949), Hollingshead (1949), and others. The reputational approach assumes that those who have a reputation for influence are indeed influential; hence status is measured by attribution of knowledgeable others. Investigators who have used this approach – in addition to Hunter – include Olmstead (1954), Form and D'Antonio (1959), D'Antonio et al. (1961), and Belknap and Steinle (1963).

A persistent criticism of the reputational approach, beginning with Kaufman and Jones's review (1954) of Hunter's book, is that reputational techniques measure options about influence rather than influence itself (see also Danzger 1964, Rose 1967). Most sustained criticism of the theoretical assumptions of the reputational approach has come from a group of political scientists known as the "Yale pluralists," including Dahl (1955, 1961), Polsby (1962), and Wolfinger (1962). Several researchers of community influence networks have defended the reputational approach (Ehrlich 1961, D'Antonio and Erickson 1962, Gamson 1966b); for example, Gamson argues that reputation is not only an indicator of resources, but a resource itself, one that has relevance and effect in community activities.

The main difference between the positional and reputational approaches, as seen by Laumann and Pappi (1976), is that the reputational (and decisional) ones ask, "Who are the powerful people?," whereas the positional ones ask, "which positions possess authority or generalized influence in the sense that their incumbents can make decisions in their respective institutional sectors or will be consequential in the resolution of community-level issues?" (p. 96). Controversy thus centers on the question of external validity, but in the theoretical sense of which question ought to be asked (and answered), rather than in the methodological sense of which approach better locates the "true influentials."

The external validation of information and referral flow patterns, in terms of individual status, is precisely what is required to establish Proposition 3.1, which states that high-status individuals tend to be information sources and referral sinks, relative to other professions, whereas the opposite relations hold for individuals of low status. Because of the need for the external validation of individual status, there will be no attempt here to resolve the various controversies surrounding the positional and reputational approaches to the identification of high-status individuals. Instead, both positional and reputational measures will be employed.[5]

The NIDA data set contains two measures of formal organizational position in the Baltimore and San Francisco drug-abuse communities. One measure distinguishes what will here be called "treatment administrators," those who have planned or administered a drug-treatment program.[6] The other measure distinguishes "prevention administrators," those who have planned or implemented a drug-prevention program, including one relying primarily upon generalized information or education.[7] Included among these "positional influentials" are directors of drug-training centers and community-health centers, heads of drug-education programs, chairpersons of local drug-abuse councils, and members of drug-problems committees of professional societies.

The NIDA data set also distinguishes "specialists" and nonspecialists or "generalists" in the drug-abuse field. Although some positional considerations were employed in the early stages of identifying drug specialists, this is primarily a reputational measure. Local people knowledgeable about the "drug scene" and well-known members of each profession were asked to suggest specialists in the drug-abuse field. In addition, members of each profession sampled were asked to nominate specialists; 45 percent of respondents offered one or more names.[8] The results of these two approaches were cross-tallied and the frequency of mentions used to determine the approximately 10 to 15 specialists in each profession in each city (there was no attempt to make this status equivalent across professions). Included among these specialists are community organizers, researchers who have published or lectured on the subject of drugs, drug resource teachers and counselors in school systems, professionals employed in drug-treatment and -rehabilitation centers, and supervisory personnel involved in service to drug users.

These specialists are not the equivalent of the "influentials" determined by reputational techniques in studies of community influence. Reputations as drug specialists can derive from "high-visibility" activities like television appearances, publication, activities in professional organizations, etc. This implies status relative to others in the same profession, but not necessarily status comparable to specialists in other professions. Particularly in professions less involved with drug abuse, participation in a single well-publicized activity may lead to nomination as a "specialist"; this does not in itself connote influence in communitywide networks. At the same time, however, visibility or exposure can translate into community influence (Sears and Whitney 1973).

The joint distributions of the reputational measure (specialists) and the positional measures (treatment and prevention administrators) for the NIDA data reveal that these measures are increasingly inclusive, from specialists (8.4 percent of the respondents in the two cities) to treatment administrators (13.1 percent) to prevention administrators (28.4 percent). The relative proportions of professions with these statuses are remarkably consistent between Baltimore and San Francisco, with no difference greater than a percentage point: 8.2 (Baltimore) and 8.6 (San Francisco) percent are specialists, 13.1 and 13.1 are treatment administrators, and 27.9 and 28.9 are prevention administrators.

As might be expected, given the literature on community influence, there is considerable overlap among the reputational and positional measures, with specialists about 4.7 times as likely as generalists to be treatment administrators and about 2.9 times as likely to administer prevention programs (overlap between treatment and prevention administration is virtually nonexistent). Despite the overlap, however, 469 respondents (13.6 percent) in the total sample are *either* specialists *or* treatment administrators *but not both*; 856 respondents (24.9) are either specialists or prevention administrators but not both. These positional and reputational measures are correlated about .09, a level that – although statistically different from zero at the .01 level – is too low to arouse suspicions of separate measurements of the same status.[9] Hence the two different approaches to identifying high-status individuals provide both three distinct measures of stratification in local drug-abuse communities and separate external validation of the statuses that accrue to information and referral flow patterns as stated in Proposition 3.1.

One set of descriptive data relevant to Proposition 3.1 is the numbers of professions serving each as sources and recipients – separately for information and referrals – for high- versus low-status individuals. These data reveal that for all 24 of 24 cases (2 cities × 3 status measures × 4 types of flows), high-status individuals have more links (as measured by links per respondent) than do low-status individuals.[10] This result, which holds for *all four* types of flows (giving and receiving drug information and referrals of drug users), demonstrates the centrality of influentials in all aspects of inter-organizational professional exchange, involving both information and advice and professional referrals.

A test more relevant for Proposition 3.1, however, is the *relative* numbers of professions involved in these exchanges; these data provide considerable support for Proposition 3.1. Table 3.1 gives the differences in mean numbers of professions serving as sources versus recipients of information and referrals, in each city, between specialists and generalists (top panels), between treatment administrators and others (middle panels), and between prevention administrators and others (bottom panels). In 12 of 12 cases (2 cities × 3 status measures × 2 commodities), the differences are larger for the status category predicted by Proposition 3.1. That is, the difference (recipients over sources) is larger for high status on information exchange and for low status on referral exchange. For example, as seen in the top panel of Exhibit 3.1, Baltimore generalists exceed specialists in the same

Trafficking in drug users

Table 3.1. *Differences in mean numbers of professions serving as sources versus recipients of information and referrals*

	Baltimore						
Category of professionals	Sample size	Mean number of professions (of 12)		Predicted difference	Actual difference	t value	Prob-value
Generalists and Specialists		Give info	Receive info				
Specialists	130	5.12	3.59	−	−1.53	3.99	<.0005
Generalists	995	1.88	2.22	+	+.34	3.70	<.0005
		Give refrls	Receive refrls				
Specialists	130	2.54	2.63	+	+.09	.29	<.4*
Generalists	995	1.02	.69	−	−.33	5.13	<.0005
Administrators and planners of drug treatment programs		Give info	Receive info				
Administrators	211	4.27	3.35	−	−.92	3.17	<.001
Others	909	1.79	2.16	+	+.37	3.97	<.0005
		Give refrls	Receive refrls				
Administrators	211	2.14	2.26	+	+.12	.50	<.4*
Others	909	.98	.61	−	−.37	5.90	<.0005
Administrators and planners of drug prevention programs		Give info	Receive info				
Administrators	388	3.32	2.93	−	−.39	1.96	<.05
Others	724	1.70	2.09	+	+.39	3.84	<.0005
		Give refrls	Receive refrls				
Administrators	388	1.66	1.60	+	−.06	.38	<.4*
Others	724	.96	.56	−	−.40	5.85	<.0005

San Francisco						

Sample size	Mean number of professions (of 12)		Predicted difference	Actual difference	*t* value	Prob-value
	Give info	Receive info				
149	4.68	3.65	−	−1.03	2.86	<.0025
1097	1.92	2.33	+	+.41	4.53	<.0005
	Give refrls	Receive refrls				
149	2.34	2.68	+	+.34	1.10	<.25*
1097	1.04	.76	−	−.28	4.34	<.0005
	Give info	Receive info				
214	4.22	3.38	−	−.84	2.81	<.0025
1025	1.84	2.31	+	+.47	5.41	<.0005
	Give refrls	Receive refrls				
214	2.28	2.48	+	+.20	.76	<.25*
1025	.97	.68	−	−.29	4.76	<.0003
	Give info	Receive info				
457	3.16	2.95	−	−.21	1.17	<.25*
781	1.72	2.23	+	+.51	4.95	<.0005
	Give refrls	Receive refrls				
457	1.53	1.54	+	+.01	.07	>.4*
781	1.00	.68	−	−.32	4.45	<.0005

*Failed at .05 significance level.

city on giving versus receiving information (differences of $+.34$ versus -1.53), whereas specialists exceed generalists on giving versus receiving referrals ($+.09$ versus $-.33$).

In 11 of 12 cases, the difference (recipients over sources) predicted to be larger is *positive*, whereas the difference predicted to be smaller is *negative* (the exception: Baltimore prevention administrators with respect to referrals; bottom panels, third and fourth lines). This is a strict test of Proposition 3.1, that high-status individuals provide information to more professions than provide information to them (negative difference) and, conversely, provide referrals to fewer professions than provide referrals to them (positive difference). For example, as seen in the top panels, San Francisco specialists give information to more professions than give information to them (4.68 versus 3.65, a difference of -1.03), but provide referrals to fewer professions than provide referrals to them (2.34 versus 2.68, a difference of $+.34$).

In all 12 cases, at least one of these differences is significantly different from zero at the $.05$ level of confidence (by Student's t test for the difference in two means, independent samples with population variances unequal and unknown); in 5 cases, *both* differences are significantly different from zero. In no case is it probable, at the $.05$ level of confidence, that the order of differences for high and low status, as specified by Proposition 3.1, is reversed from the order predicted.

In short, the NIDA data lend considerable support to Proposition 3.1. The positional and reputational measures (specialists, treatment and prevention administrators) serve as three separate external validations of the relationship between individual status in local drug communities and exchange behavior in interorganizational professional networks. At the level of purposive interpersonal action, as stated in Proposition 3.1, individuals of high status provide information to more professions than provide information to them and, conversely, provide referrals to fewer professions than provide referrals to them. The opposite is true of individuals who have less status in the drug community.

Proposition 3.2: opposite flows

Information and referral exchange among professions is, to the action level, what input–output flows of goods and services among industrial sectors are to the individual firm, as in the work of Leontief (1951, 1966). Just as input–output flows are aggregates of values for individual firms, information and referral flows – among professions *qua* professions – must be aggregates of the behavior of individual professionals. Attention to system-level flows, rather than to characteristics of individuals (like positional and reputational status) and individual behavior brings survey research data back to what are central sociological questions regarding the structure of relationships among individual actors. Survey researchers have rarely concerned themselves with relationships among respondents (but see Coleman 1958), particularly in studies of influence in community networks (for a concurring view, see Laumann and Pappi 1976, p. 146). This remains true despite theoretical literature that stresses that relationships among actors, groups, and statuses, rather than characteristics of these entities per se, are the objects of special concern for social scientists (e.g., Nadel 1957; Blau 1964, 1974; Cartwright 1965). One sign of change in these attitudes is the recent interest in more macro-level implications of community networks (Mitchell 1969a, Tilly 1969, Laumann 1973, Laumann and Pappi 1976).

To test propositions about interpersonal networks at more macro levels, like that of exchanges among professions involved in the control of drug abuse, it is necessary to have a measure of *flow* comparable to value as this is used to measure goods and service flows in economics. One possible means of constructing such a system-level measure of flow is suggested by recent literature on "social networks." A simple but important property of social networks is *density*, usually defined as the ratio of the numbers of links actually observed to the number theoretically possible (Kephart 1950; Barnes 1969, pp. 61–4). For a given flow type (like information), if the amount of flow can be considered roughly constant for all possible links between any two individuals, then density can serve as an aggregate measure of flow at the system level. Even when the motivating assumption is not realistic (as it undoubtedly is not for drug information and advice and for referrals of young drug users), if the amount of flow can be considered a monotonically increasing function of density, then density can serve as a surrogate indicator of the amount of flow; this assumption seems reasonable for the data at hand.

In addition to being a handy indicator of what might otherwise defy practical measurement, density has the additional advantage, for purposes of aggregation, of being the equivalent measure – on the aggregate-system level – of the mean numbers of links to other professions, that is, those serving as sources and recipients of information and referrals, the measure applied to exchange by individuals (in Exhibit 3.1) on the level of purposive action. That is, the number of links becomes, on the aggregate-system level, the numerator of the density ratio, where the denominator is the number of links theoretically possible.

Unfortunately, the practicality of using density as a measure of system-level flow is an inverse function of population size. Among the 1,663 respondents in the Baltimore sample, for example, there are over 1.38 million potential symmetric links and twice that number (more than 2.76 million) potential directional flows;[11] these numbers make the measurement of system flows intractable except by means of sampling. Sampling methodology in social science has been mostly confined to a peculiarly statistical concept of "population," defined by one social statistician (Stephan 1969, p. 89) as "sets of objects for which any interrelationships that exist can be ignored"; there has been relatively little work on network sampling (but see Goodman 1961; Bloemena 1964; Frank 1971, 1977, 1978; Wasserman 1977).

Granovetter (1976) has proposed a method for sampling social networks to estimate average acquaintance volume (the mean number of links per individual) and network density. His "subgraph" approach encounters practical difficulties, however, particularly in large populations, which are necessarily sparse. Density is an inverse function of population size, the square of which is the denominator of the density ratio, whereas the average acquaintance volume has a practical upper bound in the number of relations that it is possible for any one individual to maintain. This means that, in populations much larger than 100,000, the expected number of relations to be found can fall below one per interview, for interviews that might contain up to 500 yes–no relational questions (for details, see Beniger 1976, pp. 228–9; Morgan and Rytina 1976).

Data analysis here is based on the "subgroup" approach to network sampling (Beniger 1976). Using this methodology, a population is first partitioned, by criteria salient to respondents, into a manageable number of mutually exclusive and exhaustive subgroups; these subgroups are used, in place of individual names, for at least the first round of network interviewing. The NIDA survey of professionals in Baltimore and San Francisco used professions as subgroups, in effect, in its questionnaire items on information and referral exchange. This allows the estimation of information and referral flows among professions by means of a measure called "estimated-density spaces" (EDS), a practical approximation of simple network density (Beniger 1976, pp. 229–30, where EDS are referred to as "estimated upper bounds of densities"). Details on the methodology of subgroup sampling and the estimation of density spaces are presented in Appendix B.

Estimated-density spaces provide a means to test Proposition 3.2, a more macro-level extension of Proposition 3.1, which implies that information will tend to flow from high- to low-status individuals, and referrals from low- to

Table 3.2. *Directions (same and opposite) of predominant information and referral flows between all pairs of professions – Baltimore and San Francisco*

Information and referrals	No. of pairs	%
Baltimore[a]		
Flows same direction	26.5	40.2
Flows opposite directions	39.5	59.8
Totals	66.0	100.0
San Francisco[b]		
Flows same direction	20	30.3
Flows opposite directions	46	69.7
Totals	66	100.0

[a]z-value, 3.20; prob-value, .055.
[b]z-value, 3.20; prob-value, .0007.

high-status individuals. If these relationships were also to hold analogously for professions, the movement of drug information and referrals of young drug users ought to be predominantly in opposite directions – a pattern of flow necessary (though not sufficient) if cybernetic control is to obtain at this more macro level. This is the motivation for Proposition 3.2.

The relative directions of exchanges between pairs of professions can be measured by the *ratios* of EDS for flows in each direction, with the relative size of this ratio (greater or less than 1) indicating the predominant direction of flow.[12] Proposition 3.2 can be tested by a direct comparison of the ratios of EDS for all 66 possible pairs of professions. The results of these comparisons, for both Baltimore and San Francisco, are summarized in Tables 3.2 and 3.3.

In the data on Baltimore, for 39.5 (59.8 percent) of the 66 pairs of professions, the predominant movements of information and referrals are in opposite directions (the fractional 39.5 results from the tie in flows of information between psychiatrists and police). The probability (prob-value) that 39.5 of 66 cases could have resulted in opposite flows by chance alone is .055 (based on the normal approximation to the binomial distribution, parameters .5 and 66; there are two ways each that flows can be in the same and opposite directions). This lends considerable support to Proposition 3.2. Evidence is even stronger in San Francisco, where 46 (69.7 percent) of the pairs of professions manifest flows in predominantly opposite directions: the prob-value is less than .001.

Table 3.3. *Rank of professions by numbers of other professions for which predominant information and referral flows are in opposite directions – Baltimore and San Francisco*

Baltimore				San Francisco			
Rank	Professions	No. of opposite flows	%	Rank	Professions	No. of opposite flows	%
1	Psychiatrists	9.5	86.4	1	Teachers	11	100.0
t2	Nurses	9	81.8	t2	Physicians	10	90.9
t2	Teachers	9	81.8	t2	Psychologists	10	90.9
4	School administrators	8	72.7	t4	Psychiatrists	9	81.8
t5	Lawyers	7	63.6	t4	School administrators	9	81.8
t5	Physicians	7	63.6	6	Probation officers	8	72.7
t5	Probation officers	7	63.6	7	Lawyers	7	63.6
t5	Psychologists	7	63.6	t8	Clergy	6	54.5
9	Social workers	6	54.5	t8	Nurses	6	54.5
10	Clergy	5	45.5	t8	Social workers	6	54.5
11	Police	2.5	22.7	t11	Pharmacists	5	45.5
12	Pharmacists	2	18.2	t11	Police	5	45.5
Total		79.0				92	

Looking at the same data in terms of individual professions, 9 of 12 in Baltimore and 10 of 12 in San Francisco maintain predominant *exchanges* of information and referrals (rather than flows in the same direction) with a majority of other professions. Exchange is particularly characteristic of psychiatrists and teachers, who have over 80 percent of their relationships with other professions on a predominantly exchange basis in each city. Reciprocal relations are least likely among pharmacists and police, who maintain exchanges with less than half the other professions in each city. Such deviations from reciprocal flows of information and referrals will be further explained – with results that strengthen Proposition 3.2 – later in this chapter.

In summary, although there is somewhat weaker support from the data on Baltimore compared to that on San Francisco, there is nevertheless considerable evidence for Proposition 3.2, that movement of information and referrals among professions is predominantly in opposite directions. This pattern of flow is necessary (though not sufficient) if cybernetic control is to obtain at the system level.

Proposition 3.3: the stratification of professions

With Proposition 3.1, information and referral flows were established to vary inversely with status. High status, that is, tends to be associated with information sources and referral sinks, whereas the converse is true of low status. Information and referral flows were established to move in opposite directions, in Proposition 3.2, on the more macro level of exchange among professions.

Because information and referrals are associated inversely with status on the level of interpersonal action and move in opposite directions on the level of professions, it might be that professions are themselves stratified by these exchanges. Such stratification, a component of functional specialization in the control system at a still more macro level, is postulated in Proposition 3.3. In this sense, then, Proposition 3.3 represents a synthesis of the previous two propositions.

Thus it remains, in this section, to turn the previous line of reasoning back upon itself – to examine whether opposite flows of information and referrals are indeed associated with hierarchy, on the more macro level of exchange among professions, much as such patterns were associated with the status of individual actors. As a first attempt to identify such an exchange hierarchy among professions, the 12 professions in the NIDA survey might be reordered according to the number of other professions for which the density of giving exceeds the density of receiving; such an ordering is shown in Figure 3.1 (for Baltimore) and Figure 3.2 (for San Francisco). For example, in Figure 3.1, Baltimore psychologists are shown to rank fifth in information exchange; there are seven other professions for which the density of the psychologists' giving of information exceeds that of their receiving.

In all cases where two or more professions serve as relative sources for the same number of professions, they are ranked according to the direction of flow among themselves. For example, for the exchange of drug information and advice in Baltimore (Figure 3.1), both nurses and probation officers are relative sources of information for five professions. Nurses are relative sources for probation officers, however; hence the former profession is ranked just ahead of the latter. Professions tied for number of other professions served as sources are themselves in a relationship of cyclical exchange – and hence unorderable – in only a single case: Baltimore teachers

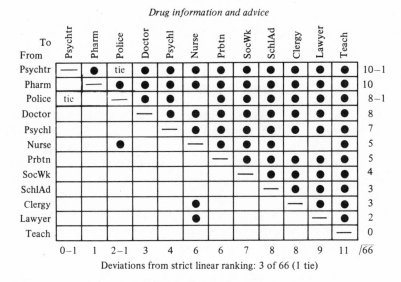

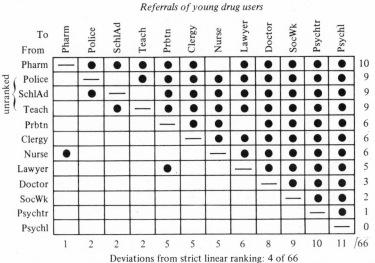

Figure 3.1. Hierarchical structure of 12 professions – Baltimore. Professions ranked by number of other professions for which density of giving exceeds density of receiving, ties decided by direct comparison.

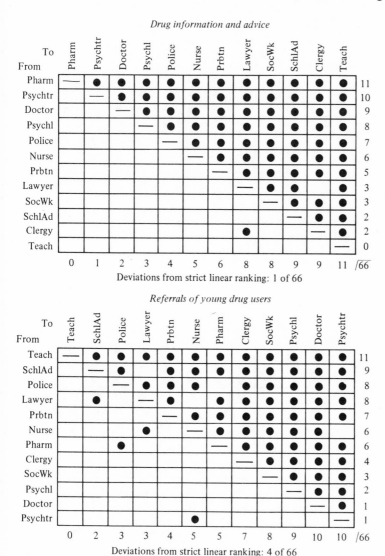

Figure 3.2. Hierarchical structure of 12 professions – San Francisco. Professions ranked by number of other professions for which density of giving exceeds density of receiving, ties decided by direct comparison.

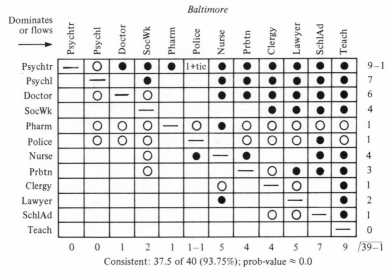

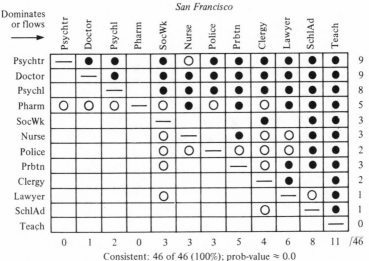

Figure 3.3. Dominance structure of 12 professions ranked by numbers of other professions dominated (give information, receive referrals); ● indicates dominance of column by row, ○ indicates row gives both information and referrals.

serve as a relative source of referrals for school administrators, administrators for police, and police for teachers (note the bracket for unranked professions in Figure 3.1, bottom matrix).

For each of the 66 pairs of different professions in Figures 3.1 and 3.2, the direction of greater flow is indicated by a heavy black dot or bullet, a graphic device for exploratory analysis and summary description of flow structures (Beniger 1976). The pattern of these bullets in the four matrices reveals – in their predominance on one side of the main diagonals – perhaps these matrices' most striking feature: the strict hierarchical structure of information and referral movement in both Baltimore and San Francisco. In none of the four matrices are there more than four deviations from strict hierarchy; the mean number of deviations is 3.0. There is also one tie, that is, one flow – of information between Baltimore psychiatrists and police – that is the same size in each direction, at least as determined by comparative EDS.

The high degree of structure represented by the matrices in Figures 3.1 and 3.2 can be tested by comparison to the null model, that is, the assumption that such patterns of relationships could have occurred by chance alone. The number of bullets below the diagonal expected under the null model is 27.5;[13] the probability of obtaining as few as four such values for referral exchange in each city (the most extreme deviation from strict hierarchy) is practically zero.[14] Even if the 12 professions were, in reality, perfectly stratified by information and referral exchange, as ranked in Figures 3.1 and 3.2, the small number of deviations would be surprising, given the crudity of estimated-density space as a measure of flow and the fact that the EDS are estimated with relatively small samples (ranging from 26 to 210).

Figures 3.1 and 3.2 thus establish a precondition for stratification by exchange on the system level, the strict linear ranking of professions on unidirectional flows of information and referrals. The next step is to determine whether the rankings are reversed for information and referrals, that is, whether information and referrals move in opposite directions in a more general hierarchical structure of professions. A first approximate test of this hypothesis would be to correlate the information and referral rankings in each city; these separate rankings are compared and correlated in Table 3.4.

Although weaker than support for unidirectional rankings, the evidence in Table 3.4 does establish a case for opposite flows. Information and referral rankings are *negatively* correlated in each city. Three professions – psychiatrists, physicians, and psychologists – in the top half of the rankings of information sources in both Baltimore and San Francisco are also in the bottom half of the rankings of referral sources in these cities. Two other

Table 3.4. *Information and referral rankings of 12 professions in each city*

	Information			Referrals	
Rank	Profession	Exceed giving	Rank	Profession	Exceed giving
Baltimore[a]					
1	Psychiatrists	10 + 1t	1	Pharmacists	10
2	Pharmacists	10	3t	Police	9
3	Police	8 + 1t	3t	School administrators	9
4	Physicians (nonpsych.)	8	3t	Teachers	9
5	Psychologists	7	5[b]	Probation officers	6
6[b]	Nurses	5	6[b]	Clergy	6
7[b]	Probation officers	5	7[b]	Nurses	6
8	Social workers	4	8	Lawyers	5
9[b]	School administrators	3	9	Physicians (nonpsych.)	3
10[b]	Clergy	3	10	Social workers	2
11	Lawyers	2	11	Psychiatrists	1
12	Teachers	0	12	Psychologists	0
	$N(N-1)/2 = 66$			$N(N-1)/2 = 66$	
San Francisco[c]					
1	Pharmacists	11	1	Teachers	11
2	Psychiatrists	10	2	School administrators	9
3	Physicians (nonpsych.)	9	3[b]	Police	8
4	Psychologists	8	4[b]	Lawyers	8
5	Police	7	5	Probation officers	7
6	Nurses	6	6[b]	Nurses	6
7	Probation officers	5	7[b]	Pharmacists	6
8[b]	Lawyers	3	8	Clergy	4
9[b]	Social workers	3	9	Social workers	3
10[b]	School administrators	2	10	Psychologists	2
11[b]	Clergy	2	11[b]	Physicians (nonpsych.)	1
12	Teachers	0	12[b]	Psychiatrists	1
	$N(N-1)/2 = 66$			$N(N-1)/2 = 66$	

Note: Ranked by number of other professions for which density of giving exceeds density of receiving.

professions – school administrators and teachers – rank in the bottom half as information sources and the top half as referral sources in both Baltimore and San Francisco.

The rank-order correlations in San Francisco are relatively high ($-.587$ Spearman's r_s, $-.485$ Kendall's tau) and significantly different from zero at the .05 level. For Baltimore, the correlations are not nearly as high ($-.140$ Spearman's r_s, $-.109$ Kendall's tau) nor significant (prob-value is .32). These less conclusive findings for Baltimore seem the result of problems with the data on pharmacists, who are relatively uninvolved with referrals of young drug users, and on police, who were not included as *respondents* in the Baltimore sample. There do not appear to be any more complex patterns of deviations from the structure of opposite flows in the Baltimore data.

Correlation coefficients are not network measures per se, however, and serve only as guides to structural investigation. A more direct test for inverse rankings of professions on information and referral flow is found by combining separate rankings into composite ones for Baltimore and San Francisco. One way in which professions might be ordered in a composite ranking is according to the number of other professions they dominate – or are dominated by – in Figures 3.1 and 3.2. This use of the term "dominate" is obviously motivated by the status implications of giving and receiving information and referrals, on the level of interpersonal exchange, as established with Proposition 3.1. Whether a similar concept of status dominance is appropriate for more macro levels, of course, remains to be seen.

The resulting "dominance structures" of professions in Baltimore and San Francisco are shown in Fig. 3.3 (page 76). For each of the 66 pairs of different professions in each city, the direction of exchange dominance is indicated by a bullet: hollow bullets (white circles) indicate the direction of giving of both information and referrals. Because there are somewhat more hollow bullets above than below the main diagonals in Figure 3.3 (14.5 versus 12 in Baltimore, 11 versus 9 in San Francisco), giving would appear to be more closely associated with exchange dominance than is receiving.

Notes to Table 3.4 *(cont.)*

[a]Rank order correlations: Spearman's $r_s = -.140$ (prob-value $= .32$); Kendall's tau $= -.109$ (prob-value $= .32$).

[b]Tied rankings, noncyclic for density of giving, decided by direct comparison, i.e., density giving/density receiving ratio with lower-ranked profession(s) is greater than 1.

[c]Rank order correlations: Spearman's r_s, $-.587$ (prob-value $= .03$); Kendall's tau $= -.485$ (prob-value $= .01$).

Exchange dominance is a concept that will be used extensively in this monograph. It indicates reverse flows of information and referrals or, more generally, any commodity valued in an exchange system, or controlled by a more macro-level cybernetic system. For any pair of actors or sectors (individuals, groups, categories like profession, etc.), the one that receives information and supplies commodities is said to be dominated by the other and, conversely, the one that gives information and receives commodities is said to dominate. Where one actor or sector supplies both information and commodities, the evidence of Figure 3.3 suggests (but does not establish with statistical significance) that the supplier will dominate, however slightly.

The professions in Figure 3.3 are ranked, separately in each city, by the number of other professions they dominate (row totals) *minus* the number they are dominated by (column totals). Both the row and column totals sum to the same numbers, which have already been shown in Tables 3.2 and 3.3 to be the total pairs of professions – 39.5 in Baltimore, 46 in San Francisco – with flows in opposite directions. Consistent with these rankings are a remarkable number of the dominance relationships in Figure 3.3, as indicated by the predominance of solid bullets above the main diagonal. In San Francisco, all 40 of 40 pure dominance relationships are consistent with the hierarchical structure of professions. Consistency is almost as great for the data from Baltimore, where 37.5 of 40 pure dominance relationships (93.75 percent) are consistent with the single hierarchical structure. The two exceptions are part of the only circle of reciprocal exchange: Lawyers dominate nurses, who dominate probation officers, who dominate lawyers. The first of these three relations, because it is the only one absent in the San Francisco data, is the most likely to be due to stochastic error.

Under the null model – the assumption that relationships between dominance and hierarchical structure could have occurred by chance alone – the probability of obtaining as much consistency in each city is practically zero.[15] This finding establishes a second precondition for stratification by exchange on the system level, that information and referrals move in opposite directions in a single hierarchical structure of professions. The fact that for giving relations, as designated by hollow bullets, the distribution about the main diagonal is not statistically significant at least leaves open the possibility that these represent random deviations from the hierarchical structure. Such lack of interaction between dominance hierarchy and nondominance relations is strong evidence that the former exists and that the latter are not due to an alternative structure (further evidence will be provided in the next section; see especially Table 3.6 and Figures 3.6 and 3.7).

	Information Baltimore		
Information San Fancisco	+.93 (+.82)	Information San Francisco	
Referrals Baltimore	−.14 (−.11)	−.21 (−.17)	Referrals Baltimore
Referrals San Francisco	−.57 (−.49)	−.59 (−.49)	+.75 (+.57)
	Prob-values .001 (.0001)		
	.32 (.32)	.24 (.23)	
	.03 (.01)	.03 (.01)	.007 (.006)

Figure 3.4. Intercorrelations of information and referral rankings of 12 professions (ranked by number of professions for which density of giving exceeds density of receiving, for information and referrals in each city).

It remains, in this test of Proposition 3.3, to determine whether there exists a unified stratification of professions, consistent across cities, that is based on the dominance of information and referral exchange, possibly resulting from the functional specialization required of a macro-level system to control deviance among youth and characterized by reciprocal flows of information and referrals. If there does exist such a hierarchical exchange structure of professions, then the four previous rankings of information and referral flows (Figures 3.1 and 3.2, summarized in Table 3.4) ought to be correlated – between Baltimore and San Francisco – in two ways: First, rankings for both information and referral flow ought to be *positively* correlated between cities. Second, rankings for information and referral flow ought to be *negatively* correlated for both intercity pairs.

Both the Spearman's and Kendall's coefficients of rank-order correlation[16] among the four rankings are listed in Figure 3.4. Rankings for both information and referral exchange are positively correlated between Baltimore and San Francisco, with information rankings highly correlated ($r_s = .930$, tau $= .818$) and those for referrals moderately correlated ($r_s = .748$, tau $= .574$). Rankings for information and referral exchange are negatively correlated in all four instances, both within cities (as already shown in Table 3.4) and between: The Baltimore information and San Francisco referral rankings are moderately negatively correlated ($r_s = -.566$, tau $= -.485$), with somewhat smaller negative correlations ($r_s = -.210$, tau $= -.171$) for San Francisco information and Baltimore referrals. Thus all the coefficients listed in Figure 3.4 support the two preconditions – positive correlations of both information and referral rankings between cities, and negative correlations of the two types of rankings for both intercity pairs – for the unified hierarchical exchange structure postulated in Proposition 3.3. For the six pairs of rankings, only two correlations – of the Baltimore referral ranking with information rankings in both cities – are not statistically significant at the .05 level; these coefficients have prob-values of .32 (for Baltimore) and .23 (for San Francisco).

Because the four separate rankings are highly intercorrelated in the predicted directions, as shown in Figure 3.4, some simple combination of these rankings might be used to approximate a unified exchange structure. The numbers of professions served as information sources and referral sinks – the two dominance relationships – were used to construct the original rankings; hence these same measures provide a natural means to extend the rankings to a unified one for exchange dominance.

Such a ranking, determined by the unweighted sum of professions dominated (as information sources and referral sinks) in both Baltimore and San Francisco, is presented in Table 3.5 and Figure 3.5. The 12 professions are strictly ranked on this basis, with psychiatrists most dominant (they have 40.5 of 44 or 92 percent of possible dominance relationships) and teachers least dominant (with 2 of 44 or 4.5 percent of dominance relationships). The one tie in unweighted sums, between physicians and psychologists, can be decided by direct comparisons: Physicians dominate psychologists in three of the four rankings.

Note that the determination of this single hierarchical structure is not, strictly speaking, an exercise in scale construction. It was decided a priori, on theoretical grounds, that the four individual rankings are equally valid estimates of the functionally prerequisite stratification of exchange in a macro-level control system; hence the four counts of professions dominated were unweighted in determining the single ranking. We shall thus resist the temptation to employ the various procedures, common in scale construction, by which the Baltimore referral counts – with their lower intercorrelations – would have been given lesser weight. This affords a stronger test of Proposition 3.3, that professions are stratified in a single hierarchy of information and referral flows, by subjecting the a priori assumption to

Table 3.5. *Dominance hierarchy of 12 professions – data from both cities combined*

| Rank | Profession | Baltimore | | San Francisco | | Total |
		Info source	Refrl sink	Info source	Refrl sink	
1	Psycht	10–1	10	10	10	40–1
2[a]	Doctor	8	8	9	10	35
3[a]	Psychl	7	11	8	9	35
4	Pharm	10	1	11	5	27
5	SocWk	4	9	3	8	24
6	Nurse	5	5	6	5	21
7	Police	8–1	2	7	3	20–1
8	Probtn	5	5	5	4	19
9	Clergy	3	5	2	7	17
10	Lawyer	2	6	3	3	14
11	SchlAd	3	2	2	2	9
12	Teach	0	2	0	0	2
Totals		66	66	66	66	264

Note: Professions ordered by numbers of professions dominated, dominated by, in each city (four numbers equally weighted).
[a]Tie decided by direct comparison.

comparative analysis, rather than by making the best fit of a linear ranking to the data at hand.

These self-imposed restrictions notwithstanding, the hypothesis of a single hierarchy of professions with respect to information and referral exchange remains tenable. As shown in the dominance matrix in Figure 3.5, of the 66 possible pairs of professions, 35 pairs (53.0 percent) are characterized by the same reverse flows of information and referrals (and hence exchange dominance) in both cities; these pairs are designated by the larger bullets. Assuming, for the null model, a binomial distribution with parameter .125 (i.e., $.5^3$) and 66, the probability (prob-value) of obtaining 35 or more flows reversed in the same way in both cities by chance alone is practically zero.

In addition, 16 more pairs (51.6 percent of the remaining 31 pairs) are characterized by opposite flows in one city; these pairs are designated by the smaller bullets in Figure 3.5. Thus of the total 51 pairs for which there is any evidence – in one city or both – of a dominance relationship, 50 pairs (98 percent) are consistent with the hypothesis of a single exchange-dominance

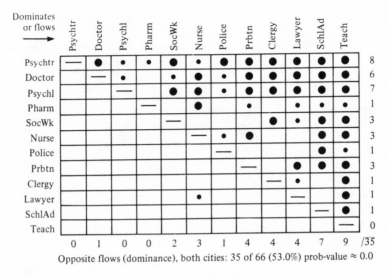

Opposite flows (dominance), both cities: 35 of 66 (53.0%) prob-value ≈ 0.0

Figure 3.5. Dominance structure – both cities combined; ● indicates opposite flows (dominance), both cities; • indicates opposite flows (dominance), one city only.

hierarchy, as shown by the predominance of bullets (large and small) above the main diagonal in Figure 3.5. Assuming, for the null model, a binomial distribution with parameters .5 and 51, the prob-value is again virtually zero. The single deviation from a strict dominance structure, among the 132 pairs of professions in Baltimore and San Francisco, involves lawyers and nurses; the former profession dominates the latter – though in Baltimore only.

To summarize this section, then, although there is again somewhat weaker support from the data on Baltimore as compared to that on San Francisco, there is nevertheless considerable evidence for Proposition 3.3, that there exists a strict dominance hierarchy of professions with respect to information and referral exchange, with the predominant flow of information down the hierarchy and the predominant movement of referrals up the same hierarchy. The four individual rankings of professions on information and referral exchange (Figures 3.1 and 3.2) are positively correlated within types between cities and negatively correlated between types, both within cities and between (Figure 3.4). These four rankings can be used to determine a single combined exchange-dominance hierarchy (Table 3.5), which is compatible with the hypothesis of reciprocal flows of information and referrals (exchange dominance) among all but one of the 132 pairs of professions in the two cities (Figure 3.5).

The validation of the exchange hierarchy

As the previous section has shown, there does exist a strict exchange-dominance hierarchy of professions with respect to information and referral flow. This hierarchy, explicated in Figure 3.5 and Table 3.5, has certain face validity. At the top are the elite of the medical sphere, psychiatrists and physicians. At the bottom is the educational sphere, including school administrators and teachers. In the middle are three counseling professions: psychologists, social workers, and clergy.

These rankings evoke hypothesized relationships between the educational, medical, and legal spheres of organizational activity. To constitute functionally separate components of a macro-level control system, as stated in the last chapter, the three spheres must manifest two types of flows: (1) a *controlled commodity flow* of referrals from the educational to the medical and legal spheres and (2) a *feedback flow* of drug information and advice back to the educational sphere. In the exchange-dominance hierarchy in Table 3.5, the four medical professions rank in the top six positions and the three legal professions occupy positions 7–10, whereas the two bottom positions are held by the educational professions. There is no overlap among the three spheres: their rankings are broken only by the three counseling professions, which the next chapter will argue play an intermediary "facilitating" role in organizational control systems. Thus the exchange-dominance hierarchy is compatible with the stratification already hypothesized for cybernetic control of authority over young drug users.

The stratification of professions is only one component, of course, in the functional specialization of a community system for the control of deviance among youth with respect to drugs. Other components will be identified in the next chapter. It remains, in this chapter, to validate further the composite ranking in Table 3.5. In addition to the certain face validity already discussed, the unified exchange-dominance hierarchy might also be given external validation. An obvious opportunity is afforded by scales of occupational prestige.

Comprehensive studies of occupational prestige have been conducted by Duncan (1961), Siegel (1971), and Temme (1975); earlier work is reviewed by Reiss (1961). What empirical evidence is available suggests that the prestige of occupations is relatively invariant, both over time (Hodge, Siegel, and Rossi 1964) and across cultures (Hodge, Treiman, and Rossi 1966).

The ratings used here are the 1960 Hodge-Siegel-Rossi prestige scores, developed at the National Opinion Research Center (NORC) from 1963 to 1965.[17] Scores for the 12 professions were adapted to the 1970 U.S. Census occupation codes as reported in the codebook for the 1976 NORC Social Survey (National Opinion Research Center 1977).

Validation is afforded by the regression of the 1960 Hodge-Siegel-Rossi prestige scores on the exchange-dominance scores (the total number of professions served as information source and referral sink, both cities combined) as computed in Table 3.5. The two rankings are correlated +.45; each accounts for about 20 percent of the variance in the other (as measured by R^2). A single point in the exchange-dominance scale is equivalent to 2.47 points in the occupational-prestige scale, a coefficient that could be expected to change were more (or other) professionals included in the exchange-dominance rankings. Both the intercept (10.49) and the slope (+2.47) are statistically significant at the .05 level.

There is no reason, of course, why occupational prestige ought to be perfectly related to exchange dominance. Many factors enter into determination of the prestige of occupations; for a discussion of four possible dimensions,[18] see Gusfield and Schwartz (1963). Conversely, stratification by information and referral exchange might be expected to depend on other factors, like functional importance in the macro-level system for control of deviance among youth, rather than on occupational prestige alone. The purpose of the regression is merely to establish the 1960 Hodge-Siegel-Rossi prestige scale as one means of externally validating the unified exchange-dominance hierarchy. Because exchange dominance is substantially positively related to occupational prestige, there is additional reason to accept Proposition 3.3, that professions are stratified by reciprocal flows of information and referrals.

Given that the composite ranking in Table 3.5 has both external and face validity, why are only 35 of the 66 possible pairs of professions (large bullets) in Figure 3.5 wholly consistent with the exchange-dominance hierarchy, with an additional 15 pairs (small bullets above the diagonal in Figure 3.5) consistent in one city only? To answer this question, or to show that inconsistencies are due to random processes, would be to give further validity to the exchange-dominance hierarchy.

One possible explanation of the inconsistency, if the stratification of professions in Figure 3.5 and Table 3.5 does indeed hold, is that random deviations occur as a function of the rank proximity of professions in each pair. That is, deviations are most likely between professions with adjacent rankings (there are 11 such pairs) and least likely between the 2 professions –

	Psychtr	Doctor	Psychl	Pharm	SocWk	Nurse	Police	Prbtn	Clergy	Lawyer	SchlAd	Teach
Doctor		Doctor										
Psychl	1	1	Psychl									
Pharm	1	2	2	Pharm								
SocWk		1		2	SocWk							
Nurse	1				2	Nurse						
Police	½	1	1	2	2	1	Police					
Prbtn				1	2		2	Prbtn				
Clergy				2		2	2	2	Clergy			
Lawyer				1	1	3	2		1	Lawyer		
SchlAd				1					2	2	SchlAd	
Teach				1			1					Teach
Totals	3½	5	5	15	10	9	14½	7	11	10	5	2 /97

Figure 3.6. Distribution of 48.5 deviations from final (combined) dominance hierarchy by rank distance between professions in pair. Cell entries are numbers of deviations from final (combined) dominance hierarchy; rank distance might be seen as number of cells diagonally from main diagonal.

psychiatrists and teachers – at opposite ends of the hierarchy. As shown in Figure 3.5 and Table 3.5, there are 48.5 deviations from a perfect exchange-dominance hierarchy. The distribution of these deviations among pairs of professions is given in Figure 3.6 and Table 3.6.[19] If the speculation is correct, deviations ought to occur predominantly near the diagonal (which represents pairs of professions with adjacent rankings), whereas deviations near the opposite (lower left) corner ought to be relatively unlikely. Inspection of Figure 3.6 reveals just such a pattern: 15 of the 48.5 deviations are in cells immediately adjoining the diagonal and an additional 19 deviations are within 3 cells of the diagonal. The opposite corner, in contrast, contains a block of empty cells; no deviation is farther than 8 cells (of a possible 11) from the diagonal and only 3.5 deviations are as far as 6 cells.

A more formal test of the relationship between deviations from the strict exchange-dominance ranking and proximity of professions in the same ranking is provided by the concept of *rank distance*. The rank distance between professions is simply the absolute difference of their ranks in the unified exchange-dominance hierarchy. Successive rank distances (from 1 to 11) are represented by successive diagonals – counting from the main diagonal – in Figure 3.6. If deviations are negatively related to rank distance

Table 3.6. *Distribution of 48.5 deviations from final (combined) dominance hierarchy by rank distance between professions in each pair*

Rank distance	No. cells	Probability	Expected number deviations	Actual number deviations	Difference expected and actual	Contribution to chi-square
1	11	.167	8.08	15	+6.92	5.92
2	10	.152	7.35	9	+1.65	.37
3	9	.136	6.61	10	+3.39	1.73
4	8	.121	5.88	5	−.88	.13
5	7	.106	5.14	6	+.86	.14
6	6	.091	4.41	1.5	−2.91	1.92
7	5	.076	3.67	1	−2.67	1.95
8	4	.061	2.94	1	−1.94	1.28
9	3	.045	2.20	0	−2.20	2.20
10	2	.030	1.47	0	−1.47	1.47
11	1	.015	.73	0	−.73	.73
Totals	66	1.000	48.50	48.5	0.0	17.84[a]

[a]Prob-value: <.075.

(so that the greater the rank distance, the less likely are deviations from the strict linear ranking), then there ought to be disproportionately as many deviations among the lesser distances (i.e., in cells on diagonals nearer the main diagonal).

The test of this hypothesis against the null model that deviations are purely random (i.e., that the number of deviations is proportionate to the number of cells in its diagonal) is presented in Table 3.6. As this table shows, the possibility that deviations from strict linear ranking are purely random can be rejected with over 92 percent confidence. An unexpectedly large number of deviations occur among professions at rank distances 1 to 3, as revealed by the patterns of signs of the differences between expected and actual numbers of deviations (second column from the right). Of these deviations, a disproportionately large number occurs among professions adjacent in the rankings (rank distance 1); 33.2 percent of the total chi-square is due to adjacent professions, compared to 45.0 percent for those at rank distances 1 to 3.

It appears, then, that the extent to which exchange between two professions deviates from that predicated by a strict exchange-dominance hierarchy varies as an inverse function of the rank distance between the

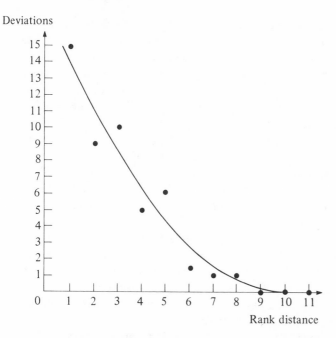

Figure 3.7. Regression fit of deviations from final (combined) dominance hierarchy as parabolic function (second-degree polynomial) of total rank distance (sum of differences in exchange-dominance ranks with all other professions).

professions, so that the greater the distance, the fewer the deviations. Nonlinear regression affords one means to fit this inverse function. The simplest such nonlinear fit, a second-degree polynomial (parabolic function) in total rank distance, is presented in Figure 3.7. Rank distance accounts for about 95 percent of the deviation from the strict exchange-dominance hierarchy (as measured by R^2); the F-statistic is significant at the .01 level. As shown by the graph of the data and parabolic fit in Figure 3.7, the number of deviations from strict linear rankings is a smoothly decreasing and decelerating function of rank distance in the same hierarchy. This is evidence that deviations are not due wholly to random variation (sampling and measurement error), but that deviation is an inverse function of the distance between professions in the exchange-dominance hierarchy. This result is precisely what would be expected if the stratification of professions by exchange dominance is strictly as shown in Figure 3.5 and Table 3.5.

The fact that deviations in predominant flows of information and referrals are a function of rank distance may account for another local variation from random error noted earlier, that is, that certain professions – particularly pharmacists and police – appear to be less precisely located in (or compatible with) a strict linear ranking. As seen in the column of totals of Table 3.6, the 12 professions vary in deviations from the exchange-dominance hierarchy, from 15 for pharmacists and 14.5 for police to 3.5 for psychiatrists and 2 for teachers. The speculation here is that this variation in the number of deviations from strict ranking might be due to the particular location of professions in the exchange hierarchy. Psychiatrists and teachers are at the two ends of the continuum, as would be expected, whereas pharmacists and police stand near the middle (at ranks 4 and 7, respectively). Perhaps professions deviate more from the strict ranking because they are nearer its middle, and hence at a lesser *total rank distance* from all other professions.

A simple measure of total rank distance is the sum of differences in exchange-dominance rankings with all other professions (there are obviously 11 such differences for each of the 12 professions). By this measure, the 2 professions in the middle of the hierarchy (nurses and police) have a total rank distance of 36, whereas the 2 at the extremes (psychiatrists and teachers) have 66 as their total rank distance.

A test of the speculation that the total rank distance of each profession from all others accounts for deviations from the strict exchange-dominance hierarchy is afforded by regression of deviations on the total rank-distance measure. As expected, the two variables are correlated negatively ($r = -.78$); each accounts for about 61 percent of the variance in the other (as measured by R^2). Ten points of total rank distance is equivalent to a decrease of 1.48 deviations from the exchange-dominance hierarchy. Both the intercept (15.13) and the slope ($-.148$) are statistically significant at the .05 level. The probability that the relationship between total rank distance and deviations from the hierarchy is *not* inverse is virtually zero. In short, this regression analysis provides further evidence that deviations are not due wholly to random variation (sampling and measurement error), but that the measurement of deviation is an inverse function of the distance between professions in the exchange-dominance hierarchy. This inverse relationship is manifest in more deviations, both for more distant pairs (as shown earlier) and for professions nearer the middle of the hierarchy.

Thus considerable validation has been provided for the unified exchange-dominance hierarchy of professions with respect to information and referral flow as explicated in Table 3.5 and Figure 3.5. The hierarchy has face validity in that the stratification of professions evokes relationships between the educational, medical, and legal spheres already hypothesized – in the previous chapter – for cybernetic control of authority over young drug users. External validation is provided by regression against occupational prestige, which is substantially positively related to exchange dominance. Deviations from this hierarchy can be attributed to stochastic error related to the proximity of professions' rankings. Each of these findings serves to validate the unified exchange-dominance hierarchy and thus to provide additional support for Proposition 3.3. Professions appear to be stratified by reciprocal flows of information and referrals, that is, with predominant movement of information down the hierarchy and predominant movement of referrals up the same hierarchy.

Summary

If deviance among youth with respect to drugs is to be controlled at the system level, it is necessary that drug information and advice and referrals of young drug users pass in opposite directions through interorganizational systems and professional networks. Authority for deviant youths must flow upward through the system to ever more specialized components: to drug administrators, specialists, and experts, on the individual level; to higher-status professions, with respect to the specialized functions of drug control, on a more macro level; to medical and legal spheres of activity, on the highest control-system level. At the same time, informational feedback about these flows must pass downward to less specialized individuals, professions, and organizational spheres.

Working against these required flows of drug information and referrals are certain organizational factors. Information is positively correlated with hierarchical standing in formal organizations, whereas people-commodities – as processed by the organization – are negatively correlated with such standing. This means that information tends to enter organizational hierarchies at the top, whereas work with people concentrates near the bottom. Within an individual organization, purposive actors have little motivation to exchange information downward or referrals upward – precisely the two flows required for cybernetic control.

Outside individual organizations, however, information and referrals serve as generalized media that translate status across formal boundaries in interorganizational networks. This provides the motivation for individuals who intend to advance in the informal drug community that they themselves generate to seek user referrals in exchange for drug information and advice. It is through these reciprocal movements of information and referrals, precisely the opposite of those expected within formal organizations, that the needs of one control-system sector translate into performance in some other sector.

This view of information and referrals as generalized media, intended as a synthesis of the autonomous-system and purposive-action approaches to change and control, was developed in the last chapter from control-system engineering and Parsonian social theory. This chapter has tested the model using data from the NIDA survey of drug professionals. Information and referral flows were found to vary inversely with status, with high status associated with information sources and referral sinks (Proposition 3.1). On the more macro level of exchange among professions, information and referral flows were found to move in opposite directions (Proposition 3.2). In an integration of these two findings, that information and referrals convey opposite statuses in interpersonal action, and move in opposite directions on the level of professions, professions were found to be themselves stratified by exchanges of information and referrals (Proposition 3.3). As predicted from the control-systems model, information tends to move down the resulting exchange-dominance hierarchy, whereas the predominant movement of referrals is up the same hierarchy.

Propositions 3.1 to 3.3 thus suggest the means by which self-interested control of information and referrals, at the level of individual action, can aggregate in the social exchanges needed for the control of illegal drug use and abuse to obtain at the system level. The answer is implied by the stratification of professionals and professions with respect to information and referral exchange. Such stratification is a necessary but not sufficient condition for cybernetic control; another necessary condition, the functional inter-relationship of various specialized system components, will be taken up in the next chapter. This will serve to reconcile stratification by information and referral exchange, based on the concept of exchange dominance, with the exchange relationships necessary for control of social change on the macro level.

4. Exchange relationships
in social-control systems

The concept of system in the social sciences might be traced back at least as far as the discussions of individual homeostatic processes in L. J. Henderson's *The Fitness of the Environment* (1913), a work that owes much to Pareto's cyclical theories (Henderson 1935); Henderson's work is acknowledged by Wiener in his text establishing the modern field of cybernetics (Wiener 1948, p. 115). Bertalanffy, an early proselyte of "general system theory," cites Lotka's classic *Elements of Physical Biology* (1925) as the first work to deal with system theory in full generality (Bertalanffy 1968, p. 11). Another foreshadowing can be found in Whitehead's philosophy of "organic mechanism" (Whitehead 1925); as late as the mid-1930s, Parsons credited Whitehead with "the most extensive analysis of the general concept of the 'organic' which is known to the author" (Parsons 1937, p. 32). Other biological precursors include Bernard's functional view of physiological processes (Bernard 1927) and Cannon's further work on homeostasis (Cannon 1929, 1932).

Renewed interest in general systems grew out of developments in servomechanisms, information and communication theory, and computers during and immediately following World War II. Instrumental in these developments were two publications, both issued in 1948, which founded two new areas of systems studies: cybernetics, formally introduced in Wiener's book by that title (Wiener 1948), and further popularized by him (Wiener 1950); and information theory, established in a paper by Shannon (1948), and popularized in a text by Shannon and Weaver (1949).[1] These two developments were not unrelated to the "organismic" biology of the 1920s: Wiener cites the influence of Cannon (Wiener 1948, pp. 1 and 17), and both Wiener and Shannon acknowledge a debt to the other (Wiener 1950, p. 24; Shannon and Weaver 1949, p. 3)

Both information theory and cybernetics linked two previously disparate concepts – those of communication and control. Wiener coined the word "cybernetics" for "the entire field of control and communication theory" (1948, p. 11), thus classifying communication and control together. He later

93

explained: "When I communicate with another person, I impart a message to him . . . if my control is to be effective I must take cognizance of any messages from him which may indicate that the order is understood and has been obeyed" (1950, pp. 24–5). Similarly, Shannon and Weaver defined "communication" in terms of control of receiver by sender (1949, p. 3), explaining that "communication either affects conduct or is without any discernible and probable effect at all" (p. 5).

The value to social scientists of studying information flow is its link – via information theory and cybernetics – to *control*, which has a venerable tradition in the behavioral sciences. Some sociologists view control as simply coterminous with society, for example, MacIver. He writes: "A very large part of sociological literature, by whatever name, treats of social control . . . To study social control we must seek out the ways in which society patterns and regulates individual behavior . . . " (as quoted by Nadel 1953, p. 265).

The promise of relationships among information flow, social control, and social structure raises the hope that sociology might be developed via the special analytic techniques of control-systems and information engineering. This possibility has not been entirely lost on sociologists; Stinchcombe, for example, discusses "the general strategy of treating a system of links among people from an information theory or cybernetic point of view . . . the basic notion that control can be no greater than the quantity of information received and transmitted by the control mechanisms can be generalized to systems consisting of links among people. Power concepts based on the notion of *the quantity of information* are very useful in analyzing administrative systems" (Stinchcombe 1968, p. 152; italics in the original).

As in other applied sciences, however, the success of such analysis rests on quantification through precise measurement. This requirement has to date precluded any wholesale borrowing of control-systems ideas by social scientists. Flows of social information and socially controlled commodities (including social deviance) have proved difficult to conceptualize and largely eluded measurement and systematic analysis. Such problems, long noted by social scientists (e.g., Deutsch 1966), are reflected in the recent decline in interest among them in the "general systems" movement, heralded as a new synthesis of the natural and social sciences only a decade earlier (Bertalanffy 1968, ch. 1).

Renewed hope for a breakthrough has recently come from an unexpected source: the rapid developments in what has been subsumed under the heading "social networks" (Barnes 1969; Mitchell 1969b; White, Boorman, and

Breiger 1976). Particularly promising, as a means to link the social-network literature to empirical work on control systems, are developments on sampling large-scale social networks for survey research (Beniger 1976; Granovetter 1976), as discussed in the last chapter. The densities of communication links among various subsectors of interpersonal networks provide an obvious means to quantify information flow – at the more macro level – among these sectors, and survey research provides a well-established means to collect such data. For large populations, subgroup sampling and estimated-density spaces (EDS) afford practical means to approximate network densities.

Because information flow is so central to control and to social-control systems, this chapter will focus on the actual *sizes* of flows. In this it differs from the previous chapter, which concerned the stratification of professions on information and referral exchange and hence confined its attention to relative or predominant *directions* of flows, which determine hierarchy based on exchange dominance. The remainder of this chapter will be devoted to testing the hypothesis that the control of deviance among youth with respect to drugs is maintained by a cybernetic system, including the division of informal networks among drug professionals into functional subsystems and the aggregation of interpersonal exchanges into control relationships among the subsystems. The latter part of the chapter will analyze simultaneously both the absolute sizes of professional exchanges and their predominant directions. Both relative and absolute flows of information and referrals, it will be seen, are essential components of any methodology for identifying and analyzing social control systems based on network-exchange data.

Exchange and control systems: three propositions

Essential to both the concepts of system and network is the notion of the interrelatedness of parts. In social networks, links between nodes do not necessarily carry causal connotations, but might represent various forms of communication and exchange. The English folk category "old-boy network," for example, describes links of patronage and communication among men who are graduates of the same exclusive schools (Frankenberg 1966, p. 253). The components of control systems, in contrast, are interrelated via "feedback," defined by Ashby as a "circularity of action between the parts of a dynamic system," whereby each part *affects* the other (1964, p. 53).

One task in the analysis of control systems, therefore, is to isolate the interrelated component parts. This is trivially easy in mechanical-engineering applications, where functional components are purposively designed, often physically discrete, units. In social systems, however, individual components (functional categories, sectors, subsystems, etc.) are aggregate, usually unintended, factors that emerge from the behavior of individuals and must be established by empirical means. For example, the notion of "profession," used extensively here as a functional category, requires no means of identification beyond the self-reporting of respondents to a questionnaire; the notion of "sectors," in contrast, which involves aggregates of professions, demands some empirical means by which individuals or professions can be grouped into sectors.

One obvious choice of means, grounded in network concepts, involves the relationship between within-group and between-group densities. Social scientists take as axiomatic that ingroup associations exceed outgroup associations (e.g., Blau 1977, p. 281). In other words, at any given level of systems analysis, sectors or subsystems ought to be distinguished by (1) a relatively high density of exchange (large flows) *within* components, and (2) a lower density of exchange (smaller flows) *between* components. Because information exchange can serve an integrative as well as feedback function and is therefore less likely than referral exchange to connote movement to a more specialized component, the two criteria for distinguishing sectors can be expected to hold more strongly for information than for commodities controlled. These hypothesized relationships may be more rigorously stated in a formal proposition:

> *Proposition 4.1.* The individual components of a social-control system (professions, sectors, subsystems, etc.) can be distinguished by relatively high densities of exchange (large flows) within the components, and lower densities of exchange (smaller flows) between the components; these relationships will be stronger for information than for other socially controlled commodities.

This is the first of three formal propositions to be tested in this chapter, in an empirical verification of the general hypothesis of the division of professions into functional subsystems, interconnected by the exchange relationships that are necessary for a social-control system.

A second task in the analysis of social-control systems is to establish the hierarchical levels of functional specialization. Individuals or commodities that do not require special control (i.e., that are not "deviant") will ordinarily be maintained at relatively low levels of specialization vis-à-vis the particular type of control. When individuals or commodities require control, however, they will usually pass to higher levels of specialization in the particular control function.

Youth who are not deviant with respect to drugs, for example, and therefore do not require restorative "control," are ordinarily part of an educational system that has primary organizational responsibility for preventing deviance through socialization. As we have seen, youth can become deviant with respect to drugs in two distinct ways – one medical, the other legal. Medical deviance is the responsibility of a specialized health sector, including psychiatrists, other physicians, pharmacists, and nurses, whereas legal deviance is the responsibility of a specialized law-enforcement sector involving police, lawyers and judges, and probation and parole officers. When youth are deviant in the legal sense, organizational responsibility for them partly shifts to this legal sector, the law-enforcement and criminal-justice system. When youth are deviant in the sense of health, responsibility for them shifts to the medical sector, including public health, pharmaceutical, and research specializations. Informational feedback, in contrast, will flow in the opposite directions, that is, from the medical and legal sectors to the educational one.

The nature of these functional subsystems is suggested by social-theoretical (rather than derivative-empirical) considerations, of course, but such a priori speculations can be tested empirically with the methodology developed here. Partial verification was presented in the last chapter, which establishes a strict exchange-dominance hierarchy among the 12 professions involved in the local drug abuse communities in Baltimore and San Francisco. As summarized in Figure 3.5 and Table 3.5, the hierarchy ranges from psychiatrists and physicians down to school administrators and teachers, with the predominant movement of referrals up the hierarchy and the predominant movement of information down the same hierarchy. This stratification of professions by virtue of their information and referral exchange might result from hierarchical levels of functional specialization: School administrators and teachers, on the lower levels, are least specialized with respect to illegal drug use and abuse; psychiatrists and other physicians, on the highest levels, are most specialized in drug problems.

Chapter 3 dealt with only the predominant *directions* of flows of information and referrals, however; absolute sizes of flows were ignored. This latter characteristic is important in the analysis of social-control systems, not only to identify individual components (as in Proposition 4.1), but also to establish interrelationships among components. In particular, if relative (predominant) directions of flows and absolute sizes of flows were highly correlated across a system, it could not function in an integrated fashion. Highly dense exchanges would characterize the upper or lower levels of the hierarchy, thus forming a sector barrier (by the principle underlying Proposition 4.1) to exchanges across hierarchical levels.

It is likely, therefore, that a specialized sector of the system, relatively dense in its exchange relationships with other sectors and at an intermediate level in the hierarchy, will serve as a kind of "facilitator" of exchanges – of both information and commodities – between higher and lower levels. Among the 12 professions involved in local drug-abuse communities in Baltimore and San Francisco, the social-service or counseling professions – including psychologists, social workers, probation officers, and clergy – are the most likely to serve this function because they have intermediate specialization in drug problems. Their hypothesized role can be formally stated in a second proposition:

> *Proposition 4.2.* The individual components of a control system will include a facilitating component characterized by (1) distinct component boundaries, (2) relatively *high absolute* exchange densities with other components, and (3) exchange-dominance status that is *intermediate* between lower (less specialized) and higher (more specialized) levels; this facilitating component will include, in systems for the control of deviance, the social-service or counseling professions.

Once the individual components of a system have been identified and the hierarchical levels of their functional specialization established, the model of a control system can be tested directly against empirical data; this is a third task in the analysis of social-control systems. Such systems will be characterized by the exchange dominance of lower levels of specialization by higher levels, that is, by flows of commodities (here referrals) from lower or less specialized to higher or more specialized levels and by flows of informational feedback – essential for system-level control of the commodity – downward in the same hierarchy. These reverse flows of information and commodities will be routed through the facilitating component, operating at an intermediate level of specialization vis-a-vis the particular type of control.

This model of the macro-level control system, again based on a priori theoretical considerations, can also be tested empirically as a formal proposition:

> *Proposition 4.3.* Commodities subject to social control are exchanged interpersonally in relationships characteristic of a macro-level control system; these will involve individual components, stratified by specialization in the control function, with exchange dominance of lower by higher levels (i.e., with commodity flow upward and information flow downward) and mediation of exchanges by a facilitating component.

This is the last of the three formal propositions to be tested in this chapter in an empirical verification of the general hypothesis that drug professionals, by virtue of their interorganizational exchanges of drug information and advice and referrals of young drug users, constitute a cybernetic system for the control of deviance among youth with respect to drugs at the community level. The next three sections of this chapter will be devoted to testing, in turn, Propositions 4.1 to 4.3. These propositions will establish the existence of a social-control system at supraindividual levels – at the level of professions *qua* professions and of groupings of professions in organizational sectors and functional subsystems.

Proposition 4.1: identifying individual sectors

The possibility that the individual components of a control system might be distinguished, in terms of the relative sizes of their within- versus between-group densities of exchange, is to be tested formally as Proposition 4.1. Differences in within- versus between-group relationships have been frequently noted by social scientists, for example, by Evans-Pritchard (1940). He writes of the Nuer: "Tribal sentiment is weaker than the sentiment of a village which is part of it" (p. 137).

Blau (1977) states this idea as a formal theorem: "The prevalence of ingroup relations in subgroups probably exceeds that in the larger groups encompassing them delineated by the same nominal parameter" (p. 130). This theorem is implied[2] by one of Blau's formal assumptions: "In-group associations are more prevalent than outgroup associations" (p. 281), which – restated for the particular associations of information and referral exchange – is the assumption motivating Proposition 4.1. The operational definitions and statistical measures Blau supplies to test his theorem are also similar to the ones employed here.[3]   2 19 3 6 1

The particular rationale Blau offers for his theorem can be extended to Proposition 4.1: "[The theorem] applies to all levels of subgroups. Thus, professionals are expected to associate disproportionately with other professionals, but not so much as physicians associate with other physicians, and the tendency of surgeons to associate with one another is expected to be still more pronounced. (Of course, other parameters modify this pattern; surgeons probably associate less with other surgeons in different cities than with internists in their hospital.)" (pp. 130–1).

If the assumption that ingroup associations are more prevalent than outgroup associations is correct, that is, if control systems are characterized

Table 4.1. *Largest one-eighth (18) of densities among 144 interprofessional flows,
12 × 12 information and referral networks, both cities*

	Baltimore		San Francisco	
Rank	Est.-density space	Professions in flow	Est.-density space	Professions in flow
Drug information and advice[a]				
1	.3709	*Within* Probtn	.3240	*Within* Probtn
2	.2004	*Within* Psycht	.2552	*Within* Police
3	.1323	*Within* Pharm	.1453	Psycht to Psychl
4	.1255	Psycht to SocWk	.1410	*Within* Nurse
5	.1196	*Within* SocWk	.1345	*Within* Pharm
6	.1157	Psycht to Doctor	.1260	SchlAd to Teach
7	.1145	*Within* Doctor	.1147	Psycht to Doctor
8	.1050	Police to Probtn	.1141	*Within* Psychl
9	.0930	Probtn to Police	.1135	*Within* Psycht
10	.0876	*Within* Clergy	.1106	Police to Probtn
11	.0804	*Within* Psychl	.1074	*Within* SchlAd
12	.0799	Psycht to Psychl	.1018	*Within* Doctor
13	.0795	Police to SchlAd	.0877	Psycht to SocWk
14	.0787	*Within* Nurse	.0769	*Within* SocWk
15	.0734	Pharm to Police	.0722	Psycht to Nurse
16	.0665	SchlAd to Teach	.0713	Psychl to Probtn
17	.0529	Pharm to Doctor	.0635	*Within* Clergy
18	.0447	Probtn to SocWk	.0575	*Within* Teach
Referrals of young drug users[b]				
1	.1419	*Within* Psycht	.1600	Doctor to Psytrt
2	.1028	Doctor to Psycht	.1197	*Within* Psycht
3	.0766	Probtn to Psycht	.0729	*Within* Probtn
4	.0647	*Within* Probtn	.0667	SocWk to Psycht
5	.0487	Probtn to Psychl	.0653	Probtn to Psycht
6	.0474	Probtn to SocWk	.0515	Police to Probtn
7	.0468	SocWk to Psycht	.0450	Probtn to Psychl
8	.0465	Psychl to Doctor	.0341	Psychl to Psycht
9	.0346	Police to Probtn	.0332	Probtn to SocWk
10	.0303	*Within* SocWk	.0279	*Within* SocWk
11	.0294	*Within* Doctor	.0273	Psycht to Psychl
12	.0263	Psycht to Psychl	.0243	*Within* Doctor
13	.0231	Psychl to Psycht	.0223	*Within* Psychl
14	.0227	Psycht to SocWk	.0222	Psycht to Doctor
15	.0187	Probtn to Doctor	.0185	SockWk to Psychl
16	.0185	SchlAd to Psychl	.0167	SchlAd to SocWk
17	.0134	Nurse to Psycht	.0158	Nurse to SocWk
18	.0128	Doctor to SocWk	.0155	*Within* Nurse

by greater densities of exchange within than between components, then this must be true – by Blau's logic – for the most disaggregated constituent units, here professions. Operationally, this means that the estimated-density spaces (EDS) of exchanges *within* professions ought to be larger than the EDS of exchanges *between* professions.

As a first approximate test of this deduction, Table 4.1 gives the largest one-eighth of the EDS (18 values) for the 144 interprofessional flows among the 12 professions in Baltimore and San Francisco, both for drug information and advice (top panel) and for referrals of young drug users (bottom panel). Because there are 12 possible intraprofessional flows (one for each profession), the expected number among the largest one-eighth, under the null model, is $12/8 = 1.5$ (this is equivalent to the denominator "statistically expected frequencies of association" in Blau's definition of "prevalence" given in note 3).

The actual number of intraprofessional densities among the largest one-eighth ranges from 4 (for Baltimore referrals) to 11 (for information in San Francisco). The probability (prob-value) that numbers this large or larger could have occurred by chance alone ranges from .017 in the former case to less than .00001 in the latter.[4] In other words, intraprofessional flows account for disproportionate numbers of the largest one-eighth of information and referral densities, with statistical significance above the .98 level, in both Baltimore and San Francisco.

Given the findings in Table 4.1, there is considerable evidence that densities of exchange are higher (and flows larger) within professions than between professions, particularly for information but also for referrals. This is sufficient encouragement to attempt to extend the results from professions to more macro-level components of a control system in a more general test of Proposition 4.1.

The individual sectors of the system for the control of deviance among youth with respect to drugs are suggested by social-theoretical considerations, as already mentioned. Individuals can be deviant with respect to drugs in two distinct ways – one medical, the other legal; those who are not deviant are ordinarily part of an educational system. Three of the professions in the

Notes to Table 4.1 *(cont.)*

Note: Ranked from largest estimated-density spaces, measured in ten thousandths.
[a]Baltimore: Expected within, 1.5; actual within, 8; prob-value, <.00001. San Francisco: Expected within, 1.5; actual within, 11; prob-value, <.00001.
[b]Baltimore: Expected within, 1.5; actual within, 4; prob-value, .017. San Francisco: Expected within, 1.5; actual within, 6; prob-value, <.0001.

NIDA survey – psychologists, social workers, and clergy – cannot be placed easily in the medical, legal, or education sectors. These professions will be grouped in a fourth sector, referred to here as the "counseling sector." The extent to which counseling approaches a true sector, in the control-system sense, will be determined in this section on empirical grounds. The extent to which the counseling sector constitutes the "facilitating" component, as introduced in Proposition 4.2, will be determined in the next section.

If the four organizational spheres – medical, legal, education, and counseling – constitute sectors of a control system, Proposition 4.1 implies that flows among these spheres (intersectorial flows) will not be as great as flows within the spheres but among different professions (intrasectorial flows); these, in turn, will not be as great as flows wholly within individual professions (intraprofessional flows). These deductions might be tested using estimated-density spaces. Mean EDS for the three types of flows – intraprofessional, other intrasectorial, and intersectorial – are listed in Table 4.2. The symbols of inequality in Table 4.2 indicate the relative sizes of flow types predicted by Proposition 4.1; violations of the predictions are indicated by diagonal slashes through the inequalities.

As Table 4.2 shows, the relative sizes of mean EDS predicted by Proposition 4.1 occur seven out of eight times (prob-value .004) for information flow in San Francisco and six out of eight times (prob-value .035) in the other three cases. All seven deviations from the predicted ordering are of two types: (1) flows within the counseling sector are smaller than flows between this and the other sectors, in all four cases; and (2) flows within the education sector are larger than those among school administrators or teachers in all cases except for information in San Francisco. The former may indicate that the residual counseling sector is not a true sector of a macro-level exchange system, a possibility that will be elaborated in the next section; the latter probably results from the organizational structure of schools, which usually have little vertical hierarchy and isolation of teachers relative to other professions.

The statistically significant fits in all four cases, the limited and patterned deviations, plus the earlier findings for professions in Table 4.1 – all provide substantial evidence for Proposition 4.1 that individual components of control systems can be distinguished by relatively high densities of exchange within components and lower densities between components. Table 4.2 also reveals surprisingly regular patterns of relationships – across cities – between ingroup and between-group densities of exchange. These regularities are summarized in Table 4.3, which gives the ratios of mean EDS for intraprofessional, interprofessional, and intersectorial flows.

Table 4.2. *Mean EDS for intraprofessional, intrasectorial, and intersectorial flows, for information and referral exchange, Baltimore and San Francisco*

Sector	Within professions		Within sector		To and from other sectors
Baltimore information[a]					
Medical	.1315	>	.0307	>	.0130
Legal	.1958	>	.0507	>	.0124
Counseling	.0959	>	.0164	≯	.0165
Education	.0412	≯	.0444	>	.0090
Mean	.1171	>	.0331	>	.0130
Baltimore referrals[b]					
Medical	.0446	>	.0120	>	.0034
Legal	.0330	>	.0083	>	.0048
Counseling	.0155	>	.0053	≯	.0067
Education	.00276	≯	.00278	>	.0017
Mean	.0269	>	.0089	>	.0043
San Francisco information[c]					
Medical	.1227	>	.0368	>	.0147
Legal	.2047	>	.0410	>	.0121
Counseling	.0848	>	.0162	≯	.0186
Education	.0824	>	.0781	>	.0117
Mean	.1270	>	.0362	>	.0145
San Francisco referrals[d]					
Medical	.0399	>	.0171	>	.0062
Legal	.0290	>	.0102	>	.0049
Counseling	.0207	>	.0052	≯	.0075
Education	.0067	≯	.0085	>	.0022
Mean	.0268	>	.0121	>	.0054

[a] 6 of 8 predicted; prob-value = .0352.
[b] 6 of 8 predicted; prob-value = .0352.
[c] 7 of 8 predicted: prob-value = .0039.
[d] 6 of 8 predicted; prob-value = .0352.

As shown in Table 4.3, the ratio of within-profession to within-sector flows is 3.5 for information in both cities; the ratio of within-sector to between-sector flows is 2.5 for information in both cities. The same ratios for referrals, slightly less consistent across cities, are a mean of 2.6 for within-profession to within sector (3.0 in Baltimore, 2.2 in San Francisco) and a mean of 2.2

Table 4.3. *Ratios of mean EDS for intraprofessional, intrasectorial, and intersectorial flows, for information and referral exchange, Baltimore and San Francisco*

	Within professions	Within sector
	Within sector	To and from other sectors
Information		
Baltimore	3.5	2.5
San Francisco	3.5	2.5
Mean ratio	3.5	2.5
Referrals		
Baltimore	3.0	2.1
San Francisco	2.2	2.2
Mean ratio	2.6	2.2

for within-sector to between-sector (2.1 in Baltimore, 2.2 in San Francisco). In three of the four cases, the ratios have themselves the same ratios, differing only in magnitudes of flows, with those for information approximately 1.4 times larger than those for referrals.

No attempt will be made here, given the approximate data on hand, further to specify these parameters. The regularity of these findings, however, suggests potentially rewarding future work – possibly using measures like EDS – in estimating parameters for models of within- and between-group relationships like those noted by Evans Pritchard (1940) and formalized by Blau (1977).

Proposition 4.2: the facilitating component

A second task in the analysis of social-control systems, after the component sectors have been identified, is to place these sectors in a hierarchy of functional specialization and interrelationship. Because absolute sizes and relative directions of flows are likely to correlate, there is a tendency for highly dense exchanges to characterize the upper and lower levels of a social-control system. Such patterns would constitute barriers to social exchanges across hierarchical levels, thereby threatening the functional integration of the system. One solution to this problem is a specialized sector, intermediate in the hierarchy but with relatively dense exchange relationships with other sectors, to serve as a kind of "facilitator" of exchanges – of both information and commodities – between higher and lower levels.

The facilitating component of social-control systems is the concern of Proposition 4.2. This describes the component as having three analytic characteristics: (1) distinct boundaries; (2) relatively high absolute exchange densities with other components; and (3) intermediate status in the exchange-dominance hierarchy. Each of these three hypothesized characteristics will be tested, in turn, using data from the NIDA survey of drug professionals.

Distinct boundaries. This characteristic has already been tested, for a "counseling" sector comprised of psychologists, social workers, and clergy, in the previous section. The attempt there was to demonstrate the relatively high density of exchange within this sector and the lower densities between it and the medical, legal, and education sectors. As was shown by the data in Table 4.2, however, flows within the counseling sector are smaller than its intersectorial flows – in both Baltimore and San Francisco, for both information and referrals. This result is compatible with the second characteristic of the facilitating component, high absolute exchange densities with other components. How might the existence of a facilitating component be established, however, without the identifying characteristic – greater within- than between-group densities of exchange – that motivates Proposition 4.1? Are the first two characteristics of the facilitating component, as stated in Proposition 4.2, necessarily incompatible?

A possible answer to these questions is that the counseling sector, really a residual category formed from professions remaining after the medical, legal, and education sectors were formed on theoretical grounds, may not be the true facilitating sector of the social-control system (a possibility raised in the previous section). Because the facilitating sector is likely to be comprised of all social-welfare and counseling professions, it might include not only psychologists, social workers, and clergy, but also probation officers (previously grouped in the legal sector), who are often social workers by training as well as by professional affiliation.

If the statistics in Table 4.2 are recomputed with probation officers moved from the legal to the counseling sector, the latter would in fact meet the requirement of distinct component boundaries. For information and referrals, in both Baltimore and San Francisco, flows within the new sector have larger mean EDS than those to and from the other sectors (data not shown here). Flows within the counseling professions, now four in number, still have a larger mean EDS than other intra- and intersectorial flows, as they did in

Table 4.2. The removal of probation officers from the legal sector also alters *its* flows, of course, and in the case of referrals in both cities, the mean EDS of intrasectorial flows exceeds those of intersectorial flows. In other words, the boundaries of the new legal sector are less well determined than those in Table 4.2. As established with Proposition 4.1 in the previous section, however, the boundaries of system components are less strongly maintained by commodity than by information exchanges because the latter can serve an integrative as well as control function.

Thus there is considerable evidence, consistent with control-system properties, that the previous counseling sector – plus probation officers – constitutes a separate component of the system for the control of deviance among youth with respect to drugs. Moreover, this component consists of social-service and counseling professions, precisely those included in the facilitating component for the control of social deviance in the formulation of Proposition 4.2.

High absolute exchange densities. The data in Table 4.2 show that the initial counseling sector, comprised of psychologists, social workers, and clergy, has lesser intra- than intersectorial flows – in both Baltimore and San Francisco, for both information and referrals. Moreover, the intersectorial flows of this sector are greater than those of the medical, legal, or education sectors, again in both cities and for both types of flows (right column, Table 4.2); these latter relationships are strengthened when probation officers are moved from the legal to the counseling sector. In other words, as hypothesized in Table 4.2, the facilitating component has the greatest mean EDS of intersectorial flows of any of the four sectors.

The same characteristic, relatively high absolute exchange densities with other components, can also be seen on the next disaggregated level – that of individual professions. A simple means to compare absolute exchange densities of professions is again via mean estimated-density spaces. For any given profession, the mean EDS is simply its estimated-density spaces averaged over all other professions. This measure has at least three advantages over upper-quartile counts as used in Table 4.1. Compared to quartile counts, mean EDS: (1) take into account all interpersonal flows, not just the upper extremes; (2) also constitute a ratio scale, but distinguish more finely among flow sizes; and (3) make the analysis of flow sizes compatible with work in other sections of this monograph.

The mean EDS for information and referral flows among professions, in each city, source and sink flows combined, are listed in Table 4.4. As

Table 4.4. *Professions ranked by mean EDS for information and referrals –
both cities*

	Information			Referrals		
Rank	Profession	Mean EDS	Flows, top quartile	Profession	Mean EDS	Flows, top quartile
Baltimore						
1	Psycht	.0264	8	Psycht	.0159	10
2	Police	.0254	7	*Probtn*	.0119	8
3	*Probtn*	.0246	8	Doctor	.0112	10
4	*SocWk*	.0234	9	*SocWk*	.0095	11
5	Doctor	.0212	7	*Psychl*	.0094	8
6	*Psychl*	.0168	7	Nurse	.0026	3
7	SchlAd	.0150	5	Police	.0026	2
8	Nurse	.0126	5	SchlAd	.0026	4
9	Pharm	.0112	4	Clergy	.0024	3
10	Teach	.0094	2	Lawyer	.0018	4
11	Clergy	.0092	2	Teach	.0010	1
12	Lawyer	.0082	2	Pharm	.0004	2
Total			66			66
San Francisco						
1	Psycht	.0331	11	Psycht	.0202	11
2	*Probtn*	.0265	8	Doctor	.0123	10
3	*Psychl*	.0236	7	*Probtn*	.0122	8
4	Doctor	.0224	10	*SocWk*	.0105	10
5	*SocWk*	.0212	10	*Psychl*	.0085	7
6	SchlAd	.0202	5	Nurse	.0040	7
7	Nurse	.0196	7	SchlAd	.0038	5
8	Police	.0162	2	Police	.0037	2
9	Teach	.0154	2	Clergy	.0023	1
10	Clergy	.0098	1	Lawyer	.0018	3
11	Lawyer	.0094	3	Teach	.0017	2
12	Pharm	.0078	0	Pharm	.0002	0
Total			66			66

Note: Ranked by mean estimated-density space (EDS) over 11 other
professions, both types of flows, with number of upper quartile flows
included for reference (the three facilitating professions are italicized).

indicated by the italics, three social-service professions – psychologists, social workers, and probation officers – rank among the five professions with the greatest densities of flows for all cities and types except information in Baltimore (for which psychologists rank sixth). Only the two physician categories, psychiatrists and other doctors, rank as high as the three facilitating professions. These professions, it would appear from this evidence, have relatively high absolute exchange densities with other professions, the result predicted – for the level of professions – from those hypothesized for system components in Proposition 4.2.

The regularity and persistence of this relationship is further revealed when the mean EDS for information is regressed on that for referrals in each city; these two regressions are graphed in Figure 4.1. As seen in this figure, the mean EDS for information and referrals are highly correlated in each city ($r = .77$ in Baltimore, $r = .91$ in San Francisco). Although information densities exceed those for referrals in both cities (the intercept is .0109 in Baltimore, .0111 in San Francisco), the fitted regression slopes are estimated at approximately 1.0 (1.02 in Baltimore, 1.13 in San Francisco) and are not significantly different from unity at the .05 level (both constants and slopes are highly statistically significant in both cities).

As might be expected from the rankings in Table 4.4, the three facilitating professions – psychologists, social workers, and probation officers – cluster just below the physician category in both cities, at a clear remove from the other seven professions. The striking similarity of the graphs and regression equations for the separate cities lends additional validity to the analysis (not even discounting the police, which are poorly measured in Baltimore because they are not represented as respondents). This is further evidence that the three professions have relatively high absolute exchange densities with other components, the second characteristic of a facilitating component stated in Proposition 4.2.

Intermediate exchange dominance. This final characteristic of a facilitating component has already been tested, for individual professions, in Chapter 3. The concept of exchange dominance was introduced in Chapter 3, which developed exchange-dominance scores for each of the professions as summarized in Table 3.5. In the exchange-dominance hierarchy as shown in that table, the four facilitating professions – psychologists, social workers, probation officers, and clergy – rank third, fifth, eighth, and ninth, respectively. In other words, they span roughly the middle two-thirds of the exchange-dominance hierarchy, from the more-specialized physician cate-

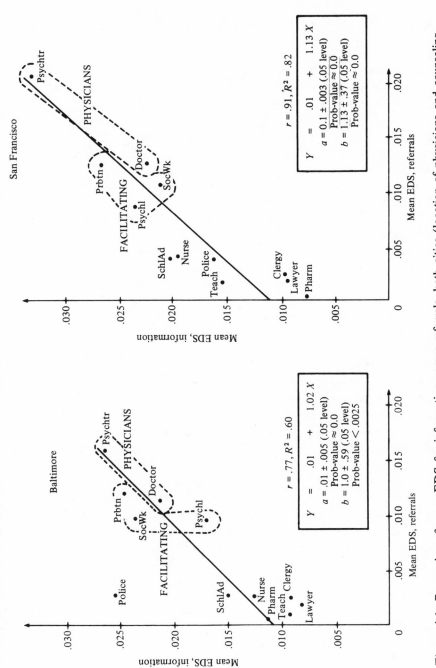

Figure 4.1. Regression of mean EDS for information versus referrals, both cities (location of physicians and counseling "facilitators" among 12 professions).

gory (ranks 1 and 2) to the less specialized education sector (ranks 11 and 12).

Similarly, on the four composite exchange-dominance rankings in Table 3.4, the four facilitating professions do not stand higher than third, with the single exception of psychologists for Baltimore referrals (rank 1), nor do they rank lower than tenth. This is the result predicted – for the level of professions – from those hypothesized in Proposition 4.2 for system components. Once again, the facilitating professions *qua* professions manifest exchange-dominance status that is intermediate between lower or less specialized and higher or more specialized levels.

To extend this finding to the facilitating component as a sector of a control system, however, which is the level of Proposition 4.2, it is necessary to assess the component's specialization in the drug problem relative to that of the medical, legal, and education sectors. The next section will attempt to demonstrate, using three independent measures of specialization – factual knowledge, information sources, and contacts – that the medical and legal sectors are more specialized than the facilitating one, at least on user referrals, whereas the education sector is less specialized. This is the final step in the verification of Proposition 4.2.

Measuring specialization: knowledge, media, contacts

The extent to which a profession or sector of the community system for socialization and social control of youth has particular specialization in the drug problem might be measured by several manifest indicators. First, factual knowledge of illegal drugs, drug use, and abuse ought to vary directly with the degree of specialization. Second, more specialized professions and sectors ought to rely more heavily on professional media – as opposed to mass media – to keep informed about drugs, whereas mass-media sources ought to prove more valuable to less specialized professionals. Finally, those in more specialized professions ought to rely more heavily on contacts within their profession, whereas less specialized professions ought to find contacts in outside (more specialized) sectors of greater usefulness.

That each of these three indicators might serve as a measure of specialization will be demonstrated empirically in this section using data from the NIDA survey of drug professionals. Each of the three indicators will be used, in turn, to test for intermediate specialization of the facilitating component of the social-control system, in this case vis-à-vis the medical, legal, and education sectors. The three indicators will reveal that the sector of greatest exchange dominance, medicine, is most specialized; that the legal sector, of intermediate exchange dominance, is more specialized than the facilitating component on information exchange, though not necessarily on referrals of young drug users; and that the sector of least exchange dominance, education, is least specialized on the drug problem. These findings will serve to confirm the third analytic characteristic of the facilitating component, as stated in Proposition 4.2, intermediate specialization to match intermediate standing in the exchange-dominance hierarchy. The findings will also move the analysis to its first glimpse of the emergent cybernetic system for the control of illegal drug use and abuse by youth.

Factual knowledge. The NIDA questionnaire includes 20 true–false questions in a section headed "Facts and Opinions about Drugs," and there is sufficient agreement among specialists on 10 of the items that they can serve as a "fact battery" to test general knowledge on drugs and drug abuse.[5] That these true–false questions constitute a valid test of specialization in control of the drug problem is borne out by the percentage differences in scores, as shown in Table 4.5 (right column), between generalists and specialists (this distinction is explained in Chapter 3). In all four sectors in both Baltimore and San Francisco, specialists scored higher (by a range of 12.3 to 25.8 points) than did generalists. Because this reputational category is an independent measure of specialization in the drug problem (Chapter 3, note 8), it serves as an external validation of the factual-knowledge questions.

Table 4.5 also supports the intermediate specialization of the counseling sector hypothesized in Proposition 4.2. As revealed in the rankings of the sectors on overall mean scores, the medical and legal sectors tend to be most knowledgeable about drugs (ranking second and first, respectively, in Baltimore, and first and third in San Francisco), and the education sector least knowledgeable (ranking last – the only sector below the grand mean – in both cities). The facilitating counseling sector ranks between these more and less knowledgeable sectors (third in Baltimore, second – but only 0.3 percentage points ahead of the legal sector – in San Francisco). Much the same patterns are seen for generalists and specialists separately.

Sources of information. The NIDA questionnaire includes 15 items on possibly helpful sources to keep the respondent informed or up-to-date in his or her professional work.[6] Of these 15 items, three can be taken – on face

Table 4.5 *Factual knowledge about drugs and drug abuse as a correlate of specialization in the problem, by generalists, specialists, and sectors – both cities*

Rank of score for all	Sector	Percentage of questions correct			Percentage difference
		All	Generalists	Specialists	
Baltimore					
1	Legal	69.5	68.3	83.5	+15.2
2	Medical	67.6	66.3	81.1	+14.8
3	Counseling	65.8	64.0	83.0	+19.0
4	Education	55.5	54.0	79.8	+25.8
All sectors		65.5	64.0	82.0	+18.0
San Francisco					
1	Medical	70.8	69.5	84.4	+14.9
2	Counseling	66.4	64.8	82.3	+17.5
3	Legal	66.1	65.1	77.4	+12.3
4	Education	57.0	56.0	69.0	+13.0
All sectors		65.3	64.0	79.0	+15.0

Note: Percentage scores on 10 true–false questions on illegal drug use and abuse. Sample sizes (generalists, specialists, total), for Baltimore, are: Medical (472, 45, 517), Legal (329, 28, 357), Counseling (415, 44, 459), Education (311, 19, 330), total (1527, 136, 1663). Sample sizes for San Francisco are: Medical (461, 44, 505), Legal (428, 38, 466), Counseling (400, 42, 442), Education (335, 30, 365), total (1624, 154, 1778).

validity – to be professional sources of information, another five as mass-media measures.[7] That the three professional sources (contacts with those receiving services, professional or technical journals or books, and regular meetings or conventions of the profession) constitute a valid test of specialization is borne out by the percentage differences between generalists and specialists as shown in Table 4.6 (right column). In all four sectors on all three items, specialists in the drug problem are more likely than generalists to find the sources helpful in keeping informed in their professional work. This is external validation of the professional source items as an independent measure of specialization.

Table 4.6 also supports the intermediate specialization of the counseling sector hypothesized in Proposition 4.2. As revealed in the rankings of the sectors on the percentages for generalists, the medical sector is the most specialized – followed, in turn, by the counseling and education sectors – on

Table 4.6. *Reliance on professional sources to keep informed on field as a correlate of specialization, by generalists, specialists, and sectors*

Rank of % for Generalists	Sector	Percentages finding helpful		Percentage difference
		Generalists	Specialists	
Contacts with those receiving professional services				
1	Legal	75.1	90.7	+15.6
2	Medical	74.4	91.9	+17.5
3	Counseling	74.3	96.7	+22.4
4	Education	61.6	85.5	+23.9
Professional or technical journals or books				
1	Medical	92.4	93.3	+ .9
2	Counseling	88.5	92.6	+ 4.1
3	Education	83.0	87.5	+ 4.5
4	Legal	82.1	92.5	+10.4
Regular meetings or conventions of profession				
1	Medical	58.3	67.6	+9.3
2	Counseling	49.7	57.7	+8.0
3	Education	46.6	55.5	+8.9
4	Legal	44.6	48.2	+3.6

Note: Percentages finding a "helpful information source" for "keeping informed or up to date" in their professional work – both cities combined. Sample sizes (generalists, specialists, total) are: Medical (874, 89, 963), Legal (727, 66, 793), Counseling (754, 84, 838), Education (607, 48, 655), total (2962, 287, 3249).

each of the three information sources. The position of the legal sector is more ambiguous; it ranks second behind the medical sector, as might be expected, on one information source (contacts with those receiving services), but last (though by no more than two percentage points) on the other two sources. This ambiguous finding results from the marginal status of police, who lack the convention and publication trappings of professionalism within the legal sector. The rankings of sectors on the percentages for specialists reveal much the same pattern as those for generalists.

This support for the intermediate specialization of the counseling sector is bolstered by the findings for the five mass-media sources: newspapers and newsmagazines, other nontechnical publications, radio, television news and documentaries, and other television programming. That these five sources constitute a valid test of specialization, in the inverse sense of the three professional sources already examined, is borne out by the percentage

Table 4.7. *Reliance on mass media to keep informed on professional field as an inverse correlate of specialization, by generalists, specialists, and sectors*

Rank of % for generalists	Sector	Percentages finding helpful		Percentage difference
		Generalists	Specialists	
Newspapers and newsmagazines				
1	Education	80.5	85.5	+ 5.0
2	Counseling	76.9	68.1	− 8.8
3	Legal	73.5	58.4	−15.1
4	Medical	63.7	55.5	− 8.2
Other nontechnical publications				
1	Education	68.5	76.5	+ 8.0
2	Counseling	59.4	46.3	−13.1
3	Legal	58.6	59.0	+ .4
4	Medical	46.5	50.5	+ 4.0
Radio				
1	Education	43.5	35.5	− 8.0
2	Counseling	35.9	29.1	− 6.8
3	Medical	33.3	28.1	− 5.2
4	Legal	30.7	31.8	+ 1.1
Television news and documentaries				
1	Education	84.0	79.5	− 4.5
2	Counseling	73.5	53.2	−20.3
3	Legal	68.3	58.7	− 9.6
4	Medical	61.5	56.4	− 5.1
Other television				
1	Education	58.5	51.0	− 7.5
2	Legal	40.8	25.8	−15.0
3	Counseling	39.0	30.5	− 8.5
4	Medical	36.7	25.1	−11.6

Note: Percentages finding "a helpful information source" for "keeping informed or up to date" in their professional work – both cities combined. Sample sizes (generalists, specialists, total) are: Medical (874, 89, 963), Legal (727, 66, 793), Counseling (754, 84, 838), Education (607, 48, 655), total (2962, 287, 3249).

differences between generalists and specialists as shown in Table 4.7 (right column). In 15 of the 20 cases, specialists in the drug problem are less likely than generalists to find the mass-media sources helpful in keeping informed or up-to-date in their professional work. Three of the five exceptions involve "other magazines, non-technical books and other printed material," a category that may not be interpreted as a mass medium by respondents. In any event, the overwhelming direction of percentage differences between generalists and specialists on the other four items constitutes external validation of the mass-media sources as an independent measure of specialization.

The rankings of the four sectors on the percentages for generalists, as shown in Table 4.7, reveal the education sector to be most likely to find helpful the mass-media sources of information in all five cases. The medical and legal sectors, in contrast, are least likely to do so in four of the five cases. The single exception is the "other television" category, which the counseling sector is less likely to find helpful than is the legal sector. For specialists, the patterns are similar – except that the legal sector is more likely than the counseling to find helpful three of the five sources.

Inter- versus intraprofessional contacts. On 2 of the 15 NIDA questionnaire items concerning helpful sources of information, the respondent was asked to judge personal contacts with people in his or her own profession and, separately, those with people in other professions.[8] Controlling for the percentage of respondents in each profession that finds contacts helpful, in general, the relative percentages of inter- versus intraprofessional contacts ought to serve as a rough indicator of specialization. One such measure is a simple plot of the percentages in each profession finding helpful intraprofessional contacts, on the x-axis, versus interprofessional contacts on the y-axis.

As revealed by this plot, shown in Figure 4.2, all six of the medical and legal professions (psychiatrists are combined with other physicians to assure sufficient sample size) favor contacts in their own professions to those in others. That is, all five of these points lie below the line $x = y$ (included for reference in the figure). Physicians, the profession most specialized by training and most of the other measures, have the most extreme preference for contacts in their own profession. The two education professions, school administrators and teachers, in contrast, favor contacts in other professions over those in their own; these two points lie above the $x = y$ line.

As might be expected of a functionally specialized component of the control system, the four counseling professions – psychologists, social workers, probation officers, and clergy – form a tight cluster in Figure 4.2. Because this facilitating component is intermediate in specialization, as hypothesized in Proposition 4.2, the component professions straddle the $x = y$ line.

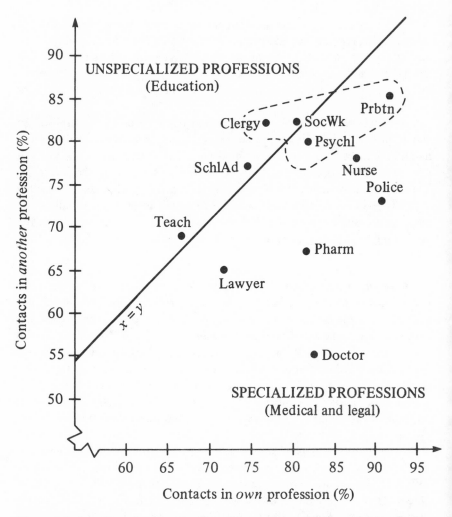

Figure 4.2. Location of sectors in plot of percentages of each profession finding helpful – as information sources to keep informed in their field – contacts in own versus other professions – both cities combined.

Because the component has relatively high absolute exchange densities with other sectors, also as hypothesized in Proposition 4.2, the component professions occupy the upper righthand corner of the graph, that is, they have relatively high approval for both types of contacts. Even though the data plotted in Figure 4.2 are based on two questionnaire items concerning helpful sources of information and are independent of the other measures used in this monograph, these data corroborate the emerging picture of the cybernetic system for the control of illegal drug use and abuse by youth. This picture will be further sharpened in the next section.

The arrangement of sectors – first approximations

Three independent measures of specialization – factual knowledge, information sources, and contacts – have established a consistent view of the functional interrelationship of sectors in the macro-level system for the control of deviance among youth with respect to drugs. Medicine is the most specialized sector of this system, followed by the legal sector; education is least specialized. The facilitating component, comprised of the counseling sectors plus probation officers, has intermediate specialization somewhere between the legal and education sectors.

Specialization is related to exchange density, as can readily be seen from the data plotted in Figure 4.2. The facilitating component, as hypothesized in Proposition 4.2, has relatively high absolute exchange density; consequently the four facilitating professions tend to value highly contacts in both their own and other professions. Figure 4.2 also reveals a tendency of professions in the same sectors to cluster on multiple variables measuring systemic aspects of the macro-level control system.

These functional interrelationships might be further specified by re-introducing exchange-dominance scores (from Chapter 3) into the picture provided by measures of specialization and exchange density. Because the analysis in the previous section indicated that especially the legal sector might differ on specialization involving information as compared to referrals, the separate exchange-dominance scores for these two types of flows constitute a logical pair of systemic variables on which to array professions. The plot of professions by the number of others dominated as referral sinks (x-axis) versus the number dominated as information sources (y-axis), separately for Baltimore and San Francisco, is shown in Figure 4.3.

Exchange-dominance scales for information and referrals are only moderately correlated ($r = .23$ in Baltimore, $r = .59$ in San Francisco), with the least-squares regression fits poorly estimated and relatively unstable. These regressions are graphed in Figure 4.3 (heavy lines) to show the deviations from $x = y$ (lighter lines) in the direction of greater dominance for referral exchange, in both Baltimore and San Francisco, as might be expected for cybernetic systems in which referrals constitute the commodity controlled. As in Figure 4.2, professions tend to cluster according to sectors

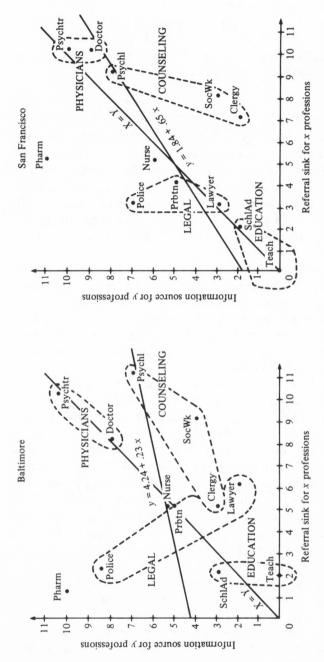

Figure 4.3. Location of sectors in plot of exchange-dominance scores (from Table 3.5), information sources versus referral sinks, both cities (numbers of professions dominated as predominant source of information, predominant sink of referrals).

(hashed lines) on the bivariate measures of systemic properties; the orientation of these sectors shows remarkable consistency between Baltimore and San Francisco.

The tilt toward referral dominance in each city is primarily the effect of the counseling sector. At the same time, both the counseling and legal sectors have exchange-dominance status intermediate between the higher exchange level and more specialized physicians and the lower and less specialized education sector. Among the two intermediate sectors, the counseling sector tends to dominate in referrals, in both cities, whereas the legal sector has the edge in information exchange; this might be expected from the findings of the previous section.

The data in Figure 4.3 are wholly compatible with the hypotheses of Proposition 4.2, that the facilitating component has distinct boundaries, high absolute exchange densities, and intermediate status in the exchange-dominance hierarchy. It is tempting to speculate that, as a general characteristic of social-control systems, the facilitating component will maintain a high density – despite intermediate specialization and exchange status – by dominating commodity exchange relative to that of information. Such a result is compatible with control-system theory, since commodities controlled (of whatever type) will have greater inertia – and consequently will require greater facilitating effort to exchange – than will informational feedback about these commodities. This speculation is derived ad hoc from the NIDA survey data, however, and cannot be independently tested with these data. Therefore the idea is simply stated here, without proof, as a corollary to Proposition 4.2:

> *Corollary 4.2.1.* The facilitating component, although of intermediate exchange dominance (Proposition 4.2), will have higher exchange dominance for commodities than for informational feedback, and will be the most unbalanced of all components toward commodity dominance.

For the system that aims to control deviance of youth with respect to drugs, for example, the number of professions that refer young drug users to the facilitating component will be fewer than the number of professions to which it gives drug information and advice. The legal sector, in contrast, as shown in Figure 4.3, will provide information and advice to more professions than give it referrals of young drug users.

To summarize this section, the two graphs in Figure 4.3 provide the first glimpse of the macro-level system for the control of illegal drug use and abuse by the young. The four sectors – medical, legal, education, and counseling – clearly emerge from the NIDA survey data; these sectors show remarkably consistent functional characteristics and interrelationships between Baltimore and San Francisco. The exchange dominance of the physicians is clear in Figure 4.3; it is comparable to their high degree of specialization in Figure 4.2. Analogously, the relatively subordinate position of the education sector on exchange dominance in Figure 4.3 corresponds to the low degree of specialization of school administrators and teachers in Figure 4.2. Both the legal and counseling sectors have more intermediate standing, on both exchange dominance and degree of specialization, with the legal sector dominating more in information exchange and the counseling sector more in user referrals. Despite this intermediate specialization and exchange status, however, the counseling sector – which is largely the facilitating component of the control system – maintains relatively high exchange density.

The importance of this latter fact, for the integrated functioning of a control system, can hardly be overstated. Were the absolute sizes of information and referral flows highly correlated with the predominant directions of these flows, and hence with exchange dominance, highly dense exchanges would characterize the upper or lower levels of the dominance ranking, thereby forming a sector barrier – by the principle underlying Proposition 4.1 – to exchanges across hierarchical levels. Were the facilitating component, in particular, not specialized in moving referrals from lower to higher levels (i.e., from the education to the legal and medical sectors), there would be much less intersectorial movement of user referrals, the commodity controlled by the cybernetic system. This would threaten the functional integration of the system itself.

The first two tasks in the analysis of social-control systems have now been completed. The component sectors have been identified and arranged in a hierarchy of functional specialization and interrelationships. It remains, in the next section, to establish directly the higher-level social-control system as specified in Proposition 4.3.

Proposition 4.3: the social-control system

If deviance among youth with respect to drugs is to be controlled, Chapter 3 argues, authority for deviant youths must pass upward through the interorganizational system – in the form of professional referrals – to ever more specialized components: to drug specialists, on the individual level; to higher-status professions, with respect to the specialized functions of drug control; to medical and legal spheres of activity, on the highest control-system level. At the same time, informational feedback about these flows must pass downward to less specialized individuals, professions, and organizational spheres.

Proposition 4.3 serves to integrate this cybernetic view of social control with the specific findings of this chapter. Based on data from the NIDA survey of drug professionals, community systems for the control of illegal drug use and abuse by youth have been shown to have four distinct sectors: medical, legal, counseling, and education. The sectors rank more or less in this way, both in exchange dominance and in their specialization in the drug problem. Applying control-system theory to this hierarchy, referrals of young users ought to pass upward from the educational to the legal and medical sectors, whereas drug information and advice ought to pass downward in the opposite direction. Between higher and lower levels of the hierarchy, exchanges of drug information and referrals of users ought to be routed through a facilitating component, largely the counseling sector of psychologists, social workers, and clergy, which has intermediate exchange status and specialization and relatively high densities of exchanges, particularly for referrals.

This model of the interorganizational system for the control of deviance among youth with respect to drugs, grounded in purposive, interpersonal exchanges of drug information and advice and referrals of users at the action level, will be used to test the more general control-system hypotheses of Proposition 4.3. This states that commodities subject to social control will be exchanged interpersonally in relations that aggregate as individual components of a larger system. This larger system is stratified by specialization in the control function; that is, exchange will be dominated by the higher levels (with commodity flow upward and information flow downward in the hierarchy), and the exchanges will be mediated by a facilitating component.

The various relationships implied by Proposition 4.3 for the drug control system are presented diagrammatically in the top panel of Figure 4.4. Given the new methodology of subgroup sampling and estimated density spaces, the empirical testing of control-system models like the one in this figure is relatively straightforward. Of the 24 possible flows of information and referrals among the four sectors of professional activity,[9] the NIDA survey data ought to support the predominance of six flows: of user referrals from education to counseling, and from counseling to medical and legal, and of informational feedback in the opposite directions, that is, from medical and legal to counseling, and from counseling to education. It follows that the six reverse flows ought to be least predominant, with the 12 flows (6 each of information and referrals) between the medical and legal sectors – and

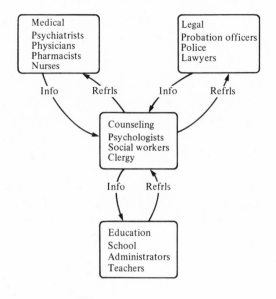

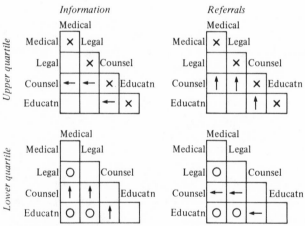

Figure 4.4. Hypothesized control system among four sectors and its quartile predictions.

between those sectors and the educational one – of intermediate importance.

To these predictions must be added the implications of Proposition 4.1, that within-group flows – of both drug information and advice, and referrals of young drug users – will tend to be larger than between-group flows. This

Table 4.8. *Summary of the predicted relative sizes of the 40 information and referral flows among the four sectors*

For information (20 flows)	For referrals (20 flows)
Largest flows (11 flows)	*Largest flows (11 flows)*
Intrasectorial (8 flows)	Intrasectorial (8 flows)
Medical to Counseling	Counseling to Medical
Legal to Counseling	Counseling to Legal
Counseling to Education	Education to Counseling
Smallest flows (9 flows)	*Smallest flows (9 flows)*
Counseling to Medical	Medical to Counseling
Counseling to Legal	Legal to Counseling
Education to Counseling	Counseling to Education
Medical & Legal (both ways)	Medical & Legal (both ways)
Medical & Education (both ways)	Medical & Education (both ways)
Legal & Education (both ways)	Legal & Education (both ways)

means that the 16 intrasectorial flows (8 each of the two types) will be among the largest of all flows. These predictions for the 40 total flows[10] can be summarized in tabular form (see Table 4.8).

The same predictions are shown graphically for sectorial-exchange matrices in the bottom portion of Figure 4.4. Arrows represent the direction of flow (to the row or column sector) that is predicted to be upper or lower quartiles – a handy means of preliminary investigation. The symbol "X" denotes flows predicted to be large (upper quartile) in both directions: "O" means that both directions are predicted to be small.

A rough idea of the accuracy of these predictions for the NIDA data set can be gained via sociograms, a technique popularized by Moreno in the 1940s and early 1950s (Moreno 1953). Sociograms are highly arbitrary in form[11] and can therefore be misleading. Firth cautions that representation of persons, groups, or categories as nodes, and of complex relationships as lines, is nothing more than a metaphor, one that ought not be reified (Firth 1954, pp. 4–5; compare Reader 1964, p. 22); what Whitehead calls the "fallacy of misplaced concreteness" is also relevant in this regard (Whitehead 1925, p. 75; Parsons 1937, pp. 29 and 476–7). Despite the sociogram's limitations, however, in the words of recent practitioners, "it provides an unusually rich means of providing a broadly grounded first approximation (i.e., a 'good intuitive feel') for the basic empirical materials" (Laumann and Pappi 1976, p. 109). It is for this purpose of exploratory data analysis, and with all the caveats listed above, that sociograms are included in the analysis here.

Figure 4.5 gives sociograms of the 33 largest (upper-quartile) inter-professional flows, that is, excluding intraprofessional ones, of both information and referrals in Baltimore and San Francisco. These sociograms reveal at least six of the characteristics predicted for macro-level systems of social control by Proposition 4.3, including:

1. *Predominance of flows within sectors.* These range from 7 (21.2 percent) of the upper-quartile flows for referrals in San Francisco to 15 (45.5) of the flows of information in the same city. All exceed the number of upper-quartile flows (6.5) expected within sectors under the null model.[12]

2. *Predominance of referral flows upward.* In both Baltimore and San Francisco, upward flows of referrals exceed those downward – 9 to 8 in the former case, 11 to 8 in the latter. Under the null model, probabilities are equal.

3. *Predominance of information flows downward.* Downward flows of information exceed those upward in both cities – 11 to 5 in Baltimore, 12 to 4 in San Francisco. Probabilities are again equal under the null model.

4. *Scarcity of lateral flows* (i.e., those between the medical and legal sectors). These range from 2 (6.1 percent) of the upper-quartile flows for San Francisco information to 7 (21.2) for referrals in the same city. In only the latter of 4 cases does the number exceed that expected (6) under the null model.[13] In all 4 cases, the number of lateral flows is less than the number of flows either within sectors or upward or downward.

5. *Prominance of the counseling sector in mediating flows* (as seen by the predominance of arrowheads in this intermediate sector). This relationship is presented more formally in Table 4.9, which lists the number of upper-quartile flows received by each of the 4 sectors for each of the 4 types of flows (information and referrals, in Baltimore and San Francisco). As seen in the top portion of this table, of the 84 intersectorial flows of the four types, 39 (46.4 percent) are to the counseling sector. This sector receives as many or more of the upper-quartile flows as any other sector (including the medical, which – because it has more professions – has a greater probability under the null model).[14] The counseling sector also makes the greatest contribution to chi-square (shown in the bottom panel of Table 4.9) in 3 of 4 cases (the exception: San Francisco information).

6. *Prominance of the medical sector as a referral sink.* Table 4.9 shows that the medical professions receive a disproportionate number of upper-quartile flows of referrals in both cities: 10 in Baltimore and 11 in

Information–Baltimore

Within sector	14	42.4 %
Between sectors–upward	5	15.2
Between sectors–lateral	3	9.1
Between sectors–downward	11	33.3
Total flows	33	100.0

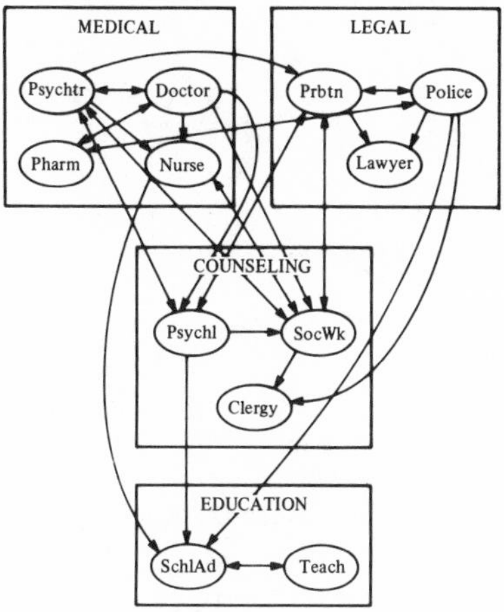

Referrals–Baltimore

Within sector	12	36.4 %
Between sectors–upward	9	27.3
Between sectors–lateral	4	12.1
Between sectors–downward	8	24.2
Total flows	33	100.0

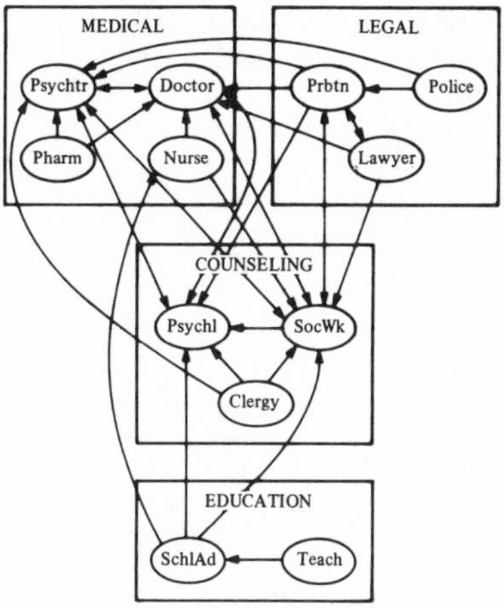

Information–San Francisco

Within sector	15	45.5 %
Between sectors–upward	4	12.1
Between sectors–lateral	2	6.1
Between sectors–downward	12	36.4
Total flows	33	100.0

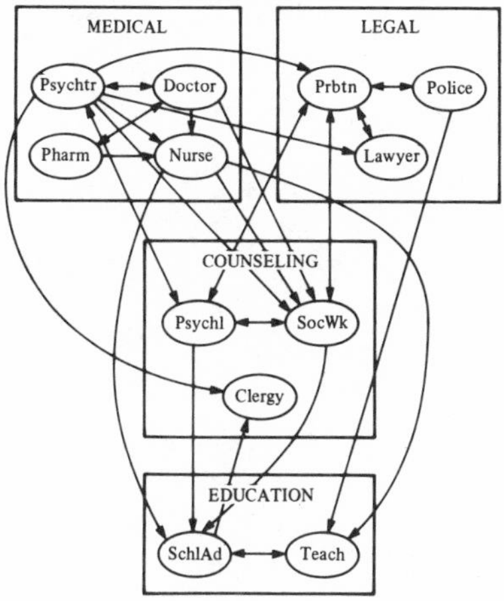

Referrals–San Francisco

Within sector	7	21.2 %
Between sectors–upward	11	33.3
Between sectors–lateral	7	21.2
Between sectors–downward	8	24.2
Total flows	33	100.0

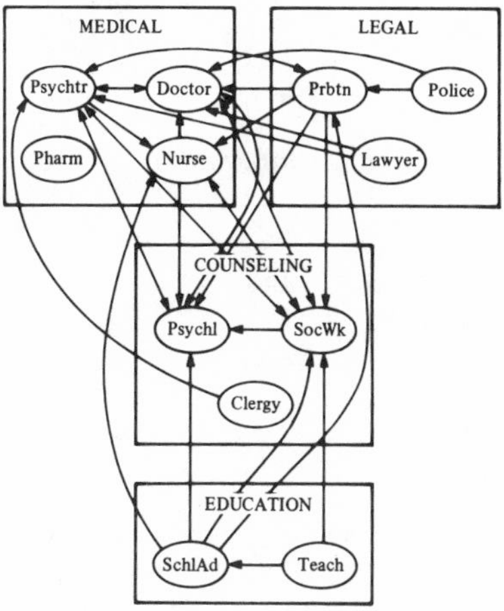

Figure 4.5. Thirty-three largest (upper quartile) interprofessional flows.

Table 4.9. *Thirty-three largest (upper-quartile) flows received by sectors –
both cities*

Receiving sector	Baltimore		San Francisco		
	Information	Referrals	Information	Referrals	Totals
Total no. received, each type					
Medical	4	10	1	11	26
Legal	4	1	4	2	11
Counseling	8	10	8	13	39
Education	3	0	5	0	8
Total	19	21	18	26	84

Receiving sector	Probability	Expected number	Predicted deviation	Actual number	Difference expected and actual	Contri-bution to chi-square
Baltimore information						
Medical	.302	5.736	−	4	−1.736	.525
Legal	.255	4.840	−	4	− .840	.146
Counseling	.255	4.840	+	8	+3.160	2.064
Education	.189	3.585	+	3	− .585	.095
Total	1.000	19.000		19	0.0	2.830[a]
Baltimore referrals						
Medical	.302	6.340	+	10	+3.660	2.113
Legal	.255	5.349	+	1	−4.349	3.536
Counseling	.255	5.349	+	10	+4.651	4.044
Education	.189	3.962	−	0	−3.962	3.962
Total	1.000	21.000		21	0.0	13.655[b]
San Francisco information						
Medical	.302	5.434	−	1	−4.434	3.618
Legal	.255	4.585	−	4	− .585	.075
Counseling	.255	4.585	+	8	+3.415	2.544
Education	.189	3.396	+	5	+1.604	.757
Total	1.000	18.000		18	0.0	6.994[c]
San Francisco referrals						
Medical	.302	7.849	+	11	+3.151	1.265
Legal	.255	6.623	+	2	−4.623	3.226
Counseling	.255	6.623	+	13	+6.377	6.141
Education	.189	4.906	−	0	−4.906	4.906
Total	1.000	26.000		26	0.0	15.538[d]

[a]Prob-value $< .50$.
[b]Prob-value $< .005$.
[c]Prob-value $< .10$.
[d]Prob-value $< .005$.

San Francisco, compared to expected numbers (under the null model) of 6.3 and 7.8, respectively.

This preliminary test using upper-quartile flows received, and the sociograms in Figure 4.5, lend considerable support to the hypothesized model of a macro-level social-control system provided by Proposition 4.3. As shown in Table 4.9, deviations of the actual from expected numbers of upper-quartile flows are in the directions predicted by Proposition 4.3 in 13 of 16 cases (the prob-value is .011).[15] Distributions in 3 of the 4 cases (the exception: Baltimore information) are statistically significant at the .10 level despite only 3 degrees of freedom. Large flows of referrals are particularly predominant in the medical and counseling professions; 44 of 47 intersectorial flows in the 2 cities are recieved by these 2 sectors.

In addition to the patterns of flows among sectors, the directions of flows – within sectors, upward, laterally, or downward – can also be tested using chi-square methods. Distributions of upper-quartile flows among the four directional types are tabulated for the sociograms in Figure 4.5 and discussed above in points 1–4. Chi-square statistics of the significance of these distributions, for information and referrals in both Baltimore and San Francisco, are given in Table 4.10. Tested are the cybernetic hypotheses, based on Proposition 4.3, that upper-quartile flows of information ought to predominate within sectors, and downward between sectors, whereas upper-quartile flows of referrals ought to predominate within sectors and upward between sectors.

As shown in Table 4.10, deviations of the actual from expected numbers of flows are in the predicted directions in 7 of 8 cases in both Baltimore and San Francisco. The two failures of prediction are seemingly random: Upward movement of referrals is underrepresented in Baltimore, lateral movement of referrals is overrepresented in San Francisco. The prob-value for 7 of 8 correct predictions, assuming a binomial distribution with $p = .5$ and $n = 8$ for the null model, is .035. Distributions of upper-quartile flows are significantly different from random at the .005 level in 2 of the 4 cases (those for information) despite only 3 degrees of freedom. Predicted deviations contribute over three quarters of the total chi-square values in all 4 cases.

These tests of the cybernetic-system model – tests based exclusively on upper-quartile interprofessional flows – are admittedly preliminary. A more formal test of the model, as specified by Proposition 4.3, might proceed along several lines. Individual types of flows among sectors (as represented by the matrices in the bottom portion of Figure 4.4) would specify more precisely

Table 4.10. *Chi-square tests of significance of distribution of 33 largest (upper-quartile) interprofessional flows among four categories of sector flows*

| Category | Null Model | | | | Difference expected and actual | Contri-bution to chi-square |
	Probability	Expected number	Predicted deviation	Actual number		
Baltimore information						
Within	.197	6.5	+	14	+7.5	8.65
Upward	.311	10.25	−	5	−5.25	2.69
Lateral	.182	6.0	−	3	−3.0	1.50
Downward	.311	10.25	+	11	+ .75	.05
Total	1.000	33.00		33	0.0	12.89[a]
Baltimore referrals						
Within	.197	6.5	+	12	+5.5	4.65
Upward	.311	10.25	+	9	−1.25	.15
Lateral	.182	6.0	−	4	−2.0	.67
Downward	.311	10.25	−	8	−2.25	.49
Total	1.000	33.00		33	0.0	5.96[b]
San Francisco information						
Within	.197	6.5	+	15	+8.5	11.12
Upward	.311	10.25	−	4	−6.25	3.81
Lateral	.182	6.0	−	2	−4.0	2.67
Downward	.311	10.25	+	12	+1.75	.30
Total	1.000	33.00		33	0.0	17.90[c]
San Francisco referrals						
Within	.197	6.5	+	7	+ .5	.04
Upward	.311	10.25	+	11	+ .75	.05
Lateral	.182	6.0	−	7	+1.0	.17
Downward	.311	10.25	−	8	−2.25	.49
Total	1.000	33.00		33	0.0	.75[d]

[a]Prob-value <.005; Predicted deviations contribute 100% of chi-square.
[b]Prob-value <.25; Predicted deviations contribute 97.5% of chi-square.
[c]Prob-value <.001; Predicted deviations contribute 100% of chi-square.
[d]Prob-value <.9; Predicted deviations contribute 77.3% of chi-square.

the control-system model. Mean estimated-density space affords a more exact measure than quartile counts of the sizes of flows. These two more formal methods to test Proposition 4.3 will be employed in the next section.

Testing the control-system model

Both information and commodity flows in a control system are one of four types: (1) flows that maintain boundaries, by the principle underlying Proposition 4.1, such as the intrasectorial flows already discussed; (2) control-direction flows, that is, opposite flows of commodities and information; (3) flows orthogonal to the direction of control; and (4) flows opposite to the control direction. These four flow types are listed in order of decreasing density, at least if the control-system model implied by Proposition 4.3 is correct. That is, control-direction flows ought to predominate in a cybernetic system, exceeded in density only by boundary-maintaining flows; flows opposite to the control direction ought to be sparse or nonexistent.

This reasoning might be extended to the community system for the control of deviance among youth with respect to drugs that is diagrammed in Figure 4.4 (top panel). As predicted by Proposition 4.3, larger flows of information ought to predominate within sectors and from higher to lower levels of specialization in the drug problem. Smaller flows of information, in contrast, ought to predominate from lower to higher levels and among sectors not *directly* related functionally, here called "noninteracting" sectors. The medical and legal sectors, which are horizontally separated, and these two sectors and education, which are vertically separated by the intermediate counseling sector, are the three pairs of noninteracting sectors in the drug-control system. For referrals, large flows ought to predominate within sectors and from lower to higher levels. Smaller flows of referrals, in contrast, ought to predominate from higher to lower levels and among the same non-interacting sectors.

These predictions can be specified for an exhaustive set of 40 flow types. Each of the 4 sectors has both intraprofessional and interprofessional but intrasectorial flows, for a total of 8 types; to these must be added $\binom{4}{2} = 6$ intersectorial flows in each direction, making a total of 20 flow types each for information and referrals. Reasoning from the general control-system model underlying Proposition 4.3, the 20 flow types might be ranked according to densities in 7 categories: (1) intraprofessional (4 types); (2) interprofessional but intrasectorial (4 types); (3) control-direction, interacting levels (3 types);

(4) control-direction, but skipping a level (2 types); (5) orthogonal to control, that is, intersectorial but within a level (2 types); (6) opposite to control, adjacent levels (3 types); and (7) opposite to control, skipping a level (2 types).

These predictions can be tested via mean estimated-density spaces, a more precise measure of flow size than the quartile counts employed in the last section. The 20 flow types are listed, in the seven categories ranked by predicted density, in Table 4.11 (for Baltimore) and 4.12 (San Francisco), along with the mean EDS for each flow type. Mean EDS is here estimated-density space averaged over the cells of each flow type in the 12×12 interprofessional matrix. The number of cells of each of the 20 types (total 144 cells),[16] plus the actual rank of the mean EDS, is also listed in Tables 4.11 and 4.12.

Predicted and actual rankings were correlated by means of both Spearman's and Kendall's coefficients of rank-order correlation. The Spearman's r_s coefficients range from .60 (for Baltimore referrals) to .93 (Baltimore information); Kendall's tau coefficients range from .47 to .81 for the same two cases. These substantial correlations between predicted and actual rankings of flow types (all coefficients are significant at the .005 level) constitute further evidence for the predictive value of Proposition 4.3 and for the fit of the control-system model to the NIDA survey data.

Examination of deviations from the predicted rankings reveals many of the poorest fits of the model to involve the counseling sector. For information, flows tend to be smaller than expected within the sector, whereas exchanges with the legal sector are poorly predicted in both directions. For referrals, flows from both the medical and legal sectors to counseling are relatively larger than predicted. Given the high absolute exchange density of the counseling sector and the fact that probation officers join the sector as part of a facilitating component, these deviations from predicted rankings in Tables 4.11 and 4.12 are not unusually troublesome. Indeed, considering the crudeness of the statistical test, the robustness of the control-system predictions are cause for surprise.

To assess the validity of estimated-density spaces for groupings of flows, the mean EDS for flow types can be compared between Baltimore and San Francisco. Pearson's r is $+.97$ for both information and referrals. Regression of the types for San Francisco on those of Baltimore produces intercepts of approximately zero (.0044 for information, .0021 for referrals), exactly as expected if the densities of flow types were in fact identical in the two cities (discounting sampling and measurement errors). Similarly, the slopes of the fitted regression lines are approximately equal to 1.0 (.99 for information, .88 for referrals). The former slope does not differ from 1.0 at the .05 level of confidence; the latter just barely does (it ranges between .78 and .98 at the .05 level).

In addition to the validity implied by these regressions, the mean EDS in Tables 4.11 and 4.12 also have a certain face validity in their correspondence to the predicted control-system model. Of the dozen largest flow types, in each of the four cases, between 9 and 11 are among the 11 boundary-maintaining or control-direction types – the only flows that exist in the theoretical model. Among the intraprofessional flows, the largest occur in the two most specialized sectors, medical and legal, in all four cases; the least specialized education sector has the smallest intraprofessional flows in all cases. Indeed, incorporation of finer rank distinctions based on degree of specialization could significantly improve the rank-order correlations in Tables 4.11 and 4.12.

Even the results derived straightforwardly from Proposition 4.3, however, provide substantial verification of the control-system model. The rankings of the mean EDS for the 20 flow types, closely predicted by cybernetic considerations, provide a more formal test of the control-system model than those of the previous section. Combined with these tests based on upper-quartile interprofessional flows, the results of this section strongly support Proposition 4.3, that socially controlled commodities are exchanged inter-personally in relationships characteristic of a macro-level control system.

Summary

This chapter has continued development of what for this monograph is a central theoretical task: reconciliation of the autonomous-system and purposive-action approaches to social control. Such a synthesis of the two perspectives, as applied to community systems for the control of deviance among youth with respect to drugs, must resolve a crucial question: How does the self-interested control of drug information and advice and referrals of young drug users at the level of individual action aggregate in the social exchanges required for the control of illegal drug use and abuse to obtain at the system level, at least to the extent that user referrals pass to more specialized sectors with informational feedback to the less specialized sector of origin?

A partial answer to this question, developed in the last chapter, involves the stratification of professionals and professions with respect to information and referral exchange. In the informal drug community generated by professionals themselves, through their exchange behavior, information is

Table 4.11. *Predicted and actual rankings, sizes of flows among the four sectors (as measured by EDS averaged over component cells).* Baltimore

Information[a]

Within each of the 12 professions

Predicted rank	Types of sectorial flows	No. of cells	Average EDS	Actual rank
2.5	Medical-self	4	.1315	2
2.5	Legal-self	3(2)	.1958	1
2.5	Counseling-self	3	.0959	3
2.5	Education-self	2	.0412	6

Within each of the 4 sectors

Predicted rank	Types of sectorial flows	No. of cells	Average EDS	Actual rank
6.5	Medical-within	12	.0307	7
6.5	Legal-within	6	.0507	4
6.5	Counseling-within	6	.0164	11
6.5	Education-within	2	.0444	5

In the primary directions necessary for control

Predicted rank	Types of sectorial flows	No. of cells	Average EDS	Actual rank
10	Medical to Counseling	12	.0278	8
10	Legal to Counseling	9	.0157	12
10	Counseling to Education	6	.0176	10

In the control directions, skipping one level

Predicted rank	Types of sectorial flows	No. of cells	Average EDS	Actual rank
12.5	Medical to Education	8	.0094	16
12.5	Legal to Education	6	.0203	9

Referrals[b]

Within each of the 12 professions

Predicted rank	Types of sectorial flows	No. of cells	Average EDS	Actual rank
2.5	Medical-self	4	.0446	1
2.5	Legal-self	3(2)	.0330	2
2.5	Counseling-self	3	.0155	3
2.5	Education-self	2	.00276	13

Within each of the 4 sectors

Predicted rank	Types of sectorial flows	No. of cells	Average EDS	Actual rank
6.5	Medical-within	12	.0120	5
6.5	Legal-within	6	.0083	8
6.5	Counseling-within	6	.0053	11
6.5	Education-within	2	.00278	12

In the primary directions necessary for control

Predicted rank	Types of sectorial flows	No. of cells	Average EDS	Actual rank
10	Counseling to Medical	12	.0089	7
10	Counseling to Legal	9	.0016	15
10	Education to Counseling	6	.0064	10

In the control directions, skipping one level

Predicted rank	Types of sectorial flows	No. of cells	Average EDS	Actual rank
12.5	Education to Medical	8	.0024	14
12.5	Education to Legal	6	.00058	16

Laterally between sectors not connected for control

14.5	Medical to Legal	12	.00055	17
14.5	Legal to Medical	12	.0095	6

Opposite the primary directions necessary for control

17	Medical to Counseling	12	.0071	9
17	Legal to Counseling	9	.0130	4
17	Counseling to Education	6	.0004	19

Opposite the control directions, skipping one level

19.5	Medical to Education	8	.0002	20
19.5	Legal to Education	6	.0005	18
	Total	144(143)		

Laterally between sectors not connected for control

14.5	Medical to Legal	12	.0152	13
14.5	Legal to Medical	12	.0063	17

Opposite the primary directions necessary for control

17	Counseling to Medical	12	.0127	15
17	Counseling to Legal	9	.0146	14
17	Education to Counseling	6	.0041	18

Opposite the control directions, skipping one level

19.5	Education to Medical	8	.0019	19
19.5	Education to Legal	6	.0026	20
	Total	144(143)		

[a]Spearman's r_s: .93 ($z = 4.03$, prob-value $<.0001$). Kendall's tau: .81 ($z = 4.70$, prob-value $<.00001$).
[b]Spearman's r_s: .60 ($z = 2.61$, prob-value $= .0045$). Kendall's tau: .47 ($z = 2.76$, prob-value $= .0029$).

Table 4.12. *Predicted and actual rankings, sizes of flows among the four sectors (as measured by EDS averaged over component cells), San Francisco*

Information[a]

Predicted rank	Types of sectoral flows	No. of cells	Average EDS	Actual rank
Within each of the 12 professions				
2.5	Medical-self	4	.1227	2
2.5	Legal-self	3	.2047	1
2.5	Counseling-self	3	.0848	3
2.5	Education-self	2	.0824	4
Within each of the 4 sectors				
6.5	Medical-within	12	.0368	7
6.5	Legal-within	6	.0410	6
6.5	Counseling-within	6	.0162	10
6.5	Education-within	2	.0781	5
In the primary directions necessary for control				
10	Medical to Counseling	12	.0358	8
10	Legal to Counseling	9	.0126	16
10	Counseling to Education	6	.0198	9
In the control directions, skipping one level				
12.5	Medical to Education	8	.0136	14
12.5	Legal to Education	6	.0160	12

Referrals[b]

Predicted rank	Types of sectoral flows	No. of cells	Average EDS	Actual rank
Within each of the 12 professions				
2.5	Medical-self	4	.0399	1
2.5	Legal-self	3	.0290	2
2.5	Counseling-self	3	.0207	3
2.5	Education-self	2	.0067	11
Within each of the 4 sectors				
6.5	Medical-within	12	.0171	4
6.5	Legal-within	6	.0102	7
6.5	Counseling-within	6	.0052	13
6.5	Education-within	2	.0085	9
In the primary directions necessary for control				
10	Counseling to Medical	12	.0125	5
10	Counseling to Legal	9	.0014	16
10	Education to Counseling	6	.0066	12
In the control directions, skipping one level				
12.5	Education to Medical	8	.0031	14
12.5	Education to Legal	6	.0026	15

Laterally between sectors not connected for control

14.5	Medical to Legal	12	.0150	13
14.5	Legal to Medical	12	.0063	19

Opposite the primary directions necessary for control

17	Counseling to Medical	12	.0102	17
17	Counseling to Legal	9	.0161	11
17	Education to Counseling	6	.0130	15

Opposite the control directions, skipping one level

19.5	Education to Medical	8	.0029	20
19.5	Education to Legal	6	.0072	18
Total		144		

Laterally between sectors not connected for control

14.5	Medical to Legal	12	.0010	17
14.5	Legal to Medical	12	.0096	8

Opposite the primary directions necessary for control

17	Medical to Counseling	12	.0080	10
17	Legal to Counseling	9	.0117	6
17	Counseling to Education	6	.0005	19

Opposite the control directions, skipping one level

19.5	Medical to Education	8	.0002	20
19.5	Legal to Education	6	.0006	18
Total		144		

[a] Spearman's r_s: .90 ($z = 3.94$, prob-value $<.0001$). Kendall's tau: .76 ($z = 4.51$, prob-value $<.0001$).
[b] Spearman's r_s: .68 ($z = 2.95$, prob-value $= .0016$). Kendall's tau: .55 ($z = 3.21$, prob-value $= .0007$).

beneficial to give away, whereas referrals are beneficial to receive. Formal positions can assure network centrality, in local drug-abuse networks, but so too can extra-organizational maneuvering – and these informal roles may serve as criteria of subsequent hiring in formal positions. Professionals will therefore attempt to establish themselves as information sources, whether formal or informal, and authority for deviants will readily pass – in the form of professional referrals – to those more specialized in the drug problem. In this way, the interorganizational network establishes referral flows and reciprocal feedback channels – the exchanges needed for control of deviance at the system level.

The stratification of professionals and professions on information and referral exchange is thus an important precondition for the control of deviance by the macro-level system. It is not a sufficient condition, however. Also essential to the concept of system is the interrelatedness of its component parts. At the network level, interpersonal relations represent communication and exchange; as constituents of higher-level control systems, they might represent boundary maintenance, controlled inter-sectorial flows, or informational feedback. This second precondition of macro-level control, the aggregation of social exchanges into the functional interrelationships of various specialized system components, has been the particular topic of this chapter.

A first step, therefore, was to identify the functional subsystems of the drug-control system. The obvious means, grounded in network concepts, involved the relationship between ingroup and outgroup densities of exchange – and the hypothesis that the former exceed the latter. This idea was confirmed as Proposition 4.1, which extends the ingroup–outgroup distinction to control-system components: professions, sectors, subsystems, etc.

Because the concept of control is so integrally tied to information flow, this chapter has focused on flow sizes. In this it differs from the previous chapter, which concerned stratification and hence confined attention to predominant directions of flows that, in turn, determine a hierarchy based on exchange dominance. If these two characteristics of flows, absolute size and pre-dominant direction, were highly correlated across a given system, it would be unable to function in an integrated fashion. For this reason, a specialized sector of social-control systems was hypothesized to serve as a kind of "facilitator" of exchanges between higher and lower levels. This hypothesis was confirmed as Proposition 4.2, which establishes a facilitating component with distinct analytic characteristics: definite boundaries, high absolute exchange density, and intermediate specialization and status. Thus Proposition 4.2 establishes another precondition for social-control systems.

It remained, in the final sections of this chapter, to test directly the hypothesis that drug professionals, by virtue of their inter-organizational exchanges, constitute a macro-level social-control system. This cybernetic model was confirmed as Proposition 4.3. Interpersonal exchanges of drug information and user referrals were found to aggregate in four distinct sectors – medical, legal, counseling, and education – stratified by specialization in the control function, with exchange dominance of lower by higher levels. Authority for young drug users, in the form of professional referrals, tends to pass upward from the education to the legal and medical sectors, whereas informational feedback passes downward in the opposite directions. Both flows are routed through the facilitating component, comprised of the counseling sector plus probation officers.

The establishment of even so simple a cybernetic model, with such piecemeal statistical procedures, marks an advance in social-science goals long ago set but not previously achieved. The general notion of a control system dates back at least three generations, and information theory and cybernetics from the end of World War II. The general systems movement, however, heralded as a new synthesis of the natural and social sciences a decade ago, has thus far failed to produce quantitative empirical results for macro-level social systems. The modest advances of this chapter were made possible by two new concepts, subgroup sampling and estimated-density spaces, which afford practical means to approximate network density and related features using survey-research methods. Under this method, interpersonal exchange relations, measured as densities in a social network, are treated as flows of information and commodities controlled in a cybernetic system.

In this way, the chapter has reconciled self-interested exchange, at the action level, with the social exchanges needed for control to obtain at the autonomous-system level. Through the confirmation of Propositions 4.1 to 4.3, stratification of individual professions, based on the interpersonal exchange of information and referrals, has been integrated with the specialization and exchange dominance of intersectorial flows. This establishes the preconditions for cybernetic control and thus completes the elementary analysis of social-control systems as exchange relationships.

Success in the piecemeal testing of various propositions does not, however, necessarily assure the overall fit of a control-system model. What may pass undetected as local deviations, in the test of one proposition or dimension of the model, may contribute to a favorable test of another proposition or dimension. This, in turn, obscures other important deviations. What remains to be accomplished to round out this analysis of social-control systems is a more straightforward testing of all simultaneous aspects of the cybernetic model.

5. The social system: boundary maintenance and hierarchical control

One shortcoming of the progressive development of the control-system model in Chapters 3 and 4 is that its various aspects and dimensions were considered in relative isolation. Chapter 3 concerned the stratification of professions and hence confined its attention to *relative or predominant directions* of information and referral flows (which determine the exchange-dominance hierarchy). Chapter 4, in contrast, was concerned with the division of interpersonal exchanges into subsystems and the analysis of relationships among these subsystems; hence it focused on the *absolute sizes* of flows.

These two distinctly different approaches of Chapters 3 and 4 are justified because the chapters set out to establish two quite separate conditions for cybernetic control at the level of autonomous systems – at the level of professions *qua* professions, and of groupings of professions in organizational sectors and functional subsystems. Chapter 3 demonstrated that information and referrals convey opposite statuses in exchange relationships, thus establishing *hierarchy* within the system. The other necessary conditions for a cybernetic system, *boundary maintenance* and the *functional interrelationship* of various specialized components, were established in Chapter 4.

Success in the piecemeal testing of various propositions in Chapters 3 and 4, however, does not necessarily assure the overall fit of the control-system model. What are undetected local deviations, in the test of one proposition or dimension of the model, may contribute to a favorable test of another proposition or dimension – which itself obscures other important local deviations (just as, for example, the correlational tests in Tables 4.11 and 4.12 may obscure local deviations among commodity-sector-directional types).

What is still needed to round out this analysis of social-control systems and their response to exogenous social change is a more straightforward test of the control-system model, which is the purpose of this chapter. Using more formal statistical procedures than those of previous chapters, this chapter will

139

examine the joint distribution of dyadic relations – between all pairs of professions on four types of flows – on measures of both hierarchy and boundary maintenance. Such an approach will improve upon that of Chapters 3 and 4 in at least four ways:

1. Analysis will be pitched at a lower system level, that of all possible dyadic relationships on all flows rather than at the level of the 40 commodity-sector-direction types.

2. Relationships will be considered simultaneously on both boundary maintenance and stratification, via joint distribution on separate measures of these two dimensions, rather than separately for relative and absolute densities.

3. Finer distinctions of local variations will be made than was possible using correlational tests.

4. Data will be considered simultaneously for both Baltimore and San Francisco, thus permitting generalization of the control-system structure independent of local-community variations.

Four simultaneous flows

Perhaps the single greatest problem in the construction of control-system models from networks of social exchange is the complexity of the data. Even a single-commodity control system involves 4 simultaneous flows – of information and commodities in two directions – between each 2 nodes. With only 12 such nodes, as with the drug-related professions in the NIDA study, the number of possible pairs (dyads) is $\binom{12}{2}$ or 66. Thus a model of the entire interprofessional exchange system must simultaneously assess 66×4 or 264 flows.

It is in the face of such analytic complexities,[1] for systems still relatively simple compared to those routinely discussed by social theorists (e.g., Parsons 1951), that the methodology of this chapter is advanced. The first step is a simplified measure of the 264 flows of drug information and advice, and referrals of young drug users, in the Baltimore and San Francisco inter-organizational control systems. One such measure is the quartile score for the estimated-density space (EDS) introduced in Chapter 3.

If quartile scores are to be useful in revealing a control structure underlying the data, as will be tested below, then the scores ought to be highly correlated between Baltimore and San Francisco. Cross-tabulations of the scores, with gamma coefficients[2] of intercity correlations, are presented in Figure 5.1. As Figure 5.1 reveals, the quartile scores for the EDS are highly correlated between Baltimore and San Francisco, both for flows of drug information

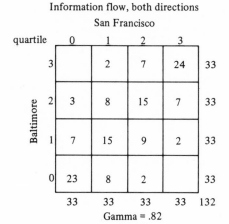

Information flow, both directions
San Francisco

quartile	0	1	2	3	
3		2	7	24	33
2	3	8	15	7	33
1	7	15	9	2	33
0	23	8	2		33
	33	33	33	33	132

Gamma = .82

Referral flows, both directions
San Francisco

quartile	0	1	2	3	
3	2		7	24	33
2	1	8	16	8	33
1	9	13	10	1	33
0	21	12			33
	33	33	33	33	132

Gamma = .83

(Baltimore on vertical axis for both tables.)

Figure 5.1. Intercity correlations of quartile scores, information and referrals (quartiles for flows in both directions in 66 dyads among 12 professions).

and advice and referrals of young drug users; the corresponding gamma coefficients are .82 (for information) and .83 (for referrals).

The congruence of the distribution of EDS among quartiles between Baltimore and San Francisco is also revealed in the similarity of classification of the dyad-directional flows in the two cities, as represented by the lower-left to upper-right diagonals in Figure 5.1 and summarized in Table 5.1.

Table 5.1. *Comparison of Baltimore and San Francisco on dyad-directional flow quartiles – information and referrals*

Baltimore vs. San Francisco	Quartile scores: information flows		Quartile scores: referral flows	
	No.	%	No.	%
Same quartile	77	58.3	74	56.1
One-quartile difference	46	34.8	54	40.9
Two-quartile difference	9	6.8	2	1.5
Three-quartile difference	0	0.0	2	1.5
Total	132	100.0	132	100.0

Of the 132 *information* flows in Figure 5.1, 77 (58.3 percent) are found in the same quartile in both cities, compared to 33 (25) expected under the null model; 74 (56.1) of the *referral* flows are found in the same quartile. The probability of congruences this great or greater, under the null model of independence of flow structures in the two cities, is virtually zero for both information and referrals.[3] In short, quartile scores for the EDS are highly correlated between Baltimore and San Francisco, both for flows of drug information and advice and for referrals of young drug users – a necessary condition if these scores are to reflect a control structure underlying the data.

Stratification and boundary maintenance

To apply quartile measures to test control-system models, the analytic variables of such models must first be specified. One such variable, that of *exchange dominance*, was introduced in Chapter 3. Using the social-science axiom that ingroup associations exceed outgroup ones, Chapter 4 added the variable of *boundary maintenance*, an application of information and commodity flows not incompatible with the boundary-maintenance function of Parsonian action theory (Parsons and Shils 1962) in that both involve the problems of integrating constituents of a sector to maintain its particular functions against changes elsewhere in the system.[4]

Taken together, the variables of exchange dominance and boundary maintenance determine mostly consistent requirements of control systems. Exchange dominance correlates with the predominance of information flows out of – and commodity flows into – sectors of relatively higher status.

Table 5.2. *Comparison of exchange dominance and boundary maintenance on predicted sizes of information and commodity flows between two nodes of different status*[a]

Type of flow (with respect to the higher status node)	Implications for flow size of:	
	Boundary Maintenance	Stratification
Information-in	Low	Low
Information-out	Low	High
Referrals-in	Low	High
Referrals-out	Low	Low

[a]For any dyadic relationship (i.e., for a relation between any pair of nodes, whether individual actors, aggregates, sectors, subsystems, etc.).

Boundary maintenance, in contrast, correlates with the predominance of large flows within sectors and relatively smaller flows between sectors. That these two requirements are partly (but only partly) consistent can be seen from Table 5.2.

In other words, the system-level requirements of boundary maintenance and stratification crosscut lower-level exchanges of information and commodities. Boundary maintenance requires exchanges within and not between sectors; stratification, in contrast, requires the movement of information downward *across* sector boundaries and of commodities upward across the same boundaries.[5]

Quartile scores for the estimated-density spaces (EDS) permit construction of *compatible* quantitative measures of both boundary maintenance by individual professions, sectors, subsystems, etc. (analogous to the work of Chapter 4), and of their stratification through exchange dominance (analogous to the work of Chapter 3). One obvious measure of boundary maintenance, one that shall hereafter be referred to as the sparse–dense scale, is the simple sum of the four quartile scores.[6] For pairs of functionally distinct sectors, this measure is *inversely* related to boundary maintenance, which requires all exchanges between distinct sectors to be *small*; for pairs within sectors the measure is *directly* related to boundary maintenance. The obvious equivalent for stratification, a measure hereafter referred to as the dominant–subordinate scale, is the sum of quartile scores for information-in and referrals-out (the two subordinate categories) *minus* the sum of quartile scores for information-out and referrals-in (the two dominant categories). The resulting measure is directly related to subordination and inversely related to dominance.

Under these definitions, both the sparse–dense and dominant–subordinate scales conveniently range through 13 possible discrete values. The former scale ranges from 0 (the "sparse" extreme) to 12 (the "dense" extreme); the latter ranges from −6 (for greatest dominance) to +6 (for greatest subordination). The presence of signed values in the dominant–subordinate scale is a useful reminder that the *direction* of dominance is completely arbitrary, an artifact of the choice of a node in a dyad to serve as the "row-node."

To reapply the reasoning of the previous section, if the sparse–dense and dominant–subordinate scores are to be useful in revealing a control structure underlying the data, the scores ought to be highly correlated between Baltimore and San Francisco. Cross-tabulations of the scores, in a graphical table designed to expose patterns of intercity correlations summarized by gamma coefficients, are presented in Figure 5.2.

As Figure 5.2 reveals, both scales are highly correlated between Baltimore and San Francisco. The corresponding gamma coefficients are .75 (for the sparse–dense scales) and .63 (for the dominant–subordinate scales). The congruence of the two scale scores between Baltimore and San Francisco is also revealed in the similarity of scores in the two cities, as represented by the predominance of values along the lower-left to upper-right diagonals and summarized in Table 5.3.

Of the 66 dyads represented in Figure 5.2, 42 (63.6 percent) are within a single point of the same sparse–dense score, and 53 (80.3) are within a single point of the same dominant–subordinate score. Computation of the probabilities of congruences this great, under the null model of independence of flow structures in the two cities, awaits elaboration of the underlying statistical model.

A statistical test

To interpret the magnitude of the congruence between measures of the sparse–dense and dominant–subordinate variables, it is necessary to determine their joint distribution under statistical independence. This distribution will be constrained by the uniform distribution of the component quartile scores. Fortunately, computation of the joint distribution is relatively straightforward.

The 4 quartiles of the EDS for each of the 4 types of flows determine 4^4 or 256 possible combinations – all equally likely under the null model of statistical independence. The distribution of these 256 combinations jointly on the sum of their 4 individual quartile scores (the sparse–dense scale) and

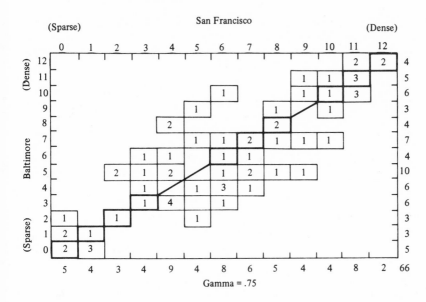

Gamma = .75

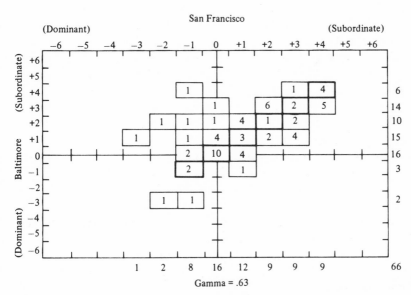

Gamma = .63

Figure 5.2. Intercity correlations of sparse–dense and dominant–subordinate ratings for 66 dyads among 12 professions. *Top*: Sparse–dense ratings (sum of 4 quartile scores). *Bottom*: Dominant–subordinate ratings (difference of 2 sums of quartile scores); rating is sum "information-in/referrals-out" minus sum "information-out/ referrals-in" (range is −6 to +6).

Table 5.3. *Comparison of Baltimore and San Francisco on sparse–dense and dominant–subordinate scale scores*

Baltimore vs. San Francisco	Sparse–dense scales		Dominant–subordinate scales	
	No.	%	No.	%
Same	16	24.2	22	33.3
Difference of 1	26	39.4	31	47.0
Difference of 2	11	16.7	8	12.1
Difference of 3	8	12.1	2	3.0
Difference of 4	5	7.6	2	3.0
Difference of 5	0	0.0	1	1.5
Difference of 6 to 12	0	0.0	0	0.0
Totals	66	100.0	66	100.0

the differences of the sums of 2 pairs of the same quartile scores (the dominant–subordinate scale) is given in the top portion of Figure 5.3. As shown in the figure, joint distribution on the 2 scales – under complete independence of component quartile scores – is symmetric about a peak at 6, 0 (values on the sparse–dense and dominant–subordinate scales, respectively). The probability of the modal values occurring, under the null model, is 16/256, or .0625.

Using this joint distribution, it is possible to evaluate the statistical significance of the congruences between scale scores in Baltimore and San Francisco as tabulated in Figure 5.2. The expected degree of congruence, under the null model that exchange structures in the cities differ randomly on the two scales, is (for either scale) given in Table 5.4.

The proportion of dyads expected to be within a single point of the same score on either scale in the two cities is thus 35.9 percent, compared to the 63.6 percent at least that congruent on the sparse–dense scale and the 80.3 percent actually that congruent on the dominant–subordinate scale (Figure 5.2). The probability of congruence this great or greater, under the null model of independence of flow structures in the two cities, is virtually zero for both information and referrals.[7]

The bottom portion of Figure 5.3 shows that the joint distribution of the sparse–dense and dominant–subordinate scores determines four equally probable categories, hereafter referred to as the dense, sparse, subordinate, and dominant categories. Actually, the discrete nature of the sparse–dense

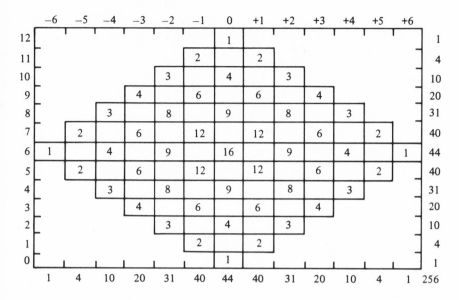

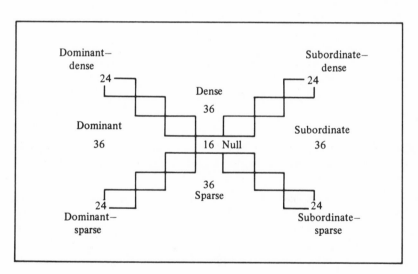

Figure 5.3. Joint distribution of sum and difference of quartile scores – all combinations. There are ($4^4 = 256$ possible combinations: the sum is sparse–dense axis (range 0–12); difference of the sum "information-in/referrals-out" minus the sum "information-out/referrals-in" is dominant–subordinate axis (range is −6 to +6).

Table 5.4. *Predicted probabilities of differences between Baltimore and San Francisco in either sparse–dense or dominant–subordinate scale scores under the null model of random distribution of scores*

Baltimore vs. San Francisco	Probability	Cumulative
Same	.123	.123
Difference of 1	.236	.359
Difference of 2	.205	.564
Difference of 3	.163	.727
Difference of 4	.117	.844
Difference of 5	.075	.919
Difference of 6 to 12	.081	1.000

and dominant–subordinate scales (constructed, as they are, from sums and differences of quartile scores) means that there will also be ambiguous areas among the four categories; these areas, divided into five intermediate categories, are also shown in the bottom portion of Figure 5.3. The five intermediate categories account for 112/256 or 43.75 percent of the combinations of quartile scores expected under independence.

The actual distributions of the 66 possible pairs of professions reveal that most fall into just three categories: dense, sparse, and subordinate. In Baltimore, 48 of 66 dyads (72.7 percent) are in these three categories; 50 of 66 dyads (75.8) are in them in San Francisco. As before, the predominance of subordinate over dominant dyads (15 to 1 in Baltimore, 18 to 1 in San Francisco) is purely artifactual; it is due to the ranking of "row nodes" from a relatively dominant sector (medical) to a relatively subordinate one (education), as well as to the approximate ranking of professions within each sector by relative dominance.

Using the joint distribution of the sparse–dense and dominant–subordinate scales in Figure 5.3 and the actual distributions of the 66 possible pairs of professions, tests of the statistical significance of the professional exchange structures in Baltimore and San Francisco are now possible. One such test, which exploits the chi-square statistic, is shown in Table 5.5. As the table reveals, the exchange structures in both cities deviate substantially from that expected under the null model and in the expected directions: toward a predominance of relations in sparse, dense, and subordinate categories. The chi-square values are statistically significant at even the .001 level in both cities; in both cities the predicted deviations account for a majority of the chi-square value (62.6 percent in Baltimore, 79.1 in San Francisco).

Table 5.5. *Chi-square tests of significance of distribution among nine categories jointly on sparse–dense and dominant–subordinate axes – each city*

Type	Null model					Contri-
					Difference	bution
		Expected	Predicted	Actual	expected	to chi-
	Probability	number	deviation	number	and actual	square
Baltimore						
Sparse	.1406	9.28	+	15	+5.72	3.53
Dense	.1406	9.28	+	18	+8.72	8.19
Subordinate	.1406	9.28	+	15	+5.72	3.53
Dominant	.1406	9.28	−	1	−8.28	7.39
Dominant–dense	.0938	6.19		0	−6.19	6.19
Dominant–sparse	.0938	6.19		1	−5.19	4.35
Subordinate–dense	.0938	6.19		7	+ .81	.11
Subordinate–sparse	.0938	6.19		8	+1.81	.53
Null	.0625	4.12		1	−3.12	2.36
Totals	1.0000	66.00		66	0.0	36.18[a]
San Francisco						
Sparse	.1406	9.28	+	15	+5.72	3.53
Dense	.1406	9.28	+	17	+7.72	6.42
Subordinate	.1406	9.28	+	18	+8.72	8.19
Dominant	.1406	9.28	−	0	−9.28	9.28
Dominant–dense	.0938	6.19		2	−4.19	2.84
Dominant–sparse	.0938	6.19		4	−2.19	.77
Subordinate–dense	.0938	6.19		2	−4.19	2.84
Subordinate–sparse	.0938	6.19		5	−1.19	.23
Null	.0625	4.12		3	−1.12	.30
Totals	1.0000	66.00		66	0.0	34.40[b]

[a]Prob-value <.001; predicted deviations contribute 62.6% of chi-square.
[b]Prob-value <.001; predicted deviations contribute 79.7% of chi-square.

Thus the chi-square test in Table 5.5 establishes that the inter-organizational-exchange structures in Baltimore and San Francisco are substantially different – in the predominance of sparse, dense, and subordinate relationships among pairs of professions – from what would be expected by chance alone. This test does *not* show, however, that the exchange structures are what might be expected under the control-system model postulated in Chapter 4. This model will be tested using the joint distribution of dyadic relationships on the sparse–dense and dominant–subordinate scales. First, however, it is necessary to reintroduce the control-system model in terms of the new categories: dense, sparse, subordinate, and dominant.

The control-system model

A system model for the inter-organizational control of deviance among youth with respect to drugs was successfully tested in Chapter 4 as Proposition 4.3. This four-sector model, summarized in Figure 4.4, can be restated in terms of boundary maintenance and stratification and the categories determined by the joint distribution of these variables. The matrix of flows in the top portion of Figure 5.4, derived directly from the control system shown in Figure 4.4, is "folded" into Figure 5.4 – in which each cell contains four flow values – in the lower left portion of the figure. The patterns of high and low values of the four flows in this figure reflect the four boundary-maintenance and stratification categories: dense (all high), sparse (none high), subordinate (high on information in and referrals out) and dominant (high on information out and referrals in).

As Figure 5.4 reveals, the control-system model determines three general classes of predictions for the relationships among pairs of professions on boundary maintenance and stratification. These general classes of predictions are:

1. Relationships contained within one sector – medical, legal, counseling, or education – will be *dense*.

2. Relationships between different sectors on the same hierarchical level (medical and legal), or between sectors separated by two levels (both medical and legal and the education sector) will be *sparse*.

3. Relationships between sectors on adjoining hierarchical levels (both medical and legal and the counseling sector, and counseling and education) will be *subordinate*.

Because of the arbitrary ranking of sectors from relatively dominant (medical) to relatively subordinate (education), none of the relationships

	Medical	Legal	Counseling	Education
Medical	Info Refl Hi Hi	Info Refl Lo Lo	Info Refl Hi Lo	Info Refl Lo Lo
Legal	Info Refl Lo Lo	Info Refl Hi Hi	Info Refl Hi Lo	Info Refl Lo Lo
Counseling	Info Refl Lo Hi	Info Refl Lo Hi	Info Refl Hi Hi	Info Refl Hi Lo
Education	Info Refl Lo Lo	Info Refl Lo Lo	Info Refl Lo Hi	Info Refl Hi Hi

Medical

Medical — Dense (X)

Info		Refl	
In	Out	In	Out
Hi	Hi	Hi	Hi

Definitions

	Info		Refl	
	In	Out	In	Out
Dense	Hi	Hi	Hi	Hi
Sparse	Lo	Lo	Lo	Lo
Subord	Hi	Lo	Lo	Hi
Domin	Lo	Hi	Hi	Lo

Other four not defined

Legal

Legal — Medical: Sparse (O) | Legal: Dense (X)

Info		Refl		Info		Refl	
In	Out	In	Out	In	Out	In	Out
Lo	Lo	Lo	Lo	Hi	Hi	Hi	Hi

Counseling

Medical: Subordinate (S) | Legal: Subordinate (S) | Counseling: Dense (X)

Info		Refl		Info		Refl		Info		Refl	
In	Out	In	Out	In	Out	In	Out	In	Out	In	Out
Hi	Lo	Lo	Hi	Hi	Lo	Lo	Hi	Hi	Hi	Hi	Hi

Education

Medical: Sparse (O) | Legal: Sparse (O) | Counseling: Subordinate (S) | Education: Dense (X)

Info		Refl		Info		Refl		Info		Refl		Info		Refl	
In	Out	In	Out	In	Out	In	Out	In	Out	In	Out	In	Out	In	Out
Lo	Lo	Lo	Lo	Lo	Lo	Lo	Lo	Hi	Lo	Lo	Hi	Hi	Hi	Hi	Hi

Figure 5.4. Predicted information and referral patterns based on control-system model.

between sectors are predicted to be dominant. As already seen, this is simply an artifact of the particular methods employed; the substantive point is that both the boundary-maintenance and stratification dimensions of control systems are represented in the three general classes of predictions for sectorial flows listed here.

Strictly speaking, of course, four binary-flow distinctions determine not four but 16 boundary-maintenance and stratification categories.[8] At least four categories not determined by the general predictions are likely to have substantive meaning in control-system models. These additional categories might be defined in terms of the four flow values in Figure 5.4: high on all flows in (universal sinks), high on all flows out (universal sources), high on information in and out (information-bounded), and high on referrals in and out (referral-bounded). The first two categories suggest the generalization of functions beyond the system-level hierarchy; the latter two suggest the specialization of boundaries rather than of functional interrelationships. Although neither of these dimensions is significant in the analysis here, the theoretical possibility suggests a possible use of higher-dimensional joint distributions for testing more complex control-system models.[9]

The other 8 of the 16 possible boundary-maintenance and stratification categories are all characterized by patterns with three of one value of flow (high or low) and one of the other value (e.g., low-low-low-high). In the absence of a convincing substantive interpretation for these categories, it seems better to treat such patterns – when they arise in control-system analysis – as statistical deviations from the 8 categories that *can* be given substantive interpretation.

Testing the model

Now that the control-system model developed in Chapter 4 has been reformulated in terms of boundary maintenance and stratification and the categories determined by the joint distribution of these variables, it remains to test this model using the distributions of relationships among the new categories: dense, sparse, subordinate, and dominant. Those dyadic relations correctly predicted by the control-system model, as represented at the lower left of Figure 5.4, are located in matrices of the same type and orientation – separately for Baltimore and San Francisco – in Figure 5.5. As can be seen in this figure, roughly half the 66 possible relationships between pairs of professions are correctly predicted in each city. This includes 43 (32.6 percent) exactly predicted and 25 (18.9 percent) predicted peripherally, that is, specified by an intermediate category that borders on the predicted one.

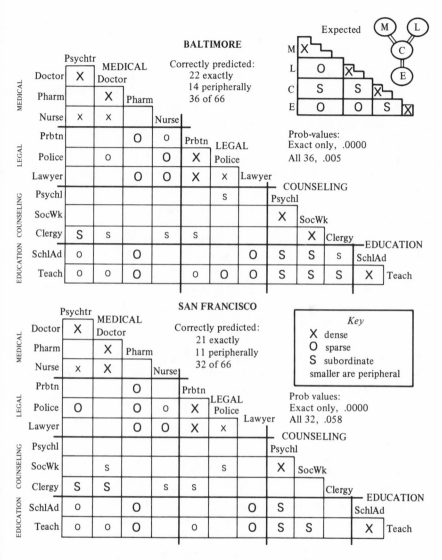

Prob-values: large letters, .14; small letters, .39

Figure 5.5. Location of cell values correctly predicted from expected sector flows.

The probability of exactly specifying a relationship by chance alone is .1406; the probability of peripherally predicting one is .3906.[10] Based on these probabilities, the exact fit of the control-system model is statistically significant at the zero level to five decimal places in both cities, whereas the prob-value of the peripheral fit is less than .005 in Baltimore and approximately .058 in San Francisco. In other words, the fit of the control-system model is indeed good in terms of the boundary-maintenance and stratification dimensions.

A finer analysis of the fit of the control-system model, at the level of individual sector flows and based on the simultaneous consideration of data from Baltimore and San Francisco, is given in Table 5.6. As can be seen in this table, the probability of correctly predicting a dyadic relation in a given sector exchange is a direct function of the number of such relations involved in that exchange, that is, of the number of individual cells in the given submatrix. For the NIDA data, the number of cells *exactly* predicted exceeds that expected under the null model for 8 of the 10 sector flows: in 7 of 10 cases, the control-system model fit is significantly better than would be expected at the .05 level. Across the entire system, 18.56 exact predictions are expected compared to 43 actually obtained.

Despite this substantial verification of the hypothesized control-system model at high levels of statistical significance, closer examination of the classification of dyadic relations reveals two systematic ways in which the model has failed:

1. There is a tendency for exchange-dominance relationships between sectors on adjoining levels (both the medical and legal ones with counseling, and counseling with education) to be *reciprocated*; this tendency is seen in a scattering of dense relations among the subordinate ones in submatrices (3,1), (3,2), and (4,3).

2. There is a tendency for exchange-dominance relationships to "jump" both sector boundaries and hierarchical levels; this is seen in the scattering of subordinate relations among the sparse ones between different sectors on the same hierarchical level (medical and legal), and between sectors separated by two levels (both the medical and legal ones with education).

After these modifications are fitted to the model, only a single sector flow – that involving the legal and counseling sectors – remains an outlier. None of these 18 dyadic relations in the two cities is exactly predicted by the original model, although 4 are peripherally predicted (see Figure 5.5). Only 6 of the 18 are predicted by the modified model, compared to an expected number – under the null model – of 6.75.

Table 5.6. *Statistical significance of 10 predicted sector flows – Baltimore and San Francisco (pooled numbers of cells)*

Sub-matrix	Sector flows	Predicted nature	Probability of each	# Cells in submatrix	Expected number correct	Actual number correct	Difference	Prob-value
(1,1)	Medical–Medical	Dense (X)	.1406	12	1.69	5	+ 3.31	.02
(2,2)	Legal–Legal	Dense (X)	.1406	6	.84	4	+ 3.16	.005
(3,3)	Counseling–Counseling	Dense (X)	.1406	6	.84	3	+ 2.16	.04
(4,4)	Education–Education	Dense (X)	.1406	2	.28	2	+ 1.72	.02
(2,1)	Legal–Medical	Sparse (O)	.1406	24	3.38	9	+ 5.62	.001
(4,1)	Education–Medical	Sparse (O)	.1406	16	2.25	4	+ 1.75	.18[a]
(4,2)	Education–Legal	Sparse (O)	.1406	12	1.69	5	+ 3.31	.02
(3,1)	Counseling–Medical	Subordinate (S)	.1406	24	3.38	3	− 0.38	.4[a]
(3,2)	Counseling–Legal	Subordinate (S)	.1406	18	2.53	0	− 2.53	1.0[a]
(4,3)	Education–Counseling	Subordinate (S)	.1406	12	1.69	8	+ 6.31	.0001
Totals				132	18.56	43	+24.44	

[a]Failed at .05 significance level.

The difficulty in accounting for these sector flows is probably related to the special characteristics – noted in Chapter 4 – of the "facilitating" counseling sector. These include comparatively high absolute exchange densities with other sectors.[11] Indeed, the model predicting that dyadic relations in the counseling-legal submatrix will be dense in joint distribution on the boundary-maintenance and stratification dimensions is supported at the .03 level of statistical significance.

Summary

The purpose of this chapter has been to develop a straightforward test of the cybernetic model of the control of illegal drug use and abuse by youth and – by extension – all such autonomous social-control systems emerging from interpersonal exchange at the action level. Using more formal statistical procedures than those of previous chapters, this chapter has considered all four types of flows among all 66 possible pairs of 12 professions, simultaneously on both the boundary-maintenance and stratification dimensions of a social-control system.

This work has remedied a major shortcoming of the previous two chapters, that the various aspects and dimensions of the control-system model were considered in relative isolation. Chapter 3 dealt with the stratification of professions and hence confined itself to *relative or predominant directions* of flows (which determine the exchange-dominance hierarchy). Chapter 4, in contrast, was concerned with the division of interpersonal exchanges into subsystems and the analysis of relationships among these subsystems; hence it focused on the *absolute sizes* of information and referral flows.

There has been a finer discrimination of local variations in this chapter than was possible with the correlational tests of Chapters 3 and 4. The analysis here has been pitched at a lower system level, that of the 66 dyadic relationships, simultaneously on four flows, compared to the 40 commodity-sector-direction types used in Chapter 4. Data were also considered simultaneously for both Baltimore and San Francisco, thus permitting generalization of the control-system structure independent of local-community variations.

A control-system model, first introduced in Chapter 4, was reformulated in terms of the stratification and boundary-maintenance categories. Using these categories, plus the joint distribution of their underlying scales, the interprofessional systems for the control of drug abuse by youth were found to be structured with a high degree of statistical significance in both Baltimore and San Francisco. Although the original control-system model was substantiated at a high level of statistical significance, a modified model – accommodating tendencies toward the "jump" of dominance over several hierarchical levels and the reciprocity of subordinate relationships – improved the fit somewhat. This structure persists amid city, organizational, and individual variations.

Chapter 5 has thus completed the work of Chapters 3 and 4 by formally establishing the autonomous system for the control of deviance by youth with respect to drugs at supraindividual levels – at the level of professions *qua* professions and of groupings of professions in organizational sectors and functional subsystems. This system suggests the means by which the self-interested control of information and referrals, at the level of individual action, can aggregate in the social exchanges needed for the control of drug abuse to obtain at the system level.

6. Summary:
the control system in context

The emergence of a so-called drug problem among American youth in the latter half of the 1960s remains one of the most rapid and dramatic social changes in U.S. history. In a period of only a few years, the use of psychoactive drugs spread from a deviant activity of the socially marginal to a major societal problem thought to afflict – or at least to threaten – the nation's youth in general. As we have seen, this sudden emergence of a national drug problem had a profound impact on community systems for the control of deviance among youth, with increasing pressures for change on three organizational systems: the health system, the law-enforcement and criminal-justice system, and the educational system.

The response of this total system for the social control of youth to the sudden "disturbance" constituted by the drug problem has been the central focus of this study. Although the disturbance to the control system was eventually contained by it, this did not occur without strain on various organizational facilities, strains that reverberated upward from facilities to mobilization channels to norms until the tension finally eased under a new balance of "control" relationships. The details of precisely how this occurred constitute an excellent case study of a much more general sociological phenomenon: the control by organizational systems of exogenous social change.

Much of the organizational response to social change, for example, the shift of government money and other resources to the new problem, may be related more to public perceptions than to more objective measures of the problem. For this reason, public perceptions of the drug problem, as molded by – or reflected in – coverage by the mass media, were traced through several distinct evolutionary stages. Judging from these stages, the NIDA survey of drug professionals that serves as the data base for this study was ideally timed: All objective and mass-media measures of the drug problem peaked during or shortly before the NIDA survey, while public concern for drugs as a national problem was in its sharpest ascent (about to peak only months afterward). Data on federal spending on drug programs also reveal

158

that the NIDA survey was well timed to capture the full impact of massive shifts in government resources, both in direct program spending and via block and formula grants.

Without such immediately prior social change, the cross-sectional analysis conducted here, presumably of an equilibrium state, would necessarily be confined to the structural aspects of the organizational control system. Because prior change can be assumed, however, the cross-sectional analysis informs dynamic as well as static aspects of the control system. Thus the NIDA data permit about as close an approximation of a laboratory test of system disturbance and its containment as one is likely to find in an uncontrolled and uncontrollable setting. Because system-level shifts in funding translated directly into increased resources for professionals in a wide range of specialties, including treatment and rehabilitation, research, and education, it was also possible to link system effects and individual responses to the NIDA questionnaire.

Steps in the control of change

The response to the drug problem by community systems for the control of deviance among youth has been documented – step-by-step – in the previous five chapters. This documentation took the form of a long series of causes and effects extending from the sudden appearance of the problem itself (a change assumed here to be exogenous to the system) to the final cybernetic equilibrium of the inter-organizational system. Because this causal chain has meandered through five chapters, however, and was not always presented – for the sake of exposition – in temporal order, it is worth summarizing here as a unified sequence. This includes 22 stages, each summarized from previous chapters, but here given an approximate temporal and causal ordering:

1. The use and abuse of illegal drugs sharply increased on university and secondary-school campuses, accompanied by steep rises in the rates of accidental drug poisoning, drug-related deaths, and arrests for the possession and sale of drugs, particularly in younger age categories, with a resulting strain on situational facilities beginning in the educational sector.

2. Mass-media attention shifted to the new social trend, lagging only months behind more objective indicators of the problem itself, with the "agenda-setting" result of increasing the salience of the problem for opinion leaders, government officials, and ultimately the public at large.

3. Public concern over the problem, as measured by Gallup and other national opinion polls on the most important problems facing the country, increased sharply.

4. Government money and other resources – including support for treatment, rehabilitation, research, and education – shifted to the new problem, with funds transferred to the state and local levels from the federal government through block and formula grants.

5. Local specialists in the new problem, suddenly in short supply, came to command greater salaries, relevant specialties were given higher-level positions and greater prominence in a wide range of community organizations; the prestige of these specialties rose relative to other subfields in a wide range of professions.

6. Attracted by personal rewards, including money, positions, prestige, personal autonomy, opportunity for innovation and advancement, etc., professionals scrambled to acquire specialization and credentials of "expertise" in the new problem; often this required a return to the classroom for post degree academic training.

7. As a result of personal investment in extraprofessional training, and of the personal rewards that accrue to experts in areas of expanding national importance, professionals who chose to specialize in the drug problem came to acquire a vested interest in it.

8. Continued specialization depended on a steady supply of deviants with the social problem, that is, a supply of young people who required processing by the larger system of social control; these *social* commodities, known universally among professionals as "referrals," came to acquire many of the system characteristics of scarce *economic* commodities.

9. Like other socially valued and scarce commodities (money, political power, influence, etc.), referrals became a generalized medium of exchange, one that translates status and rewards across organizational and system boundaries.

10. Strain developed on the channels of communication between the education sector and others (medical and legal) more specialized in the control of deviance; professionals in the schools increased their demands on the legal system, for example, for legal advice from lawyers and for working contacts with law-enforcement officials.

11. Component sectors and subsystems of the more macro-level control system came to be distinguished by strains on communication channels, that is, by relatively high densities of exchange within the components and much lower ones between them.

12. This strain on channels of communication was felt by professionals as a perceived lack of contacts for information on other organizations, particularly those in functionally distinct subsystems.

13. Professionals enjoying local reputations as specialists in the problem provided information to nonspecialists in a wide range of other organizations, thus countering the strain on channels of communication, in exchange for the referrals that conveyed status and rewards as a generalized medium.

14. Professionals seeking to achieve specialist status attempted to manipulate events to become central nodes in information and referral networks; they ordinarily began by providing information to a wide range of other professions and professionals who presumably reciprocated with referrals at a later time (at least the former status is temporally prior to the latter).

15. Despite the strain on situational facilities caused by the increased numbers of social deviants, referrals of young drug users were exchanged across organizational boundaries; the value to specialists of referrals as generalized media meant that individual self-interest was a sufficient (though not necessarily exclusive) cause of such interorganizational exchanges.

16. Because of the strain on interorganizational channels of communication, the demand among nonspecialists for information, and the incentives for both specialists and would-be specialists to supply information, this commodity was also exchanged across organizational boundaries for purely individual self-interests.

17. Because specialists sought to gain referrals in exchange for information, whereas nonspecialists sought information and needed to make referrals, information and referrals tended to move in opposite directions between specialists and nonspecialists.

18. These exchanges between specialists and nonspecialists meant that information and referrals came to convey opposite statuses in exchange relationships, with information flow conferring higher status on the provider, relative to the receiver, and referral flow conferring just the opposite status.

19. The relationships of information and referral exchange, at the purposive-action level of analysis, aggregated to the more macro-level control system, so that the movements of information and referrals among sectors, functional subsystems, etc., were predominantly in opposite directions.

20. As a result of the exchanges among sectors and subsystems of the more macro-level control system, these were stratified by information and referral flow, so that the predominant flow of information was down the resulting hierarchy, whereas the predominant flow of referrals was up the same hierarchy.

21. The social-service or counseling professions (psychologists, social workers, clergy, etc.), motivated by inter-organizational positions or responsibilities to achieve high absolute exchange densities with other sectors, with intermediate status in the exchange-dominance hierarchy, constituted a "facilitating" sector that helped to move referrals among other sectors and subsystems.

22. Given the necessary conditions of boundary maintenance, hierarchy, and a facilitating sector, the macro-level structure of interpersonal exchanges constituted a cybernetic control system, one that maintained the structure required for the regulation of deviance, including the movement of referrals from lower to higher levels of specialization in the control function via the intermediate facilitating sector and the flow of informational feedback downward to the lower level.

So ended a chain of causation that began with the sudden increase in illegal drug use and abuse by youth in the late 1960s and early 1970s, a social change exogenous to the inter-organizational community systems that would attempt to control it. The chain led, cause by cause, to the patterns of flows – involving boundary maintenance and hierarchical control – that characterize an autonomous social system. If the patterns of responses to the NIDA survey of participants are any indication, the system had contained the exogenous change through referrals of deviants (or institutional authority for deviants) – via the social-service or counseling professions – to functional subsystems specialized in medical or legal controls.

The control system in equilibrium

In addition to explaining the steps by which a social-control system accommodates exogenous change, this monograph also developed an idealized equilibrium model of such a system that could be tested empirically. Control, the central element of this model, is the unifying concept shared by both the autonomous-system and purposive-action approaches to social theory. Action theories address individual and collective attempts to control events, whereas system theories, in contrast, predict control relationships among system variables as well as control patterns among component subsystems. In other words, control behavior is directed at other actors and events on the level of purposive action and at changes in exogenous variables and relationships on the system level.

Feedback from the environment controlled constitutes a second concept common to both the autonomous-system and purposive-action approaches to social theory. In system theories, the environment consists of the changed exogenous variables and relationships that are either countered or result in system breakdown. In action theories, in contrast, the environment consists of actual actors (individual or collective) whose behavior is purposively attempted to be controlled. In either approach, however, the state of control at time t_0 determines the control relations at time t_1.

Particular patterns of commodity flows and feedback characterize a cybernetic control system. Commodities move from lower to higher levels of specialization, whereas information flows in the opposite direction. The opposite flows of information and commodities, between differentially specialized sectors of a social-control system, might be considered at the level of interpersonal action as social exchanges. Because exchange theory attempts to account for social phenomena at the action level, it might be seen as an alternative to other systems explanations expressed in terms of individuals.

If the emergence of the "drug problem" in the late 1960s had a profound impact on community-control systems in general, this impact would be specifically manifest as sharply increased numbers of youth who were deviant – medically, legally, or in both senses – with respect to drugs. Because the inter-organizational systems were intended to minimize deviance, deviant youth constituted the commodity to be controlled by these systems. To be controlled, the deviants themselves or authority for them had to move to ever more specialized components of the system: to drug administrators, specialists, and experts; to professions of higher status with respect to the specialized functions of drug control; and ultimately to the medical and legal spheres, which occupy the highest levels of control-system activity. At the same time, if the system-level control was to obtain, informational feedback about the movement of deviants had to pass downward to less specialized individuals, professions, and organizational spheres. Drug information and advice and referrals of young drug users would thus pass in opposite directions through the inter-organizational and professional networks.

These required flows of information and referrals faced certain organizational impedences, however. Information tends to enter organizations near the top, whereas work with people – as customers, students, patients, etc. – tends to concentrate toward the bottom. In other words, information is positively correlated with hierarchical standing in formal organizations, whereas people-commodities – as processed by the organization – are negatively correlated with such standing. This means that individual actors will have little motivation, at least within an organizational setting, to exchange information downward or referrals upward – precisely the flows required for control in a cybernetic system.

Because the drug-control system was inter-organizational, however, individuals intending to advance their standing in the system sought generalized media that transmitted status across organizational boundaries. Drug information and advice, and referrals of young drug users, constituted just such generalized media. Information and referral flows were therefore expected to vary inversely with status, with high status associated with information sources and referral sinks. On the more macro level, information and referral flows were expected to move in opposite directions among professions that were themselves stratified by such exchanges. Information would tend to move down the resulting hierarchy of the control system, whereas the predominant movement of referrals would be up the same hierarchy.

The first part of the idealized model of social control was thus the hypothesized stratification of professionals and professions in information and referral exchange. A second part of the model was the hypothesized division of informal networks among drug professionals into functional subsystems, with aggregation of interpersonal exchanges into control relationships among the subsystems.

Youth could be deviant with respect to drugs in two distinct ways – one medical, the other legal. Youth who were not deviant were ordinarily part of an education system. If these three organizational sectors did indeed constitute a functional system for the control of deviance by youth, user referrals ought to have flowed predominantly from the education sector to the medical and legal ones, with the flow of drug information and advice predominantly in the opposite directions. A fourth "facilitating" sector, that of the counseling professions, was expected to hold a position intermediate between the lower and upper levels of this control system.

Not only must information and referral flows among individual professionals aggregate to such system-level control relationships, however; they must simultaneously constitute sector boundaries. This is the third part of the idealized equilibrium model of social control, what might be called its overall "systemness," which involves boundary maintenance, exchanges of commodities between specialized sectors, and intersectorial feedback. Empirical testing of this control-system model in equilibrium, using the personal interview and self-administered mail survey data of NIDA, constituted the bulk of Chapters 3, 4, and 5.

The empirical evidence

The first part of this idealized model of social control to be tested (in Chapter 3) was the hypothesized stratification of professionals and professions in information and referral exchange, with opposite flows of these commodities down and up the hierarchy, respectively. Relatively high-status individuals – specialists in the drug field, plus treatment and prevention administrators – were found to be central to *all* aspects of interorganizational professional exchange, involving both information and advice and professional referrals. In 24 of 24 cases (2 cities $\times$ 3 status measures $\times$ 4 types of flows), there were more links per respondent among high- as compared to low-status individuals for *all four* types of flows: giving and receiving of information and referrals.

When the *relative* numbers of professions involved in these exchanges were compared, however, higher-status individuals tended to have more professions as recipients relative to sources of information and as sources relative to recipients of referrals. This finding, in accord with the hypothesized stratification on opposite flows of information and referrals, held in 12 of 12 cases (2 cities $\times$ 3 status measures $\times$ 2 commodities). In 11 of the 12 cases, the difference (recipients over sources) hypothesized to be larger was positive, whereas that hypothesized to be smaller was negative: in no case was it probable, at the .05 level of confidence, that the order of differences was other than the hypothesized one.

As for exchanges among the professions themselves, as measured by ratios of EDS, movements of information and referrals were predominantly in opposite directions in both Baltimore (60 percent of all pairs) and San Francisco (70 percent). When professions were ordered according to the number of others for which the density of giving exceeded that of receiving, a strict hierarchical structure was revealed: None of the 4 matrices (2 cities $\times$ 2 commodities) had more than 4 deviations in 66 pairs: the total number was 12. The prob-values of these results were virtually zero in all cases.

Similarly conclusive results obtained when professions were ordered according to the number of others they dominated (with respect to which they tended to give information and receive referrals). In each city, 40 of 66 pairs of professions were characterized by pure exchange-dominance relationships; virtually all these (94 percent in Baltimore, 100 in San Francisco) were consistent with a single hierarchical structure of professions. Again, the prob-values of these results were virtually zero.

Because the four separate rankings (2 cities $\times$ 2 commodities) were highly intercorrelated in the predicted directions, a simple combination of the rankings was used to approximate a unified stratification of professions that was consistent across cities. In the 51 of 66 pairs of professions for which there was evidence – in one city or both – of a dominance relationship, all but 1 (98 percent) were consistent with a single exchange-dominance hierarchy; again the prob-value was virtually zero.

Not only did this hierarchy have a certain face validity (medical elite at the top, counseling professions in the middle, educational sphere at the bottom), it was found to correlate $+.45$ with occupational prestige. Partial deviations from the hierarchy were also found to vary inversely with the rank proximity of professions on occupational prestige, a further validation of the unified stratification of professions in information and referral exchange, with the predominant movement of information down the hierarchy and the predominant movement of referrals up the same hierarchy.

The second part of the idealized model of social control to be tested (in Chapter 4) was the hypothesized division of informal networks among drug professionals into functional subsystems, with the aggregation of interpersonal exchanges into control relationships among the subsystems. Individual sectors of the control system were suggested by social-theoretical considerations. If these four organizational spheres – medical, legal, education, and counseling – constituted functional subsystems of a larger system, then flows among the spheres (intersectorial flows) would not be as great as flows within the spheres but among different professions (intrasectorial flows); the latter flows would not be as great as flows wholly within individual professions (intraprofessional flows). These predictions follow from the general principle that within-group densities of exchange exceed those between groups.

As measured by mean EDS, the relative sizes of flows in the three categories had the ranking predicted at the .05 level of confidence in all four cases (2 cities $\times$ 2 commodities). The measures also revealed surprisingly regular patterns of relationships between cities in the ingroup and between-group densities of exchange.

With the four organizational spheres established as distinct sectors, it remained to place them in a hierarchy of functional specialization and interrelationship. The counseling sector, comprised of psychologists, social workers, probation officers, and clergy, was hypothesized to serve as a kind of "facilitator" of exchanges by standing intermediate in the system hierarchy but with relatively dense exchange relationships with other sectors. These predictions were confirmed using measures of relative flow sizes and exchange-dominance status. Three independent measures of specialization – factual knowledge, information sources, and contacts – also confirmed that the medical and legal sectors were more specialized than the facilitating one, whereas the education sector was less specialized.

The four organizational sectors were also located more directly in a hierarchy of functional specialization and interrelationship that constitutes the higher-level social-control system. Of the possible flows of information and referrals among the four sectors, cybernetic theory and the relative predominance of within-group densities together predict that control-direction flows will be large, exceeded in density only by boundary-maintaining flows, and that flows opposite to the control direction will be sparse or nonexistent. These predictions were specified for an exhaustive set of 20 flow types and tested via mean EDS.

Predicted and actual rankings correlated with Spearman's r_s coefficients ranging from .60 to .93; all coefficients were significant at the .005 level. Between cities, the mean EDS for the 20 flow types correlated with a Pearson's r of .97 for both information and referrals. Regression of the types for San Francisco on those for Baltimore produced intercepts of approximately 0 and slopes approximately equal to 1.0, exactly as expected if the densities were in fact identical in the two cities. The mean EDS also had a certain face validity in their correspondence to the predicted control-system model.

The third and final part of the idealized model of social control to be tested (in Chapter 5) was its overall systemness, including simultaneous boundary maintenance and hierarchical control. Taken together, the requirements of exchange dominance and boundary maintenance determine only partially consistent flows of information and commodities. Boundary maintenance requires exchanges within and not between sectors; stratification requires movement of information downward across sector boundaries and of commodities upward across the same boundaries.

To test this unified control-system model, compatible measures of both boundary maintenance and exchange dominance had to be constructed. Two straightforward such scales, referred to as the sparse–dense and dominant–subordinate scales, were based on the sums and differences of quartile scores for EDS. Using the joint distribution of the two scales under statistical independence, the interprofessional exchange structures in Baltimore and San Francisco were both found to be significant at the .001 level, whereas deviations – toward predominantly sparse, dense, and dominant–subordinate relationships among pairs of professions – accounted for 63 and 79 percent of the chi-square value, respectively.

The hypothesized control-system model was tested using the joint distribution of dyadic relationships among pairs of professions on the two scales. Roughly half (52 percent) of the 66 possible relationships were correctly predicted in each city. These relationships were statistically significant at the 0 level to 5 decimal places. The number of relationships exactly predicted exceeded that expected under the null model for 8 of the 10 sector flows; in 7 of 10 cases, the fit of the control-system model was significantly better than would have been expected at the .05 level. After 2 minor modifications were incorporated into the model, only 1 sector flow – that involving the legal and counseling sectors – remained an outlier, a problem apparently related to the comparatively high absolute exchange densities between the facilitating counseling and other sectors.

To summarize the empirical evidence marshaled in Chapters 3, 4, and 5, there is considerable support in the NIDA data for an idealized control-system model consisting of: (1) the stratification of professionals and professions in information and referral exchange, with opposite flows of these commodities down and up the hierarchy, respectively; (2) the division of informal networks among drug professionals into functional subsystems, with the aggregation of interpersonal exchanges into control relationships among these subsystems; and (3) overall systemness, including simultaneous boundary maintenance and hierarchical control.

Toward a methodology of control systems

One purpose of the analysis just summarized was to establish a methodology for the study of social-control systems in general. The essential concept of a control system dates back at least three generations, whereas information theory and cybernetics stem from World War II. During all this time, despite a general systems movement heralded as a new synthesis of the natural and social sciences, no one has previously produced an empirical analysis of a large-scale system of social control. The explanation is simple: The analytic techniques of control-system engineering depend on quantification via precise measurement. Flows of social information and socially controlled commodities (including social deviance) have proved difficult to conceptualize and have therefore largely eluded measurement. This has precluded any wholesale borrowing of control-system ideas by social scientists.

The methods developed in this monograph were made possible by recent developments in what has come to be subsumed under the heading "social networks." Particularly useful has been the "subgroup" approach to sampling large-scale social networks, which enabled measurement of system-level flows using survey-research methods. The survey population was partitioned – by distinctions salient to all respondents – into a manageable number of mutually exclusive and exhaustive subgroups, which then served as referents for network questions.

These enabled computations of estimated-density spaces (EDS), a practical approximation of simple network density. Density, in turn, was used to measure system-level flows, much as dollar value is used to indicate input–output flows of goods and services among industrial sectors in the analyses pioneered by Leontief. As long as the amount of flow can be considered a monotonically increasing function of density, density can serve as a surrogate indicator of the amount of flow. This attention to system flows, rather than to individual characteristics and behavior, brings survey research back to what are central sociological questions regarding the structure of relationships among individual actors, as well as to more macrolevel considerations. Such questions have been increasingly ignored by survey researchers in recent years.

Once system-level flows are constructed as aggregates of exchanges among individuals, as they are using simple network density or EDS, then such flows can be analyzed via application of social-exchange theory, such as Levi-Strauss's norms of restricted and generalized exchange or Gouldner's norm of reciprocity. Here is the synthesis of system and action perspectives: Norms governing social exchange, at the purposive-action level of analysis, can be seen to regulate flows among functionally specialized components of a more macro-level control system; purposive interpersonal exchanges aggregate in control-system flows and, conversely, cybernetic requirements structure exchanges at the action level.

The procedures used in this monograph thus establish quantitative empirical means to derive and test autonomous social-control systems emergent in networks of exchanges measured via survey-research methods. Interpersonal exchange relationships – measured as densities in a social network – can be treated as intersectorial input and output flows of information and commodities controlled by a more macro-level cybernetic system. This is not only a methodological advance, it also constitutes a step toward integration of the general systems, social-network, and exchange-theory literature.

Other applications

The relative success in this study of the control-system methodology argues for its testing in other social-science applications. This work already continues in a study of favors and debts incurred among officials at various levels of state, county, and municipal government (for the methodology, see Beniger, Shrum, Ash, and Lutin 1979) and a study of exchange and innovation in the nuclear-waste management and solar-photovoltaic communities (the research design is outlined in Wuthnow, Beniger, Woolf, and Shrum 1979).

In general, the methodology might be applied to any network of individuals, working in a number of different organizations and organizational settings, who are engaged in a common social function, and whose individual status and rewards are seen in terms of the larger inter-organizational control system. One example will be immediately familiar to academics: How many of us would referee papers and research proposals, review books, organize and chair professional meetings, serve as discussants, answer correspondence, or engage in a host of other nonpaid relationships with people in other organizations if we did not believe that rewards from our own institutions somehow depend on such activities?

To extend this example, consider the entire international system for the production and distribution of scientific and other systematic knowledge. Clearly, this is an inter-organizational system, in that its members work in a wide variety of universities and colleges, technical schools, government and corporate institutes, public and private research centers, foundations, etc. The system is also interorganizational in that its major function, the production of a world body of knowledge (as recognized, for example, by the awarding of Nobel Prizes), must compete with such organizational functions as teaching, administration, fund raising, etc. Indeed, the function of the inter-organizational system and those of its component organizations may often clash, as, for example, when the scarce commodity of academic tenure is denied a talented researcher because he or she is a poor teacher (or, conversely, when a poor researcher is granted tenure on the basis of local contributions alone).

What status and other rewards this inter-organizational system has to offer its members mostly accrue, as in the commodity systems for the control of drug abuse, to those recognized as ranking "experts" in their particular fields. Just as in the drug-control system, specialists in the system of knowledge production are information sources and referral sinks relative to nonspecialists. Information supplied can be measured by the citations of other researchers, a generalized medium that transmits the status and rewards of the larger system across national and organizational boundaries.

The means by which an individual researcher attains specialist or expert status in the international system of knowledge production are precisely the same as those used by would-be specialists in local drug-abuse communities. That is, the researcher must first establish him- or herself as a source of information for other nonspecialists. This is accomplished through publication, with authority for findings bolstered by citations of already-established specialists (much as referrals bolster the position of nonspecialist drug professionals). If the researcher succeeds, that is, if the publications are cited by enough other workers, then his or her position shifts from one of information sink ("citation giver") to one of information source ("citation-receiver") and specialist status is assured.

Here citation giving is the system homologue, in knowledge production, of referral giving in the control of drug abuse. Analogously, citation receiving is the system homologue of information giving. Citations constitute commodity flows *and* informational feedback in knowledge production, because they are both valued in themselves and represent information transfer. Information is itself the valued commodity, in the system of knowledge production and distribution, and citations represent both information flow *and* informational feedback about its flow. It should be obvious that, even apart from the relatively more bountiful research funding and economies of scale to be found in larger and more developed countries, researchers there tend to have other natural system advantages: the so-called international languages of science (especially English, French, and German), major international journals, and the sites of important world meetings (to name just three of many advantages in attracting attention to one's work outside one's own country).

Attention to the exchange of citations and other communication among researchers in the international system of knowledge production suggests certain policy conclusions. Less-developed countries attempting to enhance their national standing in the system would do well to invest in measures to improve the ability of their researchers to monitor, publish in, and cite major international publications, and otherwise to communicate with colleagues in other nations. Such allocation of resources, perhaps more than any other investment or policy intervention, is likely to advance a nation's scientists in the international status hierarchy. Such advancement of individuals, in turn, is perhaps the most likely means by which the current acute status differences among countries are likely to be overcome.

All such conclusions concerning this or any other social-control system, however, will remain merely speculation until control-system concepts are further developed and tested using empirical data, one activity in which the general systems literature is notoriously lacking. One aim of this monograph has been to suggest a quantitative methodology with which cybernetic concepts, analogous to those used in control-system engineering, might be extended to social-policy applications.

The system–action synthesis

Undoubtedly the most ambitious aim of this study was to address a question of general importance to sociological theory: How might the self-interested control over events by individuals, at the purposive-action level of analysis, aggregate in precisely those relationships – represented by commodity flows and informational feedback – necessary for cybernetic control to obtain at the level of the autonomous system. This is no less than the question of how the autonomous-system and purposive-action approaches, as outlined in Chapter 2, might be reconciled in a unified theory of system response to social change. To answer the question, it was necessary to demonstrate how, as the result of macro-level changes, the alternatives and utilities of individual actors changed with the effect of restoring control at the higher level.

The key to the answer lay in the utility to professionals of giving and receiving drug information and advice and referrals of young drug users. Because of the strain on channels of communication between the educational sector and those sectors (medical and legal) more specialized in the drug problem, nonspecialists perceived a lack of contacts for information from other organizations, particularly those in functionally disparate subsystems. At the same time, nonspecialists needed to make referrals and sought to maximize the competence of the specialist to whom they were sent. Both these motives – to receive information through contacts in other organizations and subsystems and to make referrals of drug users – belong to individuals interested in controlling deviance, usually as a responsibility of their professional work.

If these were the only motives to be found at the purposive-action level of analysis, action theory alone would suffice. The restoration of inter-organizational control, disrupted by the sudden increase in drug use among youth, could be explained by the actions of individuals who planned or intended to restore system-level control, that is, to contain deviance among youth with respect to drugs. There would be no need for an autonomous-system component in such an explanation. In other words, for a synthesis of the system and action perspectives to be successful, it had to be demonstrated that macro-level control is both the cause of changes in individual alternatives and utilities and an *unintended* by-product of individual, self-interested behavior.

To accomplish this second step, it was necessary to establish additional motives for professionals to engage in control of the drug problem. These included the desire to establish oneself as a specialist or "expert" on drugs in the local drug-abuse community, for all the material and personal rewards that such status might entail. Such motives have nothing to do with the control of deviance by direct intention, but have been demonstrated here to be a direct result of changes in the macro-level control system and to be essential for the cybernetic control of deviance at the same system level. When federal-government resources suddenly shifted to the new problem, the response of drug professionals – at least the many who chose to capitalize on the opportunity – was twofold: First, they returned to the classroom for more formal training in the drug problem; second, they attempted to establish themselves as sources of drug information and advice and referral sinks of actual drug users for as wide a circle of professions and professionals as possible.

The former response to change, increased training, meant that a greatly increased number of professionals came to have a vested interest in a social problem; this meant that referrals took on many of the system characteristics of a scarce economic commodity. The latter response, attempts to become central nodes in networks of information and referral exchange, is more significant here for two reasons:

First, the exchange relationships most desired by professionals hoping to establish themselves as specialists in the new problem were exactly the opposite of those desired by nonspecialists. The nonspecialists, whose primary motives were to control deviance, needed to receive information and advice and to make referrals. The specialists and would-be specialists, in contrast, whose primary motives were to achieve or maintain specialist status for their personal gain, sought to supply drug information and advice and to receive user referrals. Although these two groups were driven by different motives, and only those of nonspecialists had control of deviance as an *intended* consequence, neither group could have succeeded without the other.

Second, the exchange relationships sought by specialists and would-be specialists were precisely those needed to overcome the organizational impediments to an inter-organizational control system. System-level information tends to concentrate at the top of organizational hierarchies, whereas work with people tends to concentrate at the bottom. Were the norms of individual organizations alone to prevail, it would be difficult indeed for an inter-organizational control system to establish the cybernetic patterns of information and referral flow identified in Chapter 5. This macro-level control system is the unintended consequence of the behavior of professionals who hope to establish themselves as drug specialists for motives having nothing directly to do with the control of deviance per se; they thus seek to supply drug information to nonspecialists in other organizations and subsystems, even at lower organizational levels, and to receive user referrals in return.

Changes in the macro-level control system – stemming from resource shifts to the drug problem – directly produced the individual choices and utilities of professionals hoping to establish themselves as specialists in the new problem. The behavior of these specialists and would-be specialists, in turn, as an unintended consequence, restored cybernetic control of the drug problem at the macro level. These two causal relationships, as established by this study, constitute the necessary components of a successful synthesis of the autonomous-system and purposive-action approaches to social change and its containment by an inter-organizational control system.

Appendix A. The data set

The data set used in this monograph is part of a National Institute on Drug Abuse personal interview and self-administered mail survey, which is described in Chapter 3. The original study, as proposed by the Office of the Assistant Secretary for Planning and Evaluation, Department of Health, Education, and Welfare, was intended to be an evaluation of drug-abuse information and education programs administered by the National Institute of Mental Health and the Office of Education. Support for the survey work originally came from the Center for Studies of Narcotics and Drug Abuse, NIMH, under contract HSM-42-71-93, and was continued in 1974 by the Behavioral and Social Sciences Branch, National Institute on Drug Abuse, under contract N01-MH-1-0093(ND). Dr. Louise Richards, Chief, Psychosocial Branch, Division of Research, NIDA, and formerly Research Psychologist at NIMH and then NIDA, was the federal-government investigator for both agency contracts.

The survey portion of the study was contracted to the Bureau of Social Science Research, Inc., a nonprofit corporation located in Washington, D.C. This contract work was directed by Albert Gollin, Principal Investigator, with the assistance of Catherine Judd, Renee Slobasky, and Carol Sosdian. Personal interviews in Baltimore were subcontracted to Sidney Hollander Associates; West Coast Community Surveys, Berkeley, California, conducted both the interview and mail surveys in San Francisco. Principal consultants to the survey work included Ira Cisin, Kenneth Lenihan, Dean Manheimer, Herbert Menzel, Laure Sharp, and Robert Somers.

The 12 professions represented in the survey – in both the sample and the four sets of 12 directed flow questions (Appendix B) used extensively here – were selected by HEW and its contractors as the professions most likely to have contact with young drug users. The samples were based on the most comprehensive listings, current in 1972, of members of each profession. The sources of the samples in each city are listed in Table A.1. Where more than one source list was used for a single profession, the lists were cross-referenced and duplications eliminated before selecting the sample.

Table A.1. *Lists used as sources for samples of the 12 professions – both cities*

Baltimore		San Francisco	
Medical		*Medical*	
Psycht	American Board of Medical Specialists (1970) American Psychiatric Association (1971)	Psycht	American Board of Medical Specialists (1971) Yellow Pages, San Francisco Telephone Directory (1971)
Doctor	American Board of Medical Specialists (1970) Medical and Chirurgical Faculty of the State of Maryland (1971)	Doctor	American Board of Medical Specialists (1971) San Francisco Medical Society (1971) Yellow Pages, San Francisco Telephone Directory (1971)
Pharm	Maryland Board of Pharmacy (1971)	Pharm	California State Board of Pharmacy (1971)
Nurse	Baltimore City Department of Health, Public Health Nurses (1971) Catholic Archdiocese High School (1971) Sinai Hospital, 5 selected wards (1972)	Nurse	San Francisco General Hospital, selected wards (1972) San Francisco Public Health Department (1971)
Legal		*Legal*	
Probtn	Maryland State Department of Health and Mental Hygiene, Department of Juvenile Services (1971) Maryland State Department of Public Safety and Correctional Services, Division of Parole and Probation (1971) U.S. District Court, Department of Probation (1971)	Probtn	California Youth Authority Regional Parole Office (1971) San Francisco Juvenile Court, Youth Guidance Center (1971) San Francisco Probation Office (1971) U.S. District Court, Probation Office (1971)
Police	Not sampled in Baltimore	Police	San Francisco Police Department (1972)
Lawyer	Maryland State Bar Association (1970)	Lawyer	Martindale-Hubbell Directory (1971)

176

Counseling

Psychl
American Psychological Association (1970)
Bay Area Psychological Association (1971)
Psychology Examining Committee of the Board of Medical Examiners (1970)
San Francisco Unified School District, school psychologists (1971)
Yellow Pages, San Francisco Telephone Directory (1971)

SocWk
Bay Area Association of Black Social Workers (1971)
California Chapter of the National Association of Social Workers (1971)
San Francisco Unified School District, school social workers (1971)
State Department of Professional and Vocational Standards, Social Work Licensing Board (1971)

Clergy
Catholic Archdiocese of San Francisco (1971)
Where It's At, directory of Black business and services (1971)
Yellow Pages, San Francisco Telephone Directory (1971)

Education

SchlAd
San Francisco Unified School District (1971)
Catholic Archdiocese School System (1971)

Teach
San Francisco Unified School District (1971)
Catholic Archdiocese School System (1971)

Counseling

Psychl
American Psychological Association (1971)
Baltimore City Public Schools, school psychologists (1971)
Catholic Archdiocese High School, school psychologists (1971)
Maryland State Board of Examiners of Psychologists (1971)

SocWk
Baltimore City Public Schools, school social workers (1971)
Maryland Chapter of the National Association of Social Workers (1971)

Clergy
Catholic Archdiocese of Baltimore (1971)
Yellow Pages, Baltimore Telephone Directory (1971)

Education

SchlAd
Baltimore City Public Schools (1971)
Catholic Archdiocese School System (1971)

Teach
Baltimore City Public Schools (1971)
Catholic Archdiocese School System (1971)

Table A.2. *Special characteristics of each professional subsample*

Medical	
Psycht	Subsamples of the samples of physicians, therefore smaller (41 in Baltimore, 26 in San Francisco) than those for other professions.
Doctor	Restricted to four specialties: general practice, internal medicine, pediatrics, and public health–preventive medicine.
Pharm	All those licensed by their state to dispense drugs; other teaching and research pharmacists and pharmacologists excluded.
Nurse	All public-health nurses, school nurses, and nurses in selected wards – emergency wards, drug/alcohol detoxification units, G-U and surgery wards, and postpartum medical wards – of a major hospital in each city.
Legal	
Probtn	Complete samples (260 in Baltimore, 209 in San Francisco) of all probation, parole, and youth-services officials at the city, state, and federal levels in each city.
Police	Sampled only in San Francisco, where distributed among five divisions: Bureau of Inspectors, Bureau of Special Services, Juvenile Bureau, Patrolmen, and Traffic Bureau; Patrolmen slightly overrepresented.
Lawyer	All lawyers whose office address is within the city limits of Baltimore or San Francisco and who are licensed to practice law in the same state.
Counseling	
Psychl	Complete samples (187 in Baltimore, 267 in San Francisco) of all certified counseling (clinical) psychologists, plus school psychologists and a few minor categories employed as counselors.
SocWk	All members of the National Association of Social Workers, all school social workers, plus others with some certified status.
Clergy	Dependence on the Yellow Pages as a source list may have produced underrepresentation of non-Catholic clergy without a telephone (e.g., those in "storefront" ministries); the most reluctant profession to respond.
Education	
SchlAd	All principals, assistant principals, and counselors in elementary, secondary, and vocational schools, public and private.
Teach	All classroom teachers in elementary, secondary, and vocational schools, public and private.

Table A.3. *Percentage distribution of 12 professions in the interorganizational system for the control of deviance – Baltimore*

	Government legal system	Welfare administration	Public school system	Public hospitals and health systems	Baltimore public totals
Psycht				18	18
Doctor				18	18
Pharm				10	10
Psychl		26	42	8	76
Police					—
Probtn	100				100
Lawyer	20				20
Nurse				87	87
Clergy		16			16
SocWk		56	10	4	70
Teach			94		94
SchlAd			94		94
City	12	10	24	13	59

	Corporate & business	Legal practices	Social consultants	Churches & synagogues	Private school systems	Small pharmacies	Private medical practices	Private hospitals	Baltimore private totals
Psycht							53	29	84
Doctor							53	29	84
Pharm	57					33			90
Psychl	16		8						24
Police									—
Probtn									0
Lawyer	26	54							80
Nurse					2			11	13
Clergy				84					84
SocWk	28		2						30
Teach					6				6
SchlAd					6				6
City	13	5	1	8	1	3	5	4	40

Table A.4. *Percentage distribution of 12 professions in the interorganizational system for control of deviance – San Francisco*

	Police Department	Government legal system	Welfare administration	Public school system	Public hospitals and health systems	San Francisco public totals
Psycht					17	17
Doctor					17	17
Pharm					19	19
Psychl			51	13		64
Police	100					100
Probtn		100				100
Lawyer		13				13
Nurse					98	98
Clergy			13			13
SocWk			49	6		55
Teach				83		88
SchlAd				88		88
City	9	10	10	18	12	59

	Corporate & business	Legal practices	Social consultants	Churches & synagogues	Private school systems	Small pharmacies	Private medical practices	Private hospitals	San Francisco private totals
Psycht							66	17	83
Doctor							66	17	83
Pharm	61					20			81
Psychl	18		18						36
Police									0
Probtn									0
Lawyer	30	57							87
Nurse								2	2
Clergy	35			87					87
SocWk	35		10						45
Teach					12				12
SchlAd					12				12
City	13	5	3	8	2	2	6	2	41

Table A.5. *Major organizational clusters, public and private sectors*

Public	Private (corporations and commercial businesses)
Health	
Public hospitals and health system	Private hospitals, health centers, and group practices
	Individual medical practices
	Small pharmacies
Legal	
Police department	Individual legal practices
Court and probation system	
Welfare	
Government welfare administration	Churches and synagogues
	Social consultantships
Education	
Public school system	Private school system

Samples of 250 were drawn for each profession in each city to optimize statistical power for interprofessional analysis. Sampling was systematic, from a random start, with sampling ratios based on the populations in the combined lists. In the case of two professions, psychologists and probation officers, the total population in each city approximated 250 or fewer; all available names were used for these professions. Samples were limited, as much as possible, to professionals working in the city itself rather than in the surrounding area; zip codes and telephone prefixes were used for this purpose. Analysis of Question 38, "What portion of your average working week is spent in Baltimore/San Francisco? [within the city limits, not the metropolitan area]," shows that the sampling was successfully confined to Baltimore and San Francisco proper. Other special characteristics of each professional subsample are given in Table A.2.

Despite the fact that respondents were sampled randomly by professions, the professions are remarkably similar in their distribution among organizational clusters in the public and private sectors of Baltimore and San Francisco, as shown by Tables A.3 and A.4. Here the public and private sectors in Baltimore (Table A.3) and San Francisco (Table A.4) are broken down into 13 major organizational clusters spanning the health, legal, welfare, and educational systems (Table A.5).

Percentaging is across professions in Tables A.3 and A.4, so that percentages for any one profession total 100 across the rows of both the public and private sectors in each city. As the exhibits show, distributions of professions vary by only a few percentage points between Baltimore and San Francisco in most instances, further evidence for the high level of generality of the interorganizational control system structure.

Appendix B. Subgroup sampling and estimated-density spaces (EDS)

In many biological and social applications, the relationships that link individual units of analysis may have more substantive importance than any property of these units themselves. In such cases, standard statistical procedures apply only by assuming a population of relations (as, for example, when inferences about divorce are based on samples from a population of people interrelated by marriage and divorce). Such diversion of substantive concerns for the sake of statistical tractability has proved increasingly unsatisfactory in a growing number of applied fields: ecology and ethology, sociometry and small-group analysis, and the studies of kinship and formal organization, interpersonal influence and power structures, the diffusion of innovations and the spread of rumors, etc. Each of these areas has begun to develop its own quantitative methodologies based on applications of mathematical graph theory (Berge 1962; Flament 1963; Harary, Norman, and Cartwright 1965) and frequently grounded in iterative computer techniques. Unfortunately, these methodologies usually require complete enumeration or census procedures; there has been relatively little work on sampling and statistical inference for graphs (but see Goodman 1961; Bloemena 1964; Frank 1971, 1977, 1978; Wasserman 1977). For this reason, social-network analysis has been largely confined to small groups.

This appendix introduces a practical large-population method, identified as "subgroup partitioning," for surveying networks of social relations. The formal treatment of statistical inference from subgraph samples of networks is summarized here, the practical limitations of subgraph surveys – as compared to the subgroup approach – are introduced, and certain inference procedures for subgroup surveys are formally developed (for details, see Beniger 1976).

Consider a population Ω, comprised of N people. Any type of relationship among these people can be described as an $N \times N$ matrix C, whose elements c_{ij} equal 0 or 1, depending upon whether a relation *from* person i *to* person j

is absent or present, respectively. The total number of directed or asymmetric relations R_1 in population Ω is

$$R_1 = \sum_{i=1}^{N} \sum_{j=1}^{N} c_{ij}, \quad 0 \leq R_1 \leq N^2. \tag{1}$$

The total number of directed *but nonreflexive* relations $R_{1'}$, (i.e., excluding those from person i to himself, represented by the elements c_{ii}) is

$$R_{1'} = \sum_{i \neq j}^{N} \sum^{N} c_{ij}, \quad 0 \leq R_{1'} \leq N(N-1). \tag{2}$$

The total number of *un*directed or symmetric relations R_2 (i.e., those satisfying $c_{ij} = c_{ji}$, so that $C' = C$) is

$$R_2 = \sum_{i \leq j}^{N} \sum^{N} c_{ij}, \quad 0 \leq R_2 \leq N(N+1)/2. \tag{3}$$

The total number of undirected *and* nonreflexive relations $R_{2'}$, (also satisfying $c_{ij} = c_{ji}$ and $C' = C$, but with $i \neq j$) is

$$R_{2'} = \sum_{i \leq j}^{N} \sum^{N} c_{ij}, \quad 0 \leq R_{2'} \leq N(N-1)/2. \tag{4}$$

For relatively small groups, the frequency of a relation is easily obtained by population (enumeration) methods. Because the number of possible relations among individuals varies proportionally to N^2, however, population methods rapidly become unwieldy as N increases. For example, complete knowledge of only a single directed relation in an apartment complex housing 1,000 people requires nearly 1 million bits of information. For this reason, sampling methods will be desirable whenever N exceeds a few hundred.

Suppose that n people are randomly chosen without replacement from the N people in population Ω. Let θ_i be an indicator variable equal to 0 or 1, the latter iff person i belongs to the sample. Then

$$E(\theta_i) = n/N; \tag{5}$$

$$E(\theta_i \theta_j) = \begin{cases} n^2/N^2 & \text{if } i = j \\ n(n-1)/N(N-1) & \text{if } i \neq j \end{cases} \tag{6}$$

Let r be the total number of relations among individuals in the sample. These relations can be described as an $n \times n$ matrix Z, whose elements z_{ab}

equal 0 or 1, depending upon whether a relation *from* sampled person *a to* sampled person *b* is absent or present, respectively. Z is the frequency matrix of the *sample subgraph* of *C*.

Counts of the four types of relations can be written as:

$$r_1 = \sum_{i=1}^{N} \sum_{j=1}^{N} c_{ij} \theta_i \theta_j = \sum_{a=1}^{N} \sum_{b=1}^{N} z_{ab}, \tag{7}$$

and analogously for $r_{1'}$, r_2, and $r_{2'}$. (8-10)

From (1–4) and (6–10), it follows that

$$E(r_t) = n^2 R_t / N^2; \tag{11}$$

$$E(r_{t'}) = n(n-1) R_{t'} / N(N-1). \tag{12}$$

Hence unbiased estimators of R are given by

$$\hat{R}_t = N^2 r_t / n^2; \tag{13}$$

$$\hat{R}_{t'} = N(N-1) r_{t'} / n(n-1). \tag{14}$$

One use for subgraph sample statistics is to estimate the density of a population, that is, the proportion of all possible relations that actually do exist. A straightforward definition of density is the ratio of actual relations to theoretically possible ones (Kephart 1950; Barnes 1969, pp. 61–4). From (1–4), the four measures of density defined in this way are:

$$D_1 = R_1 / N^2 \qquad\qquad 0 \le D_1 \le 1; \tag{15}$$

$$D_{1'} = R_{1'} / N(N-1), \qquad 0 \le D_{1'} \le 1; \tag{16}$$

$$D_2 = 2R_2 / N(N+1), \qquad 0 \le D_2 \le 1; \tag{17}$$

$$D_{2'} = 2R_{2'} / N(N-1), \qquad 0 \le D_{2'} \le 1. \tag{18}$$

Frank has shown that $\hat{R}_1$, $\hat{R}_{1'}$, and $\hat{R}_2$ are easily generalized from $\hat{R}_{2'}$, the estimated frequency of relations in the undirected *simple graph*, that is, one without reflexive relations (1971, pp. 89–91). For this reason, the discussion here can be confined to estimating $D_{2'}$ using $r_{2'}$.

Applying (14) and (18), an unbiased estimator of $D_{2'}$ is

$$\hat{D}_{2'} = \hat{R}_{2'} / \binom{N}{2} = r_{2'} / \binom{n}{2}, \tag{19}$$

which has certain intuitive appeal. The variance of this estimator is

$$\mathrm{var}\,(\hat{D}_{2'}) = 4\,\mathrm{var}\,(r_{2'}) / n^2 (n-1)^2. \tag{20}$$

To determine the sample size n for a desired confidence interval for $D_{2'}$, it is necessary to know var $(r_{2'})$. By enumerating the n^4 terms of 15 types in the sum of covariances of all estimated relations between possible pairs of sampled individuals, Frank (1971) calculates that

$$\text{var}\,(r_{2'}) = \frac{(N-n)\,n\,(n-1)}{(N-2)\,(N-3)}$$

$$\times \left(\frac{(n-2)\,\text{var}\,(a)}{(N-1)} + \frac{(N-n-1)\,\text{var}\,(C)}{2} \right), \quad (21)$$

(p. 91), where var (a) is the variance of the $N \times 1$ vector a, whose elements a_i equal the total number of relations involving individuals i,

$$a_i = \sum_{j=1}^{N} c_{ij}, \quad i = 1, 2, \ldots, N, \quad (22)$$

with mean

$$\bar{a} = \sum_{i=1}^{N} a_i/N = 2R_{2'}/N, \quad (23)$$

sometimes called the "average acquaintance volume," as by Granovetter (1976, p. 1290), and with variance

$$\text{var}\,(a) = \sum_{i=1}^{N} a_i^2/N - \bar{a}^2, \quad (24)$$

and where var (C) is the variance of the $N \times N$ matrix of relations with elements c_{ij} with mean

$$\bar{c} = \sum_{i<j}^{N} \sum^{N} c_{ij} / \binom{N}{2} = R_{2'} / \binom{N}{2}, \quad (25)$$

which is the density $D_{2'}$ as defined by (19), and with variance

$$\text{var}\,(C) = \sum_{i<j}^{N} \sum^{N} c_{ij}^2 / \binom{N}{2} - \bar{c}^2. \quad (26)$$

Because the elements c_{ij} are defined to equal only 0 or 1, this becomes

$$\text{var}\,(C) = D_{2'} - D_{2'}^2. \quad (27)$$

In other words, var $(D_{2'})$ depends on var $(r_{2'})$, which in turn – following (21) – depends on two other variances, var (a) and var (C). The former variance depends on differences in the total numbers of relations across individuals; the latter depends on the average acquaintance volume $\bar{a}$, since from (18) and (23), $\bar{a} = (N-1)D_{2'}$. To assess the sampling error of $D_{2'}$, it will be necessary to estimate the range of sum a_i^2 and $\bar{a}$ based on substantive considerations of the individuals involved.

A diary study has found the maximum number of acquaintances in 100 days to be 658 (Gurevitch 1961); Granovetter sets the practical limit on acquaintances of individuals at 2,000 (1976, p. 1292), a figure sufficiently large to serve for most types of human relations. Using this figure, the sum a_i^2 term will be maximum when every individual has either 0 or 2,000 relations, that is, when $\bar{a}N/2,000$ individuals each have 2,000 relations and the remaining $N(1 - \bar{a}/2,000)$ individuals have none. When this is logically impossible, that is, when $\bar{a}N/2,000 \leq 2,000$, then the sum a_i^2 is maximized when $(\bar{a}N)^{1/2}$ individuals each have $(\bar{a}N)^{1/2}$ relations and $N - (\bar{a}N)^{1/2}$ individuals have none. The sum a_i^2 term is minimized (equal to 0) when all N individuals have the same number $(\bar{a})$ of relations. Granovetter sets the practical range of $\bar{a}$ at $100 - 1,000$, which he claims to hold "with the exception of new towns in very early stages" (p. 1294). Armed with these estimated ranges of the sum of a_i^2 term and $\bar{a}$, it is possible to determine the sample size n necessary to achieve a desired confidence interval for $D_{2'}$.

The major implication of this work is that a single subgraph sample is more efficient than several smaller ones, in contrast to earlier work on multiple diad and triad samples (Niemeijer 1973; Tapiero, Capobianco, and Lewin 1975). In large populations, however, subgraph surveys encounter a number of practical problems.

One feature of large cities is that they are necessarily sparse, since density is an inverse function of population size N, $D_{2'} = \bar{a}/(N-1)$, whereas average acquaintance volume $\bar{a}$ has a practical upper bound in the number of relations that it is possible for any one individual to maintain. If 100–1,000 is a realistic range for $\bar{a}$, then a new town with a *minimum* acquaintance volume will nevertheless have 100 times the density of an established city of 1 million with a *maximum* $\bar{a}$ (.1 vs. .001). Conversely, it will not be unusual for towns of 1,000 to attain densities in the range .5–1.0 (for $500 \leq \bar{a} \leq 1,000$), which is 500–10,000 times the possible density of cities of 1 million or more.

In populations much larger than 100,000, the expected number of relations to be found falls below 1 per interview, for interviews that might contain up to 500 yes–no relational questions. For example, consider the most extreme case, the city of 1 million with an average acquaintance volume of 100. Here Granovetter recommends 8 samples of 500 people each, for a total of 4,000 interviews (1976, p. 1295). These interviews will contain a total of 1,996,000 yes–no questions [i.e., $I(n - 1)$ questions, where I is the number of interviews]. The expected number of relations to be found is 99.8, meaning an expected 199.6 "yes" answers, or fewer than 1 for every 20 interviews. Even at the unlikely rate of 10 queries (names of sampled individuals) per minute – certainly unattainable if, as Granovetter suggests, the stimuli also include address, occupation, and even photographs (p. 1290) – this design would yield an average of 1 positive response for every 16.7 hours of interviewing.

From the perspective of theory, of course, a "yes" response contains just as much information as a "no" response (i.e., 1 bit). As a practical matter, however, it is unlikely that a randomly selected respondent in a general city survey can be expected to respond accurately to 500 or more names, over a period of at least 50 minutes, and possibly much longer, when the chances that he will recognize even a *single* name is less than .05. Such a design invites at least the following practical problems:

1. the interview might prove tedious enough to inflate nonresponse and termination rates, with the result of jeopardizing other survey items, or at least necessitating payment of respondents;

2. a succession of hundreds of unfamiliar names might create social pressure on the respondent to claim acquaintanceships when none exist; and

3. the extremely low expectation of "yes" answers may lead interviewers to hurry respondents, to gloss over names, to miss positive responses, or even to falsify responses.

Granovetter's method for "one-way questioning" (p. 1297) would at least cut the number of questions asked in half, but only at the loss of a reliability check, that of querying both ends of a relation, a check that the above list of problems suggests is indispensible (see also Morgan and Rytina 1976).

In contrast to subgraph sampling, the subgroup approach exploits population sparsity. Because cities over 100,000 are virtually certain to contain fewer than 10 percent of all possible relations (since $\bar{a}$ has a practical upper bound of 1,000), the subgroup approach maximizes the number of "absent" relations located per question. First, the population is partitioned, by a criterion salient to respondents (sex, race, occupation, area of the city, etc.), into a manageable number of mutually exclusive and exhaustive subgroups. These subgroups are used, in place of names, for at least the first round of subgroup interviewing.

The advantage of this approach over subgraph sampling is that every negative response to a query about subgroups locates hundreds and possibly thousands of zeros in the population matrix C or, more precisely, yields information of bits equal to the total number of possible relations contained in the given subset (an improvement in efficiency over the single-bit questions of subgraph sampling).

Following the initial series of subgroup questions, a second round of name queries might be used. Only those respondents giving a positive response vis-à-vis a given subgroup need be presented with names sampled from that subgroup. Two comparatively recent developments in survey technology make such an individualized approach feasible: questionnaires unique to each respondent can be generated by computer at manageable cost, and computer-based telephone interviewing affords an inexpensive way to follow up previously interviewed respondents.

An alternative strategy to the second wave of name queries is to use only the subgroup interview and to develop as far as possible statistical inferences based on these responses. Partition the N members of population Ω into m mutually exclusive and exhaustive subgroups M_i, $i = 1, 2, \ldots, m$. Each subgroup M_i will contain N_i members, such that $1 \leq N_i \leq N$, and such that the sum of N_i equals N. The total sample of size n, $n \leq N$, will be distributed among the m subgroups, such that n_i individuals will be sampled from subgroup M_i, $n_i \leq N_i$, and such that the sum of n_i equals n. It will be convenient to label the m samples by m_i. (The earlier discussion might now be seen as the special case where $m = 1$, $M_1 = \Omega$, $N_1 = N$, and $n_1 = n$.)

Consider the $n \times m$ *to-group* matrix X, whose elements x_{ji} equal 0 or 1, depending upon whether a given relationship *from* the jth sampled individual *to any* individual in subgroup M_i is either absent or present ($j = 1, 2, \ldots, n$). Consider also the $m \times n$ *from-group* matrix Y, whose elements y_{ij} equal 0 or 1, depending upon whether a given relationship *to* the jth sampled individual *from any* individual in subgroup M_i is either absent or present (for undirected or symmetric relations, $X' = Y$). Because X and Y together contain only $2mn$ bits of information, they may be considerably easier and less expensive to obtain than the n^2 bits in the full sample subgraph, especially when the required n is large and it is feasible to use $m \ll n$.

X and Y may be used to estimate d_{ab}, the density of directed relations *from* individuals in subgroup M_a to those in M_b,

$$d_{ab} = \sum_{i=1}^{N} \sum_{j=1}^{N} \frac{c_{ij}\theta_{ai}\theta_{bj}}{N_a N_b}, \tag{28}$$

where θ_{ai} is an indicator variable equal to 0 or 1, the latter iff person i belongs to subgroup M_a. This includes the case $a = b$, where $d_{ab} = d_{ba}$ is the density of relations among members of the same subgroup. A weighted average of the

m^2 intergroup density estimates $\hat{d}_{ab}$ (a, b = 1, 2, ..., m) serves as an unbiased estimate of the directed but nonreflexive population density $D_{1'}$, namely

$$\hat{D}_{1'} = \sum_{a=1}^{m} \sum_{b=1}^{n} \hat{d}_{ab} \frac{N_a N_b}{N^2}. \tag{29}$$

Let $\delta_{i'a}$ indicate that individual i has *at least one* relation *to* subgroup M_a, that is,

$$\delta_{i'a} = \begin{cases} 1 \text{ iff } \sum_{j=1}^{N} c_{ij}\theta_{aj} \geq 1, \\ \\ 0 \text{ otherwise} \end{cases} \tag{30}$$

and analogously for $\delta_{aj'}$, which indicates that individual j has *at least one* relation *from* subgroup M_a. (31)

Now it is possible to define $K_{a'b}$, the *total* number of individuals in subgroup M_a with *at least one* relation *to* subgroup M_b, as

$$K_{a'b} = \sum_{i=1}^{N} \delta_{i'b}\theta_{ai}, \tag{32}$$

and analogously for $K_{ab'}$, the *total* number of individuals in M_b with *at least one* relation *from* subgroup M_a. (33)

For any given values of $K_{a'b}$ and $K_{ab'}$, it is possible to show that

$$\max (K_{a'b}, K_{ab'}) \leq \sum_{i=1}^{N} \sum_{j=1}^{N} c_{ij}\theta_{ai}\theta_{bj} \leq K_{a'b}K_{ab'}. \tag{34}$$

It follows from (28) that, for any given values of $K_{a'b}$ and $K_{ab'}$, the true d_{ab} has the bounds:

$$\frac{\max (K_{a'b}, K_{ab'})}{N_a N_b} \leq d_{ab} \leq \frac{K_{a'b}K_{ab'}}{N_a N_b}. \tag{35}$$

Let A_{ab} be the number of sampled individuals in subgroup M_a with directed relations *to* M_b, and let B_{ab} be the number of sampled individuals in subgroup M_b with directed relations *from* M_a, so that

$$A_{ab} = \sum_{j \in M_a} x_{jb}, \sum_{a=1}^{m} \sum_{b=1}^{m} A_{ab} = \sum_{i=1}^{m} \sum_{j=1}^{n} x_{ji}, \tag{36}$$

and analogously for B_{ab}. (37)

A_{ab} may be viewed as the sum of a sample of size n_a, drawn from a Bernoulli distribution with parameters N_a and $K_{a'b}/N$. For convenience, let the (unknown) population parameters be

$$\pi_{a'b} = K_{a'b}/N_a; \tag{38}$$

$$\pi_{ab'} = K_{ab'}/N_b. \tag{39}$$

Let the sample means be

$$P_{a'b} = A_{ab}/n_a; \tag{40}$$

$$P_{ab'} = B_{ab}/n_b. \tag{41}$$

Then

$$E(p_{a'b}) = E(A_{ab}/n_a) = K_{a'b}/N_a = \pi_{a'b}; \tag{42}$$

$$E(p_{ab'}) = E(B_{ab}/n_b) = K_{ab'}/N_b = \pi_{ab'}. \tag{43}$$

From (42) and (43), it follows that unbiased estimators of $K_{a'b}$ and $K_{ab'}$ are given by

$$\hat{K}_{a'b} = N_a A_{ab}/n_a; \tag{44}$$

$$\hat{K}_{ab'} = N_b B_{ab}/n_b. \tag{45}$$

Using (35), (40), and (41), an unbiased estimator of the lower bound of d_{ab} is given by

$$\text{lower } (\hat{d}_{ab}) = \max (\hat{K}_{a'b}, \hat{K}_{ab'})/N_a N_b$$
$$= \begin{cases} P_{a'b}/N_b, & \text{for } \hat{K}_{a'b} \geq \hat{K}_{ab'} \\ P_{ab'}/N_a, & \text{for } \hat{K}_{ab'} < \hat{K}_{ab'} \end{cases} \tag{46}$$

Similarly, an unbiased estimator of the upper bound of d_{ab} is given by

$$\text{upper } (\hat{d}_{ab}) = \frac{\hat{K}_{a'b}\hat{K}_{ab'}}{N_a N_b} = \frac{A_{ab}B_{ab}}{n_a n_b} = p_{a'b}p_{ab'}. \tag{47}$$

Using (38) and (39),

$$\text{var } [\text{lower } (\hat{d}_{ab})] = \begin{cases} N_b^2 \pi_{a'b}(1 - \pi_{a'b})/n_a, & \text{for } K_{a'b} \geq K_{ab'} \\ N_a^2 \pi_{ab'}(1 - \pi_{ab'})/n_b, & \text{for } K_{a'b} < K_{ab'} \end{cases} \tag{48}$$

and var $[\text{upper } (\hat{d}_{ab})] =$

$$\pi_{a'b}\pi_{ab'}[(1 - \pi_{a'b})(1 - \pi_{ab'})/n_a n_b + (1 - \pi_{ab'})/n_b + (1 - \pi_{a'b})/n_a].$$

(49)

For large n, (48) and (49) permit the construction of confidence intervals for lower $(\check{d}_{ab})$ and upper $(\hat{d}_{ab})$.

It is not possible to restrict $\hat{d}_{ab}$ further using subgroup information alone, unless an additional assumption is made concerning the value of the numerator of (28) as a function of $k_{a'b}$ and $k_{ab'}$. One possibility is that d_{ab} can be estimated as an inverse function of $k_{a'b}/k_{ab'}$ because of the physical and temporal constraints on multiple relations for any one individual, but this is an empirical question that must await further study.

One practical application of the subgroup approach is the estimated-density spaces (EDS) used in this monograph. For each of the pairs of directed-flow questions,

> During the past six months, have you given/did you receive information or advice related to drugs or drug users to/from anyone in any of these professions (12 listed)?

and

> Did you send or refer/were you sent or referred some young drug user(s) to/by anyone in any of these professions (12 listed) in the past six months?

the two sets of yes–no responses, coded 0–1, establish each respondent's row and column in the *to-group* and *from-group* matrices. Here $m = 12$, with each of the 12 subgroups M_i equivalent to a separate profession.

For example, in the San Francisco survey, the following data were obtained for two of the professions, pharmacists (M_1) and probation officers (M_2):

$$
\begin{array}{lll}
N_1 = 768 & A_{11} = 57 & B_{11} = 69 \\
N_2 = 216 & A_{12} = 6 & B_{12} = 6 \\
n_1 = 171 & A_{13} = 4 & B_{21} = 5 \\
n_2 = 148 & A_{14} = 74 & B_{22} = 96 \\
& U_{11} = 40 & U_{22} = 61
\end{array}
$$

Applying (44) and (45), unbiased estimates of $K_{a'b}$ and $K_{ab'}$, the total number in each profession who give and receive information, respectively, with respect to at least one member of the profession in question, are:

$$
\begin{array}{ll}
K_{1'1} = 256.0 & K_{11'} = 309.9 \\
K_{1'2} = 26.9 & K_{12'} = 8.8
\end{array}
$$

$$K_{2'1} = 5.8 \quad K_{21'} = 22.5$$
$$K_{2'2} = 108.0 \quad K_{22'} = 140.1$$

For example, an estimated 26.9 (of 768) pharmacists supply drug information to probation officers, whereas an estimated 22.5 (of 216) in the latter profession receive information from members of the former. Applying (46) and (47), the following unbiased estimates of the lower and upper bounds of the d_{ab} were obtained:

	Lower	Upper
d_{11}	.00053	.1345
d_{12}	.00016	.0014
d_{21}	.00014	.0008
d_{22}	.00300	.3240

The estimated upper bounds of the densities are called "estimated-density spaces" or "EDS" throughout this monograph, as first noted in Chapter 3.

By comparison, Granovetter (1976, pp. 1292–3) suggests that a city the size of San Francisco (population 715,000) would have an acquaintanceship density (symmetrical) of .00014 to .0014. In other words, the density of information exchange between pharmacists and probation officers (both directions) is roughly twice the density of acquaintanceship among city inhabitants in general. The estimated bounds also permit comparisons among the four densities. For example, the density of exchange among probation officers is greater than that between the two professions in either direction (.95 confidence).

These conclusions are not as precise as those that might have been obtained from a complete subgraph sample of the same size. On the other hand, the subgroup estimates obtained here required only $4n = 1,276$ questions or bits of information. A subgraph sample of the same n would require $n(n - 1) = 101,442$ questions or bits. The subgroup approach may also reveal social-structural properties not found in sampled subgraphs that have not been partitioned into subgroups, as illustrated throughout this book.

Notes

1. The emergence of the "drug problem"

1 "What we see now is a rapidly increasing tempo," Blum continued. "While it took approximately 10 years, by our estimate, for experimentation and use to shift from the older intellectual-artistic groups to graduate students, it took only an estimated 5 years to catch on among undergraduates, only 2 or 3 years to move to a significant number of high school students and, then, within no more than 2 years, to move to upper elementary grades" (Janssen 1969).

2 The NIDA survey of drug professionals in Baltimore and San Francisco began late in August 1972, when self-administered questionnaires were mailed to the general sample and interviewing was begun with specialists on drugs and the drug problem. All fieldwork was terminated early in February 1973, about five months after the starting date.

3 For a more elaborate treatment of the history and application of this idea, see Beniger (1978b).

4 The limited success of these attempts to establish the monitoring of social trends via mass-media content on a continuing basis is due more to the formidable costs of the collection efforts than to any shortcoming of the underlying idea. Analysis of media content was established as an important tool of policy research by the Kerner Commission (U.S. National Advisory Commission on Civil Disorders 1968), and its methodology has developed rapidly in a spate of recent work (e.g., Gerbner et al. 1969, Holsti 1969, Carney 1972, Markoff et al. 1974). Morris Janowitz, who as late as 1969 warned of the organizational and intellectual problems of content analysis (Janowitz 1968–9), has recently declared that "at this point in the development of the social sciences it makes sense to examine the relevance of improved procedures of content analysis for the study of socio-political change" (Janowitz 1976, p. 10). Janowitz cites sharply increased media attention to the issue of gun control during 1973–4 as one example of "the mass media's reflecting a crucial sociopolitical movement that would shortly have an effect on public opinion and legislative action" (1976, p. 19).

5 The Greenfield Index is named for journalist Meg Greenfield, who counted entries in a mass-media index (the *Readers' Guide to Periodical Literature*) to measure trends in media coverage as an indicator of social change. In investigating what her fellow journalists saw as a "current moral crisis" in the United States in the early 1960s, Greenfield counted *Readers' Guide* entries under "U.S.: Moral Conditions" and "U.S.: Religious Institutions" for the decade 1951–60. Her findings indicated what she described as the "curious fluctuations between sinfulness and virtue that we have undergone as a nation." These she debunked as faddish swings in media attention, between "the moral crisis (we are bad)" and "the religious revival (we are good)," in an article appropriately titled "The Great American Morality Play" (Greenfield 1961). For details, see Beniger 1978b.

6 This notion dates back at least to Walter Lippmann's *Public Opinion* (1922), which asserts a necessary condition between mass-media coverage and individual political cognitions. The

194

first explicit test of the hypothesis is McCombs and Shaw (1972), which finds substantial correlations between the issues that the media emphasized during the 1968 U.S. presidential campaign and those that undecided voters regarded as central to the election. This result squares with the earlier study by Arnold and Gold (1964) of an Iowa reapportionment referendum that finds stronger correlations between the proportion of the vote in favor and the population in those counties where local newspapers helped make the issue salient to voters.

7 This measure may seem particularly ill-suited as an indicator of agenda setting with respect to the drug problem, given that any one problem competes in a zero-sum relationship in the Gallup Poll with all other national and international developments. On the other hand, this poll may be the best indicator of government concern for any given problem, and therefore the climate of financial support available for its solution. Both these factors will be particularly important in assessing inter-organizational systems for the control of deviance among youth with respect to drugs.

8 Of the $58 million authorized to be distributed by the secretary of HEW, only $30.8 million was ever appropriated.

9 The amounts shown in Figure 1.3 for indirect block and formula grants are gross estimates because the degree of local discretion is such that precise figures are obtainable only a year or more after the fact.

2. Control systems from exchange in networks

1 The term *situational facilities* was introduced in sociology by Parsons and Shils (1962, p. 199): "It is convenient to distinguish *facilities* from the other components in the definition of role. The term refers to those features of the situation, outside the actual actions entailed in the performance of role itself, which are instrumentally important to the actor in the fulfillment of the expectations concerning his role. Thus one cannot be a scholar without the use of books or a farmer without the use of the land for cultivation. Facilities thus are objects of orientation which are actually or potentially of instrumental significance in the fulfillment of role-expectations. They *may* consist of physical objects, but not necessarily."

2 The NIDA survey distinguishes "specialists" and "nonspecialists" or "generalists" in the drug-abuse field. Although some positional considerations were employed in the early stages of identifying drug specialists, this is primarily a reputational measure. Local people knowledgeable about the "drug scene," and well-known members of each profession, were asked to suggest specialists in the drug-abuse field. In addition, members of each profession sampled were asked to nominate specialists; 45 percent of respondents offered one or more names (for details, see Chapter 3, note 8). Results of the two approaches were cross-tallied, and the frequency of mentions used to determine the approximately 10 to 15 specialists in each profession in each city; there was no attempt to make this status equivalent across professions.

3 Note that this larger control system, as the term is used here, is a theoretical construct, one that does not necessarily correspond to organizational or jurisdictional boundaries. For example, a school nurse is part of the community medical system if his or her primary responsibility is the control of deviance (rather than teaching) with respect to health, even though organizationally he or she is a member of the public school system. Social control is institutionalized, and institutions in this sense do not correspond to the collective level, a distinction in keeping with the warning of Parsons (1975, p. 97) that we cannot speak of being a member of an institution.

4 Smelser (1962, pp. 34–45) also provides "seven levels of specification" of the components of social action. The second type "concerns specification *within* each component," according to Smelser. "This involves a restriction of the meaning of the component itself which makes it more nearly applicable to concrete action. The first type of hierarchy deals with the addition of *different* components; the second restricts the applicability of the *same* component." The reason for this specification is that, "to produce concrete social action, every component must be progressively 'narrowed' in definition so that it can be 'consummated' in some sort of operative social act" (p. 34).

Smelser's second type of specification cannot be distinguished using the data at hand. For this reason, there will be no attempt here to utilize the seven levels nor the conceptual apparatus based upon them. Several other ramifications of the process derived from Smelser's four components of action, including the precise temporal sequence of exchange relationships and the differential normative strain at specific loci within the system, must await treatment in a subsequent work.

5 In *The Human Group* (1950), Homans still sounds in certain passages like an antiutilitarian Parsonian. For example, he writes under the heading "Sentiment": "If we examine the motives we usually call individual self-interest, we shall find that they are, for the most part, neither individual nor selfish but that they are the product of group life and serve the ends of a whole group, not just an individual . . . While sentiments of self-interest affected or influenced the behavior of the men in the room [Bank Wiring Observation Room], they did not solely determine that behavior. If these sentiments had been alone decisive, output would perhaps have been higher. That both self-interest *and* something else are satisfied by group life is the truth that is hardest for the hard-boiled – and half-baked – person to see. As Mayo says, 'If a number of individuals work together to achieve a common purpose, a harmony of interests will develop among them to which individual self-interest will be subordinated. This is a very different doctrine from the claim that individual self-interest is the solitary human motive' " (pp. 95–6).

6 This does *not* mean, however, that systems and action theorists necessarily disagree on what variables might be involved in social phenomena, only that they have chosen to analyze different aspects of those phenomena. It is impossible to theorize about – or even think about – everything at once. Even Wallace's distinction between systems and action theory can be overdrawn, however, as Smelser (1977) has reminded this author. Both approaches make what Smelser calls "guiding assumptions" about factors they choose not to attempt to explain. "There is an implied motivational link that makes the connection between system-attributes and their changes meaningful," according to Smelser. "And often individual and group purposive-action theories make certain definite assumptions about the type of institutional structure in which action occurs."

7 Merton notes that this conception of structural analysis has already found its way into "that depository of 'established knowledge,' the textbook" (Merton 1975, p. 34); for the significance of the textbook in different disciplines, see Kuhn 1962, pp. 163–5. As an example, Merton cites Turner (1974, p. 292) on "Bridging the Micro–Macro Gap": "One of the most important analytical problems facing sociological theorizing revolves around the question: To what extent are structures and processes at micro *and* macro levels of social organization subject to analysis by the same concepts and to description by the same sociological laws? At what levels of sociological organization do emergent properties require the use of additional concepts and description in terms of their own social laws?" (Merton 1975, p. 34).

8 Such an investigation of administrators and planners at the state, regional, county, and local levels of government in New Jersey is being conducted by the author in collaboration with

Princeton's Transportation Program, offered jointly by its School of Engineering and Applied Science, School of Architecture and Urban Planning, and Woodrow Wilson School of Public and International Affairs. The interview survey assesses flows of information in the form of letters, telephone calls, and face-to-face meetings, and of personal favors as a commodity controlled by the intergovernmental exchange networks (for the methodology, see Beniger, Shrum, Ash, and Lutin 1979). A similar survey has been designed by the author and several colleagues in Princeton's Department of Sociology; this study investigates the relationships between network exchange and technological innovativeness in two scientific-technical specialties, nuclear-waste management and solar-photovoltaic systems, employing a control-systems model that affords assessments of exchanges among organizational components as well as among individuals (the research design is outlined in Wuthnow, Beniger, Woolf, and Shrum 1979).

3. Stratification in information and referral exchange

1 In the opinion of at least one survey of social-exchange theory (Ekeh 1974), "Levi-Strauss' distinction between restricted exchange and generalized exchange is by far the most important development in social exchange theory" (p. 208). The distinction represents a phenotypical, qualitative difference between exchanges in pairs (dyadic exchanges) and larger groups (chain and individual-collectivity exchanges) analogous to those drawn by Simmel (1950a, 1950b) and rediscovered by Bales and Borgatta (1965). Levi-Strauss (1949/1969, p. 441) originally likened restricted and generalized exchange to mechanical and organic solidarity, respectively, after Durkheim's *Division of Labor in Society* (1933); twenty years later, responding to Homans and Schneider (1955), Levi-Strauss characterized the types of exchange as "two different forms of mechanical solidarity" (1949/1969, pp. iii–iv, n. 2).

2 Restricted exchange is part of what Gouldner (1960) calls "the norm of reciprocity." Ekeh (1974, p. 59) suggests that the "amoral familism" of Banfield's *Moral Basis of a Backward Society* (1958) exemplifies the morality of restricted exchange: "Those seeking office, for example, are presumed to be exclusively concerned with personal aggrandizement, and therefore voters seek to obtain bribes in order to vote them into office." Both Thibaut and Kelley (1959) and Homans (1961) stress the sensibilities and emotional factors in restricted exchange: It is characterized by attempts to avoid offending the other partner.

Because Homans viewed Levi-Strauss's concept of generalized exchange with contempt (Homans and Schneider 1955, p. 7), it led him to renewed emphasis on restricted exchange, particularly in his *Social Behavior: Its Elementary Forms* (1961), which interprets multiperson interactions with a restricted-exchange model. Although Blau (1964) has complained about isolated and abstracted pairs of social-exchange actors, his own work has paralleled that of Homans. Blau does give more attention than does Homans, however, to emergent collective phenomena in the development of psychological processes into complex social structures.

3 It was because Levi-Strauss found the explanatory power of mutual reciprocities between actors (i.e., restricted exchange) limited – and unable to account for his kinship data – that he introduced the concept of "generalized exchange" "in an attempt to arrive at a systematic typology and exhaustive explanation" (Levi-Strauss 1949/1969, p. 220). His generalized exchange is related to Malinowski's concept of "circular" exchange (Malinowski 1922), although the latter is more properly seen as simultaneously generalized and restricted exchange: The restricted exchange of necklace and armshell, between any two Kula

partners, fills psychological needs; the generalized circular exchange of both items emphasizes the social integration of Trobriand society.

Generalized exchange is only superficially like the concept of "indirect exchange" used by both Homans (1961) and Blau (1964). This latter concept refers to institutionalized behavior in which roles and norms replace individual actors in social exchanges, the "processes by which institutions develop out of elementary social behavior – the increasing roundaboutness of the exchange of rewards, which is sometimes called the increasing division of labor" (Homans 1961, p. 385).

4 In addition to the positional and reputational approaches, Bonjean and Olson (1964) identify a third technique – the *decisional* approach, also known as "event analysis" or the "issue" approach – to identify community leaders. This involves tracing the actions of leaders in decision making and policy formation in the context of specific issues. Investigators who have used this approach include Burgess (1960), Dahl (1961), Presthus (1964), Gamson (1966a), and Clark (1968).

Because the NIDA study did not employ decisional techniques to identify leaders in the Baltimore and San Francisco drug-abuse communities, this approach is not possible with the data at hand. The combination of positional and reputational approaches used here is adequate by standards of the field, however; as Bonjean and Olson (1964) state, "a combination of methods (any two or all three) appears to be the most satisfactory means for the study of community leadership."

5 Similar methods have been used by other investigators in the field of community influence. For example, Laumann and Pappi (1976), despite criticism of recommendations that some simple combination of positional, reputational, and decisional techniques is the best procedure for identifying community elites (p. 96), nevertheless employ a combination of the positional and reputational approaches in their own research. First they "identified prospective community influentials as incumbents of the highest positions of authority in organized collectivities" (p. 96). Then, recognizing that "not all community institutional subsystems . . . are equally likely to be organized into a structure of fully institutionalized and functionally specialized organizations with a full complement of explicitly identified leaders engaged in regularized transactions with one another" (pp. 97–8), they attempted to compensate for this bias of the positional approach by asking well-placed community informants to nominate other persons who enjoy reputations for influencing members on community affairs, but who do not presently occupy positions of authority in formally established organizations. For other studies employing a combination of positional and reputational techniques, see Burgess (1960), Belknap and Steinle (1963), Bloomberg and Sunshine (1963), and Presthus (1964).

6 As determined by all respondents including specialists in both cities who indicated either "in the past six months" or "at some earlier time" in response to Item 7K, "plan or administer a drug treatment program." The introduction to items in Question 7 reads: "PROFES-SIONALS' INVOLVEMENT WITH THE DRUG PROGRAM. Many professionals may have no involvement with drug problems. Others may become involved in various ways. For each of the following types of activities, please indicate whether you have done it either in the *past six months*, or *at some earlier time*, or *never*. [*Circle one answer for each activity*.]"

7 As determined by all respondents including specialists in both cities who indicate either "in the past six months" or "at some earlier time" in response to Item 7L, "Plan or implement a drug prevention (i.e., information or education) program." The introduction to items in Question 7 is reproduced in note 6 of this chapter.

8 Question 21 of the printed NIDA questionnaire states: "We wish to interview a few professionals in your city who are particularly knowledgeable about or actively working on

the drug problem. Can you suggest the names of individuals in your profession, or in other professions, whom we might seek to interview? [*Please feel free to nominate anyone, including yourself.*]"

Of the 3,439 respondents in the total sample (both cities), 1,543 (44.9 percent) named at least one drug-abuse specialist in his or her community; 779 (22.7) named one, 420 (12.2) named two, and 344 (10.0) named three or more. Of the 2,651 nominees, counts for the 12 professions included in the study range from 825 (31.1) for physicians (including psychiatrists) and 274 (10.3) for social workers to 83 (3.1) for nurses and 82 (3.1) for lawyers; 370 nominees (14.0) were other or unspecified professions.

9 For 2×2 tables, several standard measures of strength of relationship between nominal scales – Goodman and Kruskal's tau, standardized chi-square (χ^2/N), Tschuprow's T^2, Cramer's V^2 – are equivalent (Blalock 1972, p. 302). For specialists and treatment administrators, this coefficient is .094 in Baltimore, .089 in San Francisco, and .091 for the total sample. For specialists and prevention administrators, it is .086 in Baltimore, .077 in San Francisco, and .082 for the total sample. The prob-values, i.e., the probabilities of no correlation (zero coefficient), are all practically zero.

10 These 24 differences, as assessed by Student's t test for the differences in two means (independent samples with population variances unequal and unknown), are all significantly different from zero at the .05 level.

11 The number of potential symmetric links among N individuals is $N(N-1)/2$, the number of possible pairs of individuals; this is equivalent to half the number of cells in an $N \times N$ matrix minus the main diagonal (which represents intrapersonal or reflexive links excluded here). The number of potential directed links is $N(N-1)$, twice the number of possible pairs of individuals (because flow can be in either direction); this is equivalent to the number of cells in an $N \times N$ matrix, again excluding the main diagonal.

12 The choice of ratio for this indicator is arbitrary. *Differences* would have served equally well, in which case the *sign* of the difference (positive or negative) would have indicated the predominant direction of flow. In either case, the measure and statistical tests of it are system-level analogues of the differences in mean numbers of professions serving as sources versus recipients of information and referrals (and Student's t tests of these differences) as found in Table 3.1.

Were the interest in testing the statistical significance of the estimates of predominant flows, differences might have been the better measure because they would have permitted use of Student's t as in the previous section. Here interest is in only the direction of flow, however. Because the EDS are unbiased estimators of the amount of flow in each direction, their ratio is an unbiased estimator of the predominant direction of flow.

13 More generally, the expected number of deviations from strict hierarchy (i.e., the number of bullets on the "wrong" side of the main diagonal) is $N(N-1)/4 - (N-1)/2$, where N is the number of nodes (here 12 professions). This relationship derived from the fact that it is always possible to order a relative-flow matrix like those in Figures 3.1 and 3.2 so that $N-1$ nonzero entries (here represented by bullets) are above or below the diagonal.

14 The z-value of the normal approximation to the binomial distribution ($n = 55$, the number of free parameters) is 6.34, which has a prob-value (probability of occurrence by chance alone) of zero to at least six decimal places.

15 The z-values are 5.53 for Baltimore and 6.78 for San Francisco; their prob-values are zero to at least four significant figures.

16 Both coefficients vary between -1.0 and 1.0. The coefficient r_s (sometimes called "rho"), proposed by Spearman (1904) over 75 years ago, has long been a popular estimate of the strength of association (Lehmann 1975); it depends on squares of the differences in ranks. Tau (Kendall 1938), in contrast, depends on the numbers of pairs for which ranks are

concordant. Tau has several advantages over r_s, including that it can be used for large numbers of ties (Blalock 1972, p. 421) and that it can be extended to first-order partial correlations (Kendall 1955, ch. 8; Somers 1968). A detailed discussion of the history of tau, and of the relative advantages of this and related measures of association, is given by Kruskal (1958); for a summary comparison of r_s and tau that favors the latter, see Galtung (1969, pp. 218–22).

17 Respondents in a survey interview were asked to estimate the social standing of occupations by means of a nine-step ladder printed on cardboard and presented by the interviewer. The rungs of the ladder were numbered 1–9, from bottom to top, with the first, fifth, and ninth boxes labeled "bottom," "middle," and "top," respectively. Occupational titles were printed on small cards, which respondents were asked to sort into boxes formed by the rungs of the ladder (National Opinion Research Center 1977).

Testing the statistical significance of differences between or among prestige scores requires knowledge of their standard errors, which vary for each pair of professions. Siegel (1971) provides a few values that are likely to exceed most actual standard errors. For greater detail on the collection of prestige rankings, on translation of rankings into a standardized metric system, and on standard errors of scores, see Siegel, Rossi, and Hodge (1973).

18 The four dimensions are: (1) respondents' own perceptions; (2) respondents' perceptions of how others rank occupations: (3) the occupational prestige dimension per se; and (4) respondents' sense of distributive justice, i.e., whether the "real" order is just. For details, see Gusfield and Schwartz (1963). Siegel (1971, p. 31) examines this argument with empirical data and concludes that the first distinction (between respondents' own perceptions and their perceptions of others' perceptions) is not manifest in respondent rankings. No exhaustive effort has yet been made to discover the criteria – other than education and income – used by respondents in attributing prestige to occupations.

19 The column totals in Figure 3.6 are for *all* deviations involving the profession at the column head. This renders the table totals twice the actual number (48.5) of deviations or 97.

4. Exchange relationships in social-control systems

1 Useful introductions exist for each of these two fields. For cybernetics, in addition to Wiener (1950), see Ashby (1960, 1964). For information theory, in addition to Shannon and Weaver (1949), see Goldman (1953).

2 Blau (1977) derives the theorem from his formal assumption by the following logic: "If the prevalence of associations within subgroups exceeds that among them, it follows that the ratio of actual to expected associations within subgroups exceeds the ratio for the associations both within and among subgroups, and the latter indicates the prevalence of ingroup associations in the encompassing group" (p. 130). This logic can be 'directly translated into the language used in Proposition 4.1: If the densities of exchange within components exceeds those among them (an assumption tested empirically here as Proposition 4.1), it follows that the densities of exchange within components exceed those for the total network, and the latter indicates the exchange density in the larger system.

The theorem's stochastic nature Blau immediately reiterates: "Although [the theorem] would be a deterministic proposition when only one encompassing group and its subgroups are compared, it is probabilistic when it involves all encompassing groups and their subgroups. The theorem is probabilistic if expected frequencies are defined on the basis of the entire population distribution. If separate statistical expectations are computed for every encompassing group, [the theorem] is deterministic for all comparisons, but also rather trivial" (p. 130). The same principles hold for network densities and EDS, both in the comparison of total networks to their partitions (i.e., groups to subgroups) and in the comparison of control systems to their subsystems and components.

3 Blau defines "prevalence" as "the ratio of actual divided by statistically expected frequencies of associations" (p. 130). This makes *prevalence* a general form of the most common measure of network *density*, which is usually defined as the ratio of the number of links actually observed to the number theoretically possible (Kephart 1950; Barnes 1969, pp. 61–4). The total number of links *theoretically* possible seems an acceptable measure of "statistically expected frequencies" in the nonrigorous way that Blau employs this expression (following Mayhew and Levinger 1976, who use "expectation" in a statistical sense differing from its application here). Then EDS, the practical approximation of network density employed here as an aggregate measure of flow at the system level, is also – by extension of the definition of network density – a particular form of what Blau intends by "prevalence."

4 Assuming a binomial distribution with parameters $p = 1/12$ (the probability under the null model that *any* random density among the 144 will be one of the 12 intraprofessional ones) and $n = 18$ (the number of upper one-eighth EDS).

5 The 20 "fact and opinion" items appear in Question 6, introduced: "Even experts sometimes disagree on where to draw the line between fact and opinion in the drug field. For each of the following assertions, please circle the answer that comes closest to your rating of its truth or falsity." Items are lettered a–t, under the heading "Assertions about Drugs," with five possible response categories: certainly true, probably true, not sure, probably false, and certainly false (labeled 0–4).

The ten items selected to measure factual knowledge about drugs and drug abuse, with the correct answers and percentages giving those responses, are:

a. A majority of all marihuana users eventually becomes addicted to heroin. [False; 90 percent specialists, 67 percent generalists]

e. Heroin addiction is not as prevalent among white youths as it is among black. [True; 53 specialists, 44 generalists]

h. Methadone maintenance programs substitute one type of drug dependency for another. [True; 90 specialists, 83 generalists]

k. A baby born to an opiate-addicted mother will be addicted at birth. [True; 87 specialists, 71 generalists]

l. A person taking an excess of some opiate is likely to appear hostile and aggressive. [False; 86 specialists, 58 generalists]

m. "Speed" is a commonly used term for cocaine. [False; 90 specialists, 73 generalists]

q–t. Taken daily in large quantities over a long time, each of the four drugs listed below creates physical dependency, with marked withdrawal symptoms if stopped suddenly.

q. Barbiturates [True; 91 specialists, 72 generalists]

r. Cocaine [False; 38 specialists, 11 generalists]

s. Heroin [True; 100 specialists, 97 generalists]

t. Marihuana [False; 88 specialists, 70 generalists]

The distinction between generalists and specialists is explained in Chapter 3.

A study conducted for the National Institute of Mental Health (Gollin and Feinberg 1975) administered the questionnaire items to a panel of "expert" judges (senior staff and other selected members of NIMH's National Drug Abuse Council, each with the highest degree in his or her field and at least five years' experience in the drug specialty). The same

10 questions used here were chosen for an index of "drug knowledge levels." Correct responses among the 16 "experts" ranged from 13 (for Item e) to 16 (for Items a, m, and t).

6 The 15 items appear in Question 14, headed "Sources of Information and Communications" and introduced: "In your professional work, whether or not it has anything to do with drugs, how helpful are each of the following sources of information in keeping you informed or up to date in your field?" Items are lettered a–o, with two possible response categories: "not a helpful information source" and "a helpful information source" (labeled 0 and 1, respectively).

7 The three items that can be taken as professional sources of information are: "d. Professional or technical journals or books," "j. Personal contacts with those receiving my services (e.g., clients, patients, students, etc.)," and "m. Regular meetings or conventions of my profession." The five items that can be taken as mass-media sources of information are: "a. Television news or documentary programs." "b. Other television programs," "c. Radio," "f. Newspapers or news magazines," and "g. Other magazines, nontechnical books and other printed material." Of the other seven items, four involve personal contacts, two concern less universal professional sources (special publications or pamphlets, and training conferences, special meetings or workshops), and one is an open-ended catchall for other sources.

8 The two items are among those in Question 14 discussed in notes 6 and 7. They are: "h. Personal contacts with people *in my own profession*," and "i. Personal contacts with people *in other professions*" (italics are used in place of the underscore in the NIDA questionnaire). Note that these measures are independent of those used to estimate intraprofessional and interprofessional exchange densities.

9 There are $\binom{4}{2} = 6$ possible pairs of sectors, 2 types of flows (of information and referrals), and 2 directions of flow; hence there are $6 \times 2 \times 2 = 24$ possible flows of information and referrals among the four sectors.

10 The 40 total flows, 20 each for information and referrals, include that 24 intersectorial flows (discussed in the previous paragraph and note) plus the 16 intrasectorial flows. These 40 flows can be represented by two 4×4 matrices, one each for information and referrals, representing all possible exchanges among the 4 sectors; flows within sectors, represented by the main diagonal, can be in either of 2 directions, thus contributing an additional 4 cells in each matrix. This matrix representation is the motivation for the bottom portion of Figure 4.4.

11 Sociograms are arbitrary in the sense that two analysts can easily produce sociograms of the same relationships among the same set of individuals that provide strikingly different *visual* impressions of the underlying social structure. These differences stem from the arbitrariness of the locations of nodes in a sociogram and of the lengths and locations of the links or ties (lines that merely denote the presence of relationships and not their relative proximities). As a result of these necessarily arbitrary features of sociograms, their design is usually determined by aesthetic considerations, such as the visual appeal of minimizing the number of lines that cross or of "focal points" from which other nodes radiate.

12 Of the 132 $(144 - 12)$ interprofessional flows, 12 $(4^2 - 4)$ are within the medical sector, 6 $(3^2 - 3)$ are within each of the legal and counseling sectors, and 2 $(2^2 - 2)$ are within the education sector. These counts might be seen as the cells in a square profession-by-profession matrix for each sector minus the cells in the main diagonal (which represent intraprofessional flows). More generally, a sector with N professions will generate $N(N - 1)$ intrasectorial flows. The probability of an intrasectorial flow, under the null model of random distribution, is the ratio of these flows to the total possible: $26/132 = .197$. This probability times 33 (the number of upper-quartile flows) equals 6.5, the number of intrasectorial flows expected under the null model.

13 Of the 132 interprofessional flows, 12 are from medical to legal professions and 12 from legal to medical professions. These counts might be seen as the products of the number of professions in the sending and receiving sectors, i.e., 4×3 and 3×4. The probability of a lateral flow between the medical and legal sectors, under the null model of random distribution, is the ratio of these flows to the total possible: $24/132 = .182$. This probability times 33 (the number of upper-quartile flows) equals 6, the number of lateral flows expected under the null model.

14 Computation of the probability that a sector will send or receive a given flow under the null model of random distribution is straightforward. The 12×12 matrix of professional exchanges contains 144 cells; these represent 12 intraprofessional flows, 26 other intrasectorial flows, and 106 intersectorial flows. Of the latter, 32 are received by the medical sector, 27 each by the legal and counseling sectors, and 20 by the education sectors. These counts might be seen as the product of the number of professions in the sector and all other professions, so that, for example, the medical sector includes four professions and hence sends or receives $4 \times 8 = 32$ possible flows. The probability that a sector will receive a flow under the null model is the ratio of its flows to the total possible; hence the probability for the medical sector is $32/106 = .302$. These probabilities are used in the computations in Table 4.9.

15 Assuming for the null model that successes occur by chance alone a binomial distribution with parameters $p = .5$ and $n = 16$.

16 The Baltimore interprofessional matrix contains only 143 cells. Because police are not themselves in the NIDA survey of Baltimore, the police-to-police cell – on the main diagonal of the interprofessional matrix – cannot be estimated. All computations involving this cell have been adjusted accordingly.

5. The social system

1 The number of flows that must be simultaneously assessed reaches staggering proportions in even relatively simple systems. For example, in a system in which 100 components control only two commodities, the number of dyads is 4,950 and of flows 39,600.

2 Also known as Goodman-Kruskal's gamma, as proposed in Goodman and Kruskal 1954, especially Section 6.2. The formula for gamma is $(C - D)/(C + D)$, where C is the number of concordant pairs (i.e., pairs ordered the same way on both variables) and D is the number of discordant pairs (those oppositely ordered).

3 Assuming, for the null model that similar classification of dyad-directional flows occurs by chance alone, a binomial distribution with parameters $p = .25$ and $n = 132$. The normal approximation to this binomial yields the z-values 8.25 (for information) and 8.84 (for referrals).

4 As Parsons noted, "Every such system must by definition have an environment which is external to it, vis-à-vis which there is a boundary . . . and relative to which there is a problem of 'control,' i.e., of maintenance of the pattern of the system vis-à-vis the fluctuating features of the environment" (Parsons 1961c). For a similar view of the integrative function, see Morse 1961.

5 It is tempting to label these cross-cutting system requirements for boundary maintenance and stratification, which are inevitably contradictory on lower levels of action, the major source of tension – between functional isolation and fragmentation – in *all* social systems. Such metaphysical speculation shall be avoided here pending further more extensive quantitative studies.

6 A relevant finding of Chapter 4, as expressed in Proposition 4.1, is that boundary-maintaining relationships are stronger for information than for other socially controlled commodities. This finding implies that the sparse–dense scale, as defined here, is not an optimal measure of boundary maintenance and that the quartile scores for information ought to be given greater weight than the scores for referrals. Priority here, however, is given to keeping methodology as simple as possible to best expose the logic of analysis and to keep findings as free as possible from self-confirming manipulations of data. The full implications of the propositions in Chapters 3 and 4 might be incorporated in a more refined analysis, however, based on ratio-scale estimated-density spaces rather than the simplified quartile scores.

7 Assuming, for the null model of independence of flow structures in the two cities, a binomial distribution with parameters $p = .359$ and $n = 66$. The normal approximation to this binomial yields the z-values 4.69 (for the sparse–dense scales) and 7.52 (for the dominant–subordinate scales).

8 In general, given a control system with x commodities and $4x$ types of flows (of each commodity, and of information about its flow, in each direction), substantive interest will center on the 2^{4x-1} binary-flow patterns characterized by *even* numbers of a given value (e.g., the $2^3 = 8$ patterns with 0, 2, or 4 high-valued flows in the single-commodity system treated in this study).

9 This application of higher-dimensional joint distributions for testing more complex control-system data is currently under investigation, by the author and colleagues, in a survey of administrators and planners at the state, regional, county, and local levels of government in New Jersey, and in a study of the relationships between network exchange and technological innovativeness in two scientific-technical specialties, nuclear-waste management and solar-photovoltaic systems (see note 8 in Chapter 2).

10 These probabilities are most easily derived from Figure 5.3 (bottom section). Each of the four categories is exactly specified with probability $36/256 = .14$. The same categories are peripherally predicted with this probability plus that of the three bordering categories, $(24 + 16 + 24)/256 = .25$; $.1406 + .25 = .39$.

11 The particular problem of the relation between the counseling and legal sectors may be due to the somewhat ambiguous status of probation officers. Recall that evidence for the counseling sector's distinct boundaries was bolstered, in Chapter 4, when probation officers were moved from the legal to the counseling sector.

Bibliography

Aiken, Michael, and Paul E. Mott, eds. 1970. *The Structure of Community Power*. New York: Random House.

Aldrich, Howard E. 1979. *Organizations and Environments*. Englewood Cliffs, N.J.: Prentice-Hall.

Arnold, D., and D. Gold. 1964. "The Facilitation Effect of Social Environment." *Public Opinion Quarterly 28, 3: 513–16*.

Arrow, Kenneth. 1959. *Social Choice and Individual Values*. New York: Wiley.

Ashby, W. Ross. 1960. *Design for a Brain; The Origin of Adaptive Behavior*, 2d ed. New York: Wiley.

———. 1964. An Introduction to Cybernetics, paper ed. London: Methuen-University.

Bales, Robert F., and Edgar F. Borgatta. 1965. "Size of Group as a Factor in the Interaction Profile." Pp. 495–512 in *Small Groups: Studies in Social Interaction*, rev. ed., ed. A. Paul Hare, Edgar F. Borgatta, and Robert F. Bales. New York: Knopf.

Banfield, Edward C. 1958. *The Moral Basis of a Backward Society*. New York: Free Press.

Barbano, Filippo. 1968. "Social Structures and Social Functions: The Emancipation of Structural Analysis in Sociology." *Inquiry* 11: 40–84.

Barnes, J. A. 1969. "Networks and Political Process." Pp. 51–76 in *Social Networks in Urban Situations*, ed. J. Clyde Mitchell. Manchester, England: Manchester University Press.

Belknap, Ivan, and John G. Steinle. 1963. *The Community and Its Hospitals: A Comparative Analysis*. Syracuse, N.Y.: Syracuse University Press.

Bendix, Reinhard, and Seymour M. Lipset, eds. 1966. *Class, Status and Power*, 2d ed. New York: Free Press.

Beniger, James R. 1976. "Sampling Social Networks: The Subgroup Approach." *Proceedings of the American Statistical Association, Business and Economic Statistics Section* 11: 226–31.

———. 1978a. "Control Theory and Social Change: Toward a Synthesis of the System and Action Approaches." Ch. 1 (pp. 15–27) in *Sociocybernetics, An Actor-Oriented Social Systems Approach*, ed. R. Felix Geyer and Johannes van der Zouwen. Leiden, The Netherlands: Nijhoff.

———. 1978b. "Media Content as Social Indicators: The Greenfield Index of Agenda-Setting." *Communication Research* 5, 4 (Oct.): 437–53.

Beniger, James R., Wesley Shrum, Thomas Ash, and Jerome M. Lutin. 1979. "Designing a Survey of Information and Favor Exchange Networks among Regional, State, County and Municipal Levels of Government." *Proceedings of the American Statistical Association, Survery Research Methods Section* 2: 182–7.

Berge, Claude. 1962. *Theory of Graphs and Its Applications*. New York: Wiley.

Berger, Joseph, Morris Zelditch, and Bo Anderson, eds. 1972. *Sociological Theories in Progress*, vol. 2. Boston: Houghton Mifflin.

Bernard, Claude. 1927. *An Introduction to the Study of Experimental Medicine*. New York: Macmillan.

Bertalanffy, Ludwig von. 1968. *General System Theory*. New York: Braziller.

Black, Max, ed. 1961. *The Social Theories of Talcott Parsons, A Critical Examination*. Englewood Cliffs, N.J.: Prentice-Hall.

Blalock, Hubert M., Jr. 1972. *Social Statistics*, 2d ed. New York: McGraw-Hill.

Blau, Peter M. 1964. *Exchange and Power in Social Life*. New York: Wiley.

1974. "Parameters of Social Structure." *American Sociological Review* 39: 615–35.

1977. *Inequality and Heterogeneity, A Primitive Theory of Social Structure*. New York: Free Press, Macmillan.

Blau, Peter M., and W. R. Scott. 1962. *Formal Organizations*. San Francisco: Chandler.

Bloemena, A. R. 1964. *Sampling from a Graph*. Amsterdam: Mathematics Centrum.

Bloomberg, Warner, Jr., and Morris Sunshine. 1963. *Suburban Power Structures and Public Education*. Syracuse, N.Y.: Syracuse University Press.

Bode, H. W. 1945. *Network Analysis and Feedback Amplifier Design*. Princeton, N.J.: Van Nostrand.

Boeth, Richard. 1971. "The Heroin Plague." *Newsweek* 78 (July 5).

Boissevain, Jeremy, and J. Clyde Mitchell, eds. 1973. *Network Analysis: Studies in Human Interaction*. The Hague: Mouton.

Bonjean, Charles M., Terry N. Clark, and Robert L. Lineberry, eds. 1971. *Community Politics: A Behavioral Approach*. New York: Free Press.

Bonjean, Charles M., and David M. Olson. 1964. "Community Leadership: Directions of Research." *Administrative Science Quarterly* 9 (Dec.): 278–300.

Bott, Elizabeth. 1957. *Family and Social Network*. London: Tavistock.

Boulding, Kenneth. 1956a. *The Image*. Ann Arbor: University of Michigan Press.

1956b. "Toward a General Theory of Growth." *General Systems* 1: 66–75.

Brown, G. S., and D. P. Campbell. 1948. *Principles of Servomechanisms*. New York: Wiley.

Buckley, Walter. 1967. *Sociology and Modern Systems Theory*. Englewood Cliffs, N.J.: Prentice-Hall.

Ed. 1968. *Modern Systems Research for the Behavioral Scientist, A Sourcebook*. Chicago: Aldine.

Burgess, M. Elaine. 1960. *Negro Leadership in a Southern City*. Chapel Hill: University of North Carolina Press.

Burgess, Robert L., and Don Bushell, eds. 1969. *Behavioral Sociology*. New York: Columbia University Press.

Cannon, Walter B. 1929. "Organization for Physiological Homeostasis." *Physiological Reviews* 9, 13 (July): 399–431.

1932. *The Wisdom of the Body*. New York: Norton.

Carney, Thomas F. 1972. *Content Analysis: A Technique for Systematic Inference from Communication*. Winnipeg: University of Manitoba Press.

Cartwright, Dorwin. 1965. "Influence, Leadership and Control." Pp. 1–47 in *Handbook of Organizations*, ed. James G. March. Chicago: Rand McNally.

Clark, Matt. 1966. "LSD and the Drugs of the Mind." *Newsweek* 67 (May 9).

Clark, Terry N. 1968. "Community Structure, Decision-Making, Budget Expenditures, and Urban Renewal in 51 American Communities." *American Sociological Review* 33: 576–93.

1973. *Community Power and Policy Outputs: A Review of Urban Research.* Beverly Hills, Calif.: Sage.

Cohen, Bernard C. 1963. *The Press, the Public and Foreign Policy.* Princeton, N.J.: Princeton University Press.

Coleman, James S. 1958. "Relational Analysis: The Study of Social Organizations with Survey Methods." *Human Organization* 17 (Winter): 28–36.

1975. "Social Structure and the Theory of Action." Pp. 76–93 in *Approaches to the Study of Social Structure,* ed. Peter M. Blau. New York: Free Press.

Cory, Christopher. 1969. "Pop Drugs: The High as a Way of Life." *Time* 94, 13 (Sept. 26).

Coser, Lewis A. 1956. *The Functions of Social Conflict.* New York: Free Press.

ed. 1975. *The Idea of Social Structure,* New York: Harcourt Brace Jovanovich.

Dahl, Robert A. 1955. "Hierarchy, Democracy and Bargaining in Politics and Economics." Pp. 45–69 in *Research Frontiers in Politics and Government.* Stephen K. Bailey et al. Washington, D.C.: Brookings Institution.

1961. *Who Governs? Democracy and Power in an American City.* New Haven, Conn.: Yale University Press.

D'Antonio, William V., and Eugene C. Erickson. 1962. "The Reputational Technique as a Measure of Community Power: An Evaluation Based on Comparative and Longitudinal Studies." *American Sociological Review* 27 (June): 362–76.

D'Antonio, William V., William H. Form, Charles P. Loomis, and Eugene C. Erickson. 1961. "Institutional and Occupational Representations in Eleven Community Influence Systems." *American Sociological Review* 26 (June): 440–6.

Danzger, M. Herbert. 1964. "Community Power Structure: Problems and Continuities." *American Sociological Review* 29 (Oct.): 707–17.

Deutsch, Karl W. 1963. *The Nerves of Government.* New York: Free Press.

1966. "The Study of Political Communication and Control, 1962–1966." Pp. vii–xxiii in *The Nerves of Government, Models of Political Communication and Control,* paper ed. New York: Free Press.

Duncan, Otis Dudley. 1961. "A Sociometric Index for All Occupations." Pp. 109–38 in *Occupations and Social Status,* ed. Albert J. Reiss. New York: Free Press.

1964. "Social Organization and the Ecosystem." In *Handbook of Modern Sociology,* ed. Robert E. L. Faris. Chicago: Rand McNally.

Durkheim, Emile. 1933. *The Division of Labor in Society.* New York: Free Press.

Ehrlich, Howard J. 1961. "The Reputational Approach to the Study of Community Power." *American Sociological Review* 26 (Dec.):926–7.

Ekeh, Peter P. 1974. *Social Exchange Theory.* Cambridge, Mass.: Harvard University Press.

Emerson, Richard M. 1972. "Exchange Theory, Parts I and II." Pp. 58–87 in *Sociological Theories in Progress,* vol. 2, ed. Joseph Berger, Morris Zelditch, and Bo Anderson. Boston: Houghton Mifflin.

Etzioni, Amitai. 1964. *Modern Organizations.* Englewood Cliffs, N.J.: Prentice-Hall.

Evans-Pritchard, E.E. 1940. *The Nuer: A Description of the Modes of Livelihood and Political Institutions of a Nilotic People.* London: Oxford University Press (Clarendon Press).

Faris, Robert E. L., ed. 1964. *Handbook of Modern Sociology.* Chicago: Rand McNally.

Festinger, Leon, Stanley Schachter, and Kurt Back. 1950. *Social Pressures in Informal Groups.* New York: Harper.

Firth, Raymond W. 1954. "Social Organization and Social Change." *Journal of the Royal Anthropological Institute* 84: 1–20.

Flament, Claude. 1963. *Applications of Graph Theory to Group Structure.* Englewood Cliffs, N.J.: Prentice-Hall.

Form, William H., and William V. D'Antonio. 1959. "Integration and Cleavage Among Community Influentials in Two Border Cities." *American Sociological Review* 24 (Dec.): 804–14.

Frank, Ove. 1971. *Statistical Inference in Graphs.* Stockholm: Forsvarets Forskninganstalt.
   1977. "Survey Sampling in Graphs." *Journal of Statistical Planning and Inference* 1, 3: 235–64.
   1978. "Sampling and Estimation in Large Social Networks." *Social Networks* 1, 1:91–101.

Frankenberg, R. J. 1966. *Communities in Britain: Social Life in Town and Country.* Harmondsworth, England: Penguin.

Freeman, Linton C. 1968. *Patterns of Local Community Leadership.* Indianapolis, Ind.: Bobbs-Merrill.

Funkhouser, G. Ray. 1973a. "The Issues of the Sixties: An Exploratory Study in the Dynamics of Public Opinion." *Public Opinion Quarterly* 37: 62–75.
   1973b. "Trends in Media Coverage of the Issues of the Sixties." *Journalism Quarterly* 50: 533–8.

Galtung, Johan. 1969. *Theory and Methods of Social Research.* New York: Columbia University Press.

Gamson, William A. 1966a. "Rancorous Conflict in Community Politics." *American Sociological Review* 31: 71–81.
   1966b. "Reputation and Resources in Community Politics." *American Journal of Sociology* 72 (Sept.): 121–31.

Gerbner, George, et al., eds. 1969. *The Analysis of Communication Content.* New York: Wiley.

Goldman, S. 1953. *Information Theory.* London: Constable.

Gollin, Albert E., and Barry M. Feinberg. 1975 (Oct.). "The Professions Confront the Drug Problem; A Report Prepared for the National Institute of Mental Health Contract No. N01-MH-1-0093(ND)." Washington, D.C.: Bureau of Social Science Research.

Goodman, Leo A. 1961. "Snowball Sampling." *Annals of Mathematical Statistics* 32, 1: 148–70.

Goodman, Leo A., and William H. Kruskal. 1954. "Measures of Association for Cross Classifications." *Journal of the American Statistical Association* 49: 732–64.

Gouldner, Alvin W. 1960. "The Norm of Reciprocity: A Preliminary Statement." *American Sociological Review* 25, 2 (April): 161–78.

Granovetter, Mark. 1976. "Network Sampling: Some First Steps." *American Journal of Sociology* 81 (May): 1287–1303.

Greenfield, Meg. 1961. "The Great American Morality Play." *The Reporter* (June 8): 13–18.

Gurevitch, Michael. 1961. "The Social Structure of Acquaintanceship Networks." Ph.D. dissertation. Cambridge, Mass.: Massachusetts Institute of Technology.

Gusfield, Joseph, and Michael Schwartz. 1963. "The Meanings of Occupational Prestige: Reconsideration of the NORC Scale." *American Sociological Review* 28: 265–71.

Harary, F., R. Norman, and D. Cartwright. 1965. *Structural Models: An Introduction to the Theory of Directed Graphs.* New York: Wiley.

Hare, A. Paul, Edgar F. Borgatta, and Robert F. Bales, eds. 1965. *Small Groups: Studies in Social Interaction,* rev. ed. New York: Knopf.

Hawley, Amos H. 1950. *Human Ecology.* New York: Ronald Press.

Heise, David R., ed. 1974. *Sociological Methodology 1975.* San Francisco: Josey-Bass.

Henderson, Lawrence J. 1913. *The Fitness of the Environment.* New York: Macmillan.

1935. *Pareto's General Sociology: A Physiologist's Interpretation.* Cambridge, Mass.: Harvard University Press.

Hertzberg, Hendrik. 1982. "Washington Diarist: Misspeaking." *New Republic* 186, 10 (March 10): 42.

Hodge, Robert W., Paul M. Siegel, and Peter H. Rossi. 1964. "Occupational Prestige in the United States, 1925–63." *American Journal of Sociology* 70: 286–302.

Hodge, Robert W., Donald J. Treiman, and Peter H. Rossi. 1966. "A Comparative Study of Occupational Prestige." Pp. 309–21 in *Class, Status and Power,* 2d ed., ed. Reinhard Bendix and Seymour M. Lipset. New York: Free Press.

Hollingshead, August B. 1949. *Elmtown's Youth.* New York: Wiley.

Holsti, Ole R. 1969. *Content Analysis for the Social Sciences and Humanities.* Reading Mass.: Addison Wesley.

Homans, George C. 1950. *The Human Group.* New York: Harcourt, Brace and World.

1961. *Social Behavior: Its Elementary Forms.* New York: Harcourt, Brace and World.

1964. "Bringing Men Back In." *American Sociological Review* 29: 809–18.

1969. "The Sociological Relevance of Behaviorism." Pp. 1–24 in *Behavioral Sociology,* ed. Robert L. Burgess and Don Bushell, Jr. New York: Columbia University Press.

Homans, George C., and David M. Schneider. 1955. *Marriage, Authority and Final Causes: A Study of Unilateral Cross-Cousin Marriage.* New York: Free Press.

Hunter, Floyd. 1963. *Community Power Structure, A Study of Decision Makers.* Garden City, N.Y.: Doubleday Anchor.

James, H. M., N. B. Nichols, and R. S. Phillips. 1947. *Theory of Servomechanisms.* New York: McGraw-Hill.

Janowitz, Morris. 1968–9. "Harold Lasswell's Contribution to Content Analysis." *Public Opinion Quarterly* 32, 4 (Winter): 643–53.

1976. "Content Analysis and the Study of Sociopolitical Change." *Journal of Communication* 26, 4 (Autumn): 10–21.

Janssen, Peter, 1969. "The Drug Generation: Growing Younger." *Newsweek* 73 (April 21), 107–10.

Jennings, M. Kent. 1964. *Community Influentials: The Elites of Atlanta.* New York: Free Press.

Johnson, Keith. 1970. "Kids and Heroin: The Adolescent Epidemic." *Time* 95, 11 (March 16): 16–20, 25.

Johnston, Lloyd D., Jerald G. Bachman, and Patrick M. O'Malley. 1982. *Highlights from Student Drug Use in America, 1975–1980.* Rockville, Md.: National Institute on Drug Abuse.

Kaufman, Herbert, and Victor Jones. 1954. "The Mystery of Power." *Public Administration Review* 14 (Summer): 205–12.

Kendall, Maurice G. 1938. "A New Measure of Rank Correlation." *Biometrika* 30: 81–93.

1955. *Rank Correlation Methods.* New York: Hafner.

Kephart, W. M. 1950. "A Quantitative Analysis of Intergroup Relationships." *American Journal of Sociology* 55: 544–9.

Kruskal, William H. 1958. "Ordinal Measures of Association." *Journal of the American Statistical Association* 53: 814–61.

Kuhn, Thomas. 1962. *The Structure of Scientific Revolutions.* Chicago: University of Chicago Press.

Lasswell, Harold D. 1935. *World Politics and Personality Insecurity.* New York: McGraw-Hill.

Lasswell, Harold D., et al. 1947. *Language of Politics: Studies in Quantitative Semantics.* New York: George W. Stewart.

Laumann, Edward C. 1973. *Bonds of Pluralism: The Form and Substance of Urban Social Networks.* New York: Wiley.

Laumann, Edward C., and Franz U. Pappi. 1976. *Networks of Collective Action, A Perspective on Community Influence Systems.* New York: Academic Press.

Lehmann, E. L. 1975. *Nonparametrics, Statistical Methods Based on Ranks.* San Francisco: Holden-Day.

Leontief, Wassily. 1951. *The Structure of the American Economy, 1919–1939*, 2d ed. New York: Oxford University Press.

1966. *Input-Output Economics.* New York: Oxford University Press.

Levi-Strauss, Claude. 1969. *The Elementary Structures of Kinship.* Boston: Beacon Press.

Lippmann, Walter. 1922. *Public Opinion.* New York: Macmillan.

Loomis, Charles P., and Zona K. Loomis. 1961. *Modern Social Theories.* New York: D. Van Nostrand.

Lotka, A. J. 1925. *Elements of Physical Biology.* New York: Dover.

Lynd, Robert S., and Helen Merrell Lynd. 1937. *Middletown in Transition.* New York: Harcourt, Brace and World.

Maitland, Leslie. 1981. "The New Federalism May Be Bad for the Old Drug Problem." *New York Times* (Aug. 23): 6E.

Malinowski, Bronislaw. 1922. *Argonauts of the Western Pacific.* London: Routledge & Kegan Paul.

March, James G., and Herbert A. Simon. 1958. *Organizations.* New York: Wiley.

Markoff, John, et al. 1974. "Toward the Integration of Content Analysis and General Methodology." In *Sociological Methodology 1975*, ed. David R. Heise. San Francisco: Josey-Bass, pp. 1–58.

Marshall, Alfred. 1948. *Principles of Economics*, 8th ed. London: Macmillan.

Marx, Karl. 1963. *The Eighteenth Brumaire of Louis Bonaparte.* New York: International Publishers.

Mayer, Phillip. 1961. *Townsmen or Tribesmen?* Capetown, South Africa: Oxford University Press.

Mayhew, Bruce H., and Roger L. Levinger. 1976. "Size and Density of Interaction in Human Aggregates." *American Journal of Sociology* 82, 1 (July): 86–110.

McCombs, Maxwell. 1976. "Agenda-Setting Research: A Bibiographic Essay." *Political Communication Review* 1, 3 (Summer): 1–7.

McCombs, Maxwell, and D. L. Shaw. 1972. "The Agenda-Setting Function of the Media." *Public Opinion Quarterly* 36: 176–87.

McCombs, Maxwell, and G. Stone, eds. 1976. *Studies in Agenda-Setting.* Syracuse, N.Y.: Newhouse Communication Research Center, Syracuse University.

Mead, George Herbert. 1934. *Mind, Self and Society.* Chicago: University of Chicago Press.

1956. *The Social Psychology of George Herbert Mead.* Chicago: University of Chicago Press, Phoenix Books.

Merton, Robert K. 1968 (1957). *Social Theory and Social Structure.* New York: Free Press.

1975. "Structural Analysis in Sociology." Pp. 21–52 in *Approaches to the Study of Social Structure*, ed. Peter M. Blau. New York: Free Press.

Mill, John Stuart. 1909. *Principles of Political Economy.* London: Longmans, Green.

Miller, George A., Eugene Galanter, and Karl A. Pribram. 1960. *Plans and the Structure of Behavior.* New York: Holt.

Mitchell, J. Clyde, ed. 1969a. *Social Networks in Urban Situations*. Manchester, England: Manchester University Press.

1969b. "The Concept and Use of Social Networks." Pp. 1–50 in *Social Networks in Urban Situations*, ed. J. Clyde Mitchell. Manchester, England: Manchester University Press.

Moreno, Jacob L. 1953. *Who Shall Survive? Foundations of Sociometry, Group Psychotherapy and Sociodrama*, rev. ed. Beacon, N.Y.: Beacon House.

Morgan, David L., and Steve Rytina. 1976. "Comment on 'Network Sampling: Some First Steps' by Mark Granovetter." *American Journal of Sociology* 83, 3 (Nov.): 722–7.

Morse, Chandler. 1961. "The Functional Imperatives." Pp. 100–52 in *The Social Theories of Talcott Parsons, A Critical Examination*, ed. Max Black. Englewood Cliffs, N.J.: Prentice-Hall.

Mueller, John E. 1973. *War, Presidents and Public Opinion*. New York: Wiley.

Mulkay, M. J. 1971. *Functionalism, Exchange and Theoretical Strategy*. London: Routledge & Kegan Paul.

Nadel, S. F. 1953. "Social Control and Self-Regulation." *Social Forces* 31: 265–73.

1957. *The Theory of Social Structure*. London: Cohen and West.

Naisbitt, John. 1976. *The Trend Report: A Quarterly Forecast and Evaluation of Business and Social Developments*. Washington, D.C.: Center for Policy Process.

National Academy of Sciences. 1982. *Marijuana and Health*. Washington, D.C.: National Academy Press.

National Opinion Research Center. 1977. *National Data Program for the Social Sciences, Spring 1976 General Social Survey*. Ann Arbor, Mich.: Inter-University Consortium for Political and Social Research.

Nemy, Enid. 1982. "Mrs. Reagan Deplores a Drug Epidemic," *New York Times* (Feb. 17): C1.

Newsweek Magazine. 1969. "Top of the Week." 73 (April 21): 5.

1970. "Top of the Week." 76 (Sept. 7): 3.

1971. "Top of the Week." 78 (July 5): 3.

Neimeijer, Rudo. 1973. "Some Applications of the Notion of Density." Pp. 1–50 in *Network Analysis: Studies in Human Interaction*, ed. J. Boissevain and J. C. Mitchell. The Hague: Mouton.

Nisbet, Robert A. 1966. *The Sociological Tradition*. New York: Basic Books.

Ogburn, William. 1966. *Social Change, with Respect to Cultural and Original Nature*. New York: Dell Delta.

Olmstead, Donald W. 1954. "Organizational Leadership and Social Structure in a Small City." *American Sociological Review* 19 (June): 273–81.

Olson, Mancur. 1965. *The Logic of Collective Action*. Cambridge, Mass.: Harvard University Press.

Parsons, Talcott. 1937. *The Structure of Social Action*. New York: McGraw-Hill.

1951. *The Social System*. New York: Free Press.

1960. *Structure and Process in Modern Societies*. New York: Free Press.

1961a. "The General Interpretation of Action." Pp. 85–97 in *Theories of Society*, ed. Parsons, Edward A. Shils, Kaspar D. Naegele, and J. R. Pitts. New York: Free Press.

1961b. "An Outline of the Social System." Pp. 30–79 in *Theories of Society*, ed. Parsons, Edward A. Shils, Kaspar D. Naegele and Jesse R. Pitts. New York: Free Press.

1961c. "The Point of View of the Author." Pp. 311–63 in *The Social Theories of Talcott Parsons, A Critical Examination*, ed. Max Black. Englewood Cliffs, N.J.: Prentice-Hall.

1967. Review of Robert A. Nisbet, *The Sociological Tradition*. *American Sociological Review* 32 (Aug.): 640–3.

1975. "Social Structure and the Symbolic Media of Interchange." Pp. 94–120 in *Approaches to the Study of Social Structure*, ed. Peter M. Blau. New York: Free Press.

Parsons, Talcott, and Edward A. Shils, eds. 1962 (1951). *Toward a General Theory of Action*. New York: Harper & Row, Torchbooks, Academy Library.

Parsons, Talcott, Edward A. Shils, Kaspar D. Naegele, and Jesse R. Pitts, eds. 1961. *Theories of Society*. New York: Free Press.

Polsby, Nelson W. 1962. "Community Power: Some Reflections on the Recent Literature." *American Sociological Review* 27 (Dec.): 838–40.

Powers, William T. 1973. *Behavior: The Control of Perception*. Chicago: Aldine.

Presthus, Robert. 1964. *Men at the Top: A Study in Community Power*. New York: Oxford University Press.

Reader, D. H. 1964. "Models in Social Change with Special Reference to Southern Africa." *African Studies* 23: 11–33.

Reiss, Albert J., Jr., ed. 1961. *Occupations and Social Status*. New York: Free Press.

Riker, William, and Peter Ordeshook. 1973. *An Introduction to Positive Political Theory*. Englewood Cliffs, N.J.: Prentice-Hall.

Robbins, William. 1969. "Drug Experts Cite Disappointment over Nixon Bill on Penalties." *New York Times* (July 17): 16.

Rose, Arnold M. 1967. *The Power Structure: Political Process in American Society*. New York: Oxford University Press.

Scott, John Finley. 1963. "The Changing Foundations of the Parsonian Action Scheme." *American Sociological Review* 28 (Oct.): 716–35.

Sears, David O., and Richard E. Whitney. 1973. "Political Persuasion." Pp. 253–89 in *Handbook of Communication*, ed. Ithiel de Sola Pool, Wilbur Schramm, and collaborators. Chicago: Rand McNally.

Shannon, Claude E. 1948. "The Mathematical Theory of Communication." *Bell System Technical Journal* (July and Oct.): 379–423, 623–56.

Shannon, Claude E., and Warren Weaver. 1949. *The Mathematical Theory of Communication*. Urbana: University of Illinois Press.

Siegel, Paul M. 1971. "Prestige in the American Occupational Structure." Ph.D. dissertation. Chicago: University of Chicago.

Siegel, Paul M., Peter H. Rossi, and Robert W. Hodge. 1973. "Social Standings of Occupations." Manuscript scheduled by Seminar Press, New York, withdrawn 1974.

Simmel, Georg. 1950a. "The Isolated Individual and the Dyad." Pp. 118–44 in *The Sociology of Georg Simmel*, trans. and ed. Kurt H. Wolff. New York: Free Press-Macmillan.

1950b. *The Sociology of Georg Simmel*, trans. and ed. Kurt H. Wolff. New York: Free Press-Macmillan.

1950c. "The Triad." Pp. 145–69 in *The Sociology of Georg Simmel*, trans. and ed. Kurt H. Wolff, New York: Free Press.

1955. *Conflict and the Web of Group Affiliations*. Glencoe, Ill.: Free Press.

Simon, Herbert A. 1947. *Administrative Behavior*. New York: Macmillan.

Smelser, Neil J. 1962. *Theory of Collective Behavior*. New York: Free Press.

1977. Personal correspondence, Sept. 14.

Somers, Robert H. 1968. "An Approach to the Multivariate Analysis of Ordinal Data." *American Sociological Review* 33, 6 (Dec.): 971–7.

Stephan, Frederick. 1969. "Three Extensions of Sampling Survey Technique." Pp. 81–104 in *New Developments in Survey Sampling*, ed. N. Johnson and H. Smith. New York: Wiley.

Stinchcombe, Arthur L. 1968. *Constructing Social Theories*. New York: Harcourt, Brace and World.

1975. "Merton's Theory of Social Structure," Pp. 11–33 in *The Idea of Social Structure*, ed. Lewis A. Coser. New York: Harcourt Brace Jovanovich.

1977. Review of Peter M. Blau, ed., *Approaches to the Study of Social Structure. American Journal of Sociology* 82, 4 (Jan.): 873–6.

Stone, G. 1976. "Tracing the Time-Lag in Agenda-Setting." In *Studies in Agenda-Setting*, ed. M. McCombs and G. Stone. Syracuse, N.Y.: Newhouse Communication Research Center, Syracuse University.

Stone, Philip J. 1966. *The General Inquirer: A Computer Approach to Content Analysis.* Cambridge, Mass.: MIT Press.

Tapiero, C., M. Capobianco, and A. Lewin. 1975. "Structural Inference in Organizations." *Journal of Mathematical Sociology* 4, 1: 121–30.

Temme, Lloyd V. 1975. *Occupational Achievement: Meanings and Measures.* Washington, D.C.: Bureau of Social Science Research.

Thibaut, John W., and Harold H. Kelley. 1959. *The Social Psychology of Groups.* New York: Wiley.

Thom, Rene. 1975. *Structural Stability and Morphogenesis, An Outline of a General Theory of Models.* Reading, Mass.: Benjamin.

Tilly, Charles. 1969. "Community: City: Urbanization." Mimeographed. Ann Arbor: University of Michigan.

Turner, Jonathan. 1974. *The Structure of Sociological Theory.* Homewood, Ill.: Dorsey Press.

U.S. Council on Drug Abuse. 1973. *Federal Strategy for Drug Abuse and Drug Traffic Prevention 1973.* Washington, D.C.: U.S. Government Printing Office.

U.S. National Advisory Commission on Civil Disorders. 1968. *Report.* Washington, D.C.: U.S. Government Printing Office.

Wallace, Walter L., ed. 1969. *Sociological Theory.* Chicago: Aldine.

1975. "Structure and Action in the Theories of Coleman and Parsons." Pp. 121–34 in *Approaches to the Study of Social Structure*, ed. Peter M. Blau. New York: Free Press.

Warner, W. Lloyd, and collaborators. 1949. *Democracy in Jonesville.* New York: Harper.

Wasserman, Stanley S. 1977. "Random Directed Graph Distributions and the Triad Census in Social Networks." *Journal of Mathematical Sociology* 5: 61–86.

Weber, Max. 1947. *The Theory of Social and Economic Organization.* New York: Oxford University Press.

White, Harrison, Scott A. Boorman, and Ronald Breiger. 1976. "Social Structure from Multiple Networks. I. Blockmodels of Roles and Positions." *American Journal of Sociology* 81 (Jan.): 730–80.

Whitehead, Alfred North. 1925. *Science and the Modern World.* Lowell Lectures. New York: Macmillan.

Wiener, Norbert. 1948. *Cybernetics: or Control and Communication in the Animal and the Machine.* Cambridge, Mass.: MIT Press.

1950. *The Human Use of Human Beings; Cybernetics and Society.* Boston: Houghton Mifflin.

Wolff, Kurt H., trans. and ed. 1950. *The Sociology of Georg Simmel.* New York: Free Press-Macmillan.

Wolfinger, Raymond E. 1962. "A Plea for a Decent Burial." *American Sociological Review* 27 (Dec.): 841–7.

Wuthnow, Robert, James R. Beniger, Patricia Woolf, and Wesley Shrum. 1979. "Exchange and Innovation in Technical Networks." Research Proposal Submitted to the National Science Foundation, Division of Policy Research and Analysis. Princeton, N.J.: Department of Sociology, Princeton University.

Zimmerman, Paul. 1967. "The Marijuana Problem." *Newsweek* 70 (July 24): 46–50, 52.

Name index

Subject index

academics, 52, 170
accidents, drug-related, 7–8, 14, 15, 19, 20f, 159
acquaintances: density of, 193; volume of, 186, 187
actors: in control systems, 31, 35, 37, 162; in exchange theory, 40, 198n3; in organizations, 31, 37, 46, 91; in social action theory, 37, 38, 40, 42, 50, 162, 195n1; in survey research, 44, 169; in system-action synthesis, 35, 37, 41–6, 54, 162, 172
acts, unit social, 39, 196n4
adaptation of social systems, 39
addiction, drug, 201n5
administrative function, 94, 170
administrators, 35, 48, 63–8, 165, 204
advertising, 24
Advertising Council, 24
agenda setting, 19, 21, 159, 195n7
aggrandizement, personal, 197n2
aggression, drug-induced, 201n5
Albuquerque, 15
Alcohol, Drug Abuse and Mental Health Administration, 4
alcoholism, 3, 6, 14
Alcoholism and Drug Abuse Subcommittee, U.S. Senate, 4
alliances, 40, 41, 42
alternatives, social structuring of individual, 41, 43, 46, 54, 172–3
American Association for the Advancement of Science, 39
amphetamines, 3, 12, 23
amyl nitrite, 3
angel dust, 3
anthropology, 38
antiutilitarianism, 38, 196n5
Armed Forces Radio, 8
arrests, drug-related, 159
association: interpersonal, 99, 101, 142, 200n2; statistical, 199n16
attention, attracting, 171

attitudes toward exchange, 51
authority: of citations, 171; as commodity, 46; and control, 35, 37, 47, 120, 163; flows of, 35, 37, 47, 91, 120, 137; non-zero-sum nature, 50; positions of, 198n5; and referrals, 50, 52, 136, 137, 162, 171; symbols of, 51, 58
autonomous systems, *see* systems, social
autonomy, personal, 160

babies, drug-addicted, 201n5
balance in control relations, 158
Baltimore, 60–1, 175–82
banks, 50
barbiturates, 3, 8, 12, 22, 23, 201n5
barriers of hierarchies, 104
behavior: in control system, 31, 32, 35, 41, 43, 45, 172–3; social theories of, 36, 40–5, 94, 96, 196n5; and survey research, 44
behaviorism, 40
biology, 38, 42, 93, 183; organismic, 93
birthrate, 42
bit: measure, 53, 184, 189
books, 112, 113t, 115, 170, 195n1, 202n7
Boston Globe, 8
boundaries: community, 46, 51, 57; jurisdictional, 195n3; national, 170; network, 51, 57, 91; organizational, 46, 47, 51, 57, 58, 91, 160, 161, 164, 170, 195n3; professional, 51, 57; subsystem, 36, 98, 105–6, 119, 129, 136, 164, 167, 204n11; system, 46, 51, 160, 203n4
boundary maintenance, 131, 136, 139–43, 150–6, 162–8, 203n5, 204n6
bribes, 197n2
Britain, 38
budget, U.S. government, 6
bullets, graphical, 77, 79, 80, 83–4, 86, 199n13
Bureau of Social Science Research, 175
butyl nitrite, 3

218